16 26 52 55 60-61 63 67 82 101 103
110-111, 117 ,121 ,124 ,125 ,126. 135, 169,
171, 174, 177, 201, 204, 216, 219, 238, 248, 252
258,

M.W. Kurst

Copy 28, 99, 110-111, 128, 264.

Governing American Schools

Political Interaction in Local School Districts

L. Harmon Zeigler
*University of Oregon
and Oregon Research Institute*

M. Kent Jennings
University of Michigan

with the assistance of
G. Wayne Peak
Colorado State University

Duxbury Press
North Scituate, Massachusetts

Duxbury Press
A Division of Wadsworth Publishing Company, Inc.

This work was developed under a contract from the U.S. Office of Education,
Department of Health, Education, and Welfare. However, opinions expressed herein
do not necessarily reflect the position or policy of that agency, and no official
endorsement should be inferred.

ISBN-0-87872-067-7

L. C. Cat. Card No.-74-75716

Printed in the United States of America

1 2 3 4 5 6 7 8 9 10—78 77 76 75 74

To the Memory of David W. Minar

Table of Contents

LIST OF TABLES

LIST OF FIGURES

Foreword

The notion of a system of public schooling, responsive to the citizenry and controlled by a democratically selected governing board, is thoroughly pervasive in America. Despite constitutional and legislative provisions that vest authority for the creation and operation of schools with the various states, and in the face of a curriculum that is heavily influenced by textbook publishers and that is surprisingly uniform throughout the country, the ideology of local school control persists. It is in fact so strong that, if they are to gain approval, proposals for reorganization or for new methods of finance must meet the test of maintaining local control in the minds of the majority of voters.

Because the governing board is an essential element in the ideology of local control, school boards have been a major object of inquiry throughout the history of educational research. Studies have been undertaken to determine the age, occupation, socioeconomic status, background of public service, religious affiliation, motives for seeking office, and numerous other personal and social characteristics of individual board members. Research has also been carried out to describe school boards as collectivities: their size and composition, the procedures used to discharge their responsibilities, and the relationships of such boards to other governmental agencies.

This research has revealed a great deal about the demographic and structural characteristics of boards of education. *It has done little, however, to shed light on the actual functioning of those boards in governing American education.* Although it is possible to infer that upper middle class Caucasian males, who so thoroughly dominate American school boards, will behave differently than will individuals drawn from other groups, it is important to know how such boards do in fact behave. Moreover, the ideology of local control suggests that boards, as representatives of the citizenry, will be alert and responsive to constituent demands. But since any constituency consists of a multiplicity of interests, generating frequently conflicting demands, we need better information about the groups to whom boards respond and the mechanisms by which those groups make their demands known.

A break with the traditional approach to school board research occurred during the fifties, when Neal Gross and his associates at Harvard University undertook an investigation into the behavior and practices of boards of education and school superintendents. They interviewed both superintendents and board members and produced a number of reports, one of which dealt primarily with the behavior of school board members. That research represented a significant step in examining the general problem of school governance. A large void remained, however, since the data was collected entirely in the state of Massachusetts.

The research reported in this volume was undertaken to fill this void. A representative national sample of school districts was selected and interviews were conducted to obtain information that would respond to the general question of how local school systems are governed. School districts included in the study were located in the northeast, the midwest, the south, and the west. They represented central cities, suburbs, non-suburban communities in standard metropolitan statistical areas, and communities outside SMSAs.

The study was conceived by Harmon Zeigler of the University of Oregon and Kent Jennings of the University of Michigan. It was carried out as a project in the Center for the Advanced Study of Educational Administration, with substantial financial support from the U.S. Office of Education.

A major theme in the report is that the early reformers, who set about to remove educational governance from the political arena, succeeded only too well. Not only has the intended result of reform been achieved, but an unintended consequence has also resulted. Board members have been effectively insulated from the voting public, with the further consequence that boards have become increasingly dependent on superintendents for information on which to base decisions.

Because the volume presents a great deal of research data on educational governance, it is certain to be of interest to those who teach and conduct research in political science and educational administration. In addition, however, because of its currency and readability, the report will attract the intense interest of both school board members and superintendents. Those who are interested in data and research methodology will find sufficient detail to enable them to check the findings and conclusions and to debate the results. Yet, it is possible to follow the dialogue and to react to the substance of the report with only cursory reference to the methodological procedures and the presentation of data.

The book is highly provocative. One central finding is that boards of education function in a more representative manner when the school district is politically impregnated. Boards in more "political" districts have closer links to their constituents and are more likely to challenge the superintendent's dominance. These conclusions will certainly spark debate about the management of schools. Included in that debate will be a number of questions that are raised in this volume.

Is a democratically elected board, responsible to the citizens, an appropriate model of governance for schools? If so, how can boards determine more accurately their constituents' desires and aspirations? And how can they utilize this information?

Is it possible, on the other hand, that advancing technology has made such governance patterns obsolete? Should both technical and policy issues be determined by professional teachers and administrators who possess the requisite technical competence? If so, who is to protect the clients (pupils) from self-indulgent and self-serving acts of the professionals?

Or, should continued attempts be made to combine these two governance mechanisms? Can policy decisions be distinguished from implementing decisions, with a democratically elected board dealing with policy setting and professionals with implementation?

There are those who continue to view political processes as inimical to the welfare of students and to the integrity of the educational process. Their position is articulated by Bowers in his forword to the volume, *Education and Social Policy: Local Control of Education.* Says Bowers:

> *When the school's moral responsibility to the student is not sacrificed to political expediency, education can become a humanizing process . . . [to the contrary] as long as the "conventional wisdom" legitimizes control of the school through political strife we shall . . . have to wait for the answer to the real question: Is it possible to define the purpose of education in terms that elevate and enhance the well-being of the individual undergoing the process and not in terms of the self-proclaimed needs of contending interest groups?**

To those who hold this position the results reported by Zeigler and Jennings should be reassuring. On the other hand, however, there are also those who hold that political action is essential in guaranteeing that schools will be responsive to their clientele. The position of these people is stated clearly in the concluding chapter of this book:

> *In spite of the obvious perils, political decisions are — as long as we remain committed to democracy — logically superior to technical decisions. If we are going to maintain the trappings of democracy in education, then the*

**C.A. Bowers et al., ed., *Education and Social Policy: Local Control of Education* (New York: Random House, 1970), pp. 4–5.

realities of democracy should be achieved. School boards should govern or be abolished. In spite of occasional proposals for abolition, they will remain. It is possible that boards will become merely ceremonial . . . Such a result can — and should be — avoided.

Max G. Abbott, *Director*
Center for Educational
Policy and Management

Preface

The politics of education is a relatively new area of political inquiry. For decades the subject was relegated to a few paragraphs in textbooks. Occasionally a particular event would make starkly visible the connection between the worlds of education and politics. For the most part, however, the educational system was incorrectly viewed as apolitical. Although the political nature of educational systems has come to be recognized in recent years, the application of political theories and empirical evidence to the process of school governance has proceeded much more slowly. Studies have often been rich in insights, but limited in generalizability. Some of the best work has been carried out at the state and national levels, even though the heart of the American educational process lies in the local school district. Comparisons between the process of governance in school systems and other units of government have tended to be based on formal, legalistic distinctions.

In this book we direct our attention to the politics of education at the local level. Our focal point is local school districts and their authoritative governers, the school boards. We employ detailed information gathered from interviews with several hundred school board members and superintendents distributed across a national probability sample of school districts. We amplify this information by considering the social and political contexts in which the districts are embedded.

Three components of the governance phenomenon draw our attention, and these three parts are central to an understanding of governance in most political systems with visible constituencies and professional bureaucracies. The first component considers how office is attained, how well traditional expectations of democratic theory are met in the selection process, and what factors facilitate the meeting of these criteria. The second component centers on the ongoing relationships between school district governors and those whom they govern, the responsiveness of board members, the viability of interest group representation, and the degree to which board members and their publics share the same preferences. The third part of governance we address derives from the enormous resources lodged in the superintendent's office and the widespread tendency to label educational issues as technical and professional rather than political questions. Thus the third component consists of the ability of the public's representatives to confront the superintendent's office, the social and political elements about the district which encourage confrontation, and the characteristics of board members and superintendents which are important in this regard.

These are not the only important components of school governance, but we believe they are essential ones. By examining them and their interrelationships we seek to show, from the point of view of traditional democratic theory, both the healthy and the pathological characteristics of school district governance. We also try to demonstrate the empirical regularities involved in these components. Finally, we seek to show the unique aspects of educational governance as well as those aspects it shares with other systems of governance.

Acknowledgments

This book reports the results of six years of research. Naturally, there are many people whose assistance was critical to whatever merit the book has. At the University of Oregon Michael Baer (now of the University of Kentucky) assisted in developing the interview schedules, Michael Boss and Hendrik Van Dalen (now of the University of Georgia) carried out much of the data analysis, and Harlan Strauss assisted in numerous editorial tasks. At the University of Michigan John Scott and Tracy Berckmans of the Survey Research Center's Field Section and Joan Scheffler of the Coding Section played essential roles. Much of the credit for seeing the survey work through to its successful completion goes to Leigh Stelzer (now of the State University of New York at Albany).

Once the manuscript was semi-complete, we profited from the criticism of Martin Burlingame (National Institute of Education), Kenneth Prewitt (University of Chicago), Lawrence Pierce (University of Oregon), Michael Kirst (Stanford University), Neil Sullivan (California State University, Long Beach), and Heinz Eulau (Stanford University). Max Abbott, Director of the University of Oregon's Center for the Advanced Study of Educational Administration, spent far more hours than he should have listening to us develop our arguments, and reacting to our various drafts.

Our intellectual debt to the principal investigators of the California Bay Area City Council Study, Heinz Eulau and Kenneth Prewitt, will be obvious to readers of the book.

Amanda Zeigler helped her father.

In dedicating this book to the memory of David W. Minar, we seek to acknowledge the contributions of one of the pioneers in the field of education and politics. Again, our intellectual debt will be apparent.

Chapter 1

The Politics of

Local School Systems

Schools are political entities. Unfortunately, they have not been so regarded until
recently. True, the political impact of schools as socializing agents has been the
subject of considerable study in the last few years. Controversial educational issues
such as school desegregation and teacher militancy have also attracted some attention. However, the *governmental* aspects of school systems have been only inciden-
tal to these investigations. Occasionally one may encounter a case study or other
investigation of limited scope which approaches school district government
as a political process, but even these are few and far between. Rarer yet is the
study that inquires how and for what ends school systems are governed.[1] Such
unconcern with governance would not be especially remarkable except for the
unusually high salience attached to schools. To our knowledge, no one bemoans
the lack of systematic analysis of mosquito abatement districts! Schools, however,
generate heated intellectual and popular controversy. Critics such as Silberman
describe classrooms as virtual prisons and call for a remaking of American education.
More radical assailants, including Illich, want to abolish rather than remake schools.
Previously, Admiral Rickover blamed schools for sputnik and almost single-
handedly launched us into an era of new math, physics, social studies, and so
forth. Most recently, Jencks asserted that schools have no effect on one's income,
and therefore are ineffective agents of social change.[2] He was answered by an
irate educational establishment.

Yet, when the content of the charges and countercharges are examined,
the fact is that no one has systematically analyzed the *governing* of American
schools. For example, Silberman's treatment contains no mention of school

1

boards, the bodies legally charged with making authoritative decisions. If there is a crisis in American education, then the governors are partially responsible. Who governs American education to what end? Our study, an empirical examination of a representative national sample of school districts, does not pretend to offer definitive answers. We hope, however, that a systematic presentation of the findings will shed some light into one of the darkest areas of American politics: school districts.

In 1972 there were 15,780 school districts under the formal responsibility of approximately 90,000 board members. The services boards provide and the moneys they expend make them one of the most important classes of public bodies in the nation. In terms of formal governmental organizations and officials the school districts had one-fifth of the 78,268 units of local government in 1972.[3] When the singular functions of school systems, the salience of education to parents and children, and the large investment of financial resources are considered, there is little reason to doubt the political significance of school systems. For these reasons one would expect to find numerous political studies of school district government; yet this is far from the case.

If systematic studies of educational decision making are lacking, it is because political scientists have traditionally directed their attention toward the more obviously "political" institutions of society, for example, legislatures, courts, and political parties. In doing so they have merely reflected a more basic and pervasive tendency in this country to depoliticize education — a tendency to place school systems beyond the political sphere. Since the reform movement of the late nineteenth and early twentieth centuries which attacked governmental corruption, boss-run urban political machines, and other evils associated with local partisan politics, the prevalent attitude has been that public school systems should be sheltered from the contaminating influences of politics.

To understand more fully why schools have been singled out from the many public service institutions operated by local government for such special treatment, it is necessary to examine the unique place public education occupies in the American mind. Perhaps no single word better describes the American attitude toward education than *reverence*. Education has been the means to realize the American Dream. Not only does the school provide the knowledge necessary for success, but also it teaches discipline, the value of hard work, and patriotism — all values intimately related to The Dream. Moreover, the public school provides these things in equal measures for all. It not only transmits the democratic creed, but also is a product of that creed. The public school system, as Martin has stated, is "widely regarded as the prime exemplar and the chief defender of democracy."[4] Thus the school system has taken on a unique, sacred quality in popular mythology which sets it apart from other governmental activities. Since education is attributed reverence, reformers naturally seek to protect it from the "selfish aims and corrupt tactics of the politician."[5] Professional educators, as we shall see, have sought to perpetuate both the special status of the school and its isolation from the political system.

Motivated by a laudable concern for the integrity of education, reformers throughout the country succeeded in achieving a degree of formal independence for the school system from the broader political system. Educating America's youth was much too sacred a rite to risk its perversion through practices which reformers believed characterize the world of politics. In a sense, the educational product was politically neutral, independent of partisan considerations and superior to them. At the individual level education provided members of each successive generation with the necessary tools to realize their full potential. It did so in an egalitarian fashion — by providing everyone access to these tools. Providing these tools is not a political function in the common sense of the term. Also, the school was one of the dominant agents for socializing individuals — for indoctrinating them with the values, myths, and ethics of American democracy. Thus from this perspective also, the task of public education could not afford to be subverted by the corruptive influence of politics.

The reformers had great success in removing old-style politics from the public school system. The two aspects of educational government which are most susceptible to political influence — personnel selection procedures and financing — have been made structurally independent of other local governmental units in most instances. Not only has separation protected educational government from the schemes of political power holders, but also it made members of the academic community regard educational government as apolitical. One objective of the present study is to probe the effects of such de jure separation, in order to evaluate the qualitative impact of depoliticization upon educational governance. Control of school systems has become the special province of professional educators and a handful of interested laymen, and the study of educational government has become concentrated in schools of education. Until recently political scientists have appeared so persuaded by reformers' arguments to keep schools separate from politics that they have virtually ignored educational government as an appropriate object of study.

We should not view educational government in a politically antiseptic manner. Martin captured the sense in which the term "politics" had meaning for the early reformers — a sense that remains popular among many educators today:

> *One senses that the politics anathematized by the schoolmen is that of the big-city machine of yesterday, whose ghost continues to haunt municipal democracy long after death has departed the archetype. This is to perceive politics in the worst [sense] . . . . ; it is, moreover, to give currency to standards of public morality long since discredited and by now almost universally rejected. The habit of thought among schoolmen which places school politics at one level and urban politics on another and lower level is deserving of careful appraisal.*[6]

If politics is construed in terms other than the sordid exercise of partisan power which reformers and schoolmen rebel against, it is necessary to examine an alternative construction and to relate it to educational government. One of the first political scientists to undertake this task was Eliot, who, in 1959, observed:

> *Surely it is high time to stop being frightened by a word. Politics includes the making of governmental decisions, and the effort or struggle to gain or keep the power to make those decisions. Public schools are part of government. They are political entities. They are a fit subject for study by political scientists.*[7]

He went on to appeal for:

> *Analysis not only in terms of political institutions . . . . but in terms of voting behavior, ideological predispositions, the clash of interests, decision making, and the impact of individuals and organizations on nation-wide trends in educational policy.*[8]

The past decade of student protests, teacher strikes, and taxpayer revolts has thrown the schools into political focus. As one student of educational administration observed:

> *We "educationalists" find it most amusing to observe the contemporary discovery of local school systems by political and social scientists. It is as if thirty-five thousand local units of government have popped up unexpectedly.*[9]

In the years since Eliot issued his plea, social scientists have indeed begun to focus attention on the politics of public education.[10] However, the subject matter is so vast and has been so long ignored that more time and additional investigation is necessary if the true quality of educational governance is to be understood. The present study is undertaken to help attain this objective.

POLICY LEADERSHIP AND DEMOCRATIC THEORY

Although the school board has uncontested formal authority over local educational systems, evidence (offered below) indicates that the leadership over educational policy rests as much or more with the superintendent. This disparity between authority and leadership violates a fundamental principle of democratic institutions. Democratic theory stipulates that a representative body must be responsible to the public for decisions that emanate from the representatives. Representatives may formally delegate their authority to other political actors. When they do so, the recipients of formal authority become accountable for their decisions. Moreover, guidelines are normally included which prescribe certain limits and norms for the decision-making activities of the delegate.

The situation encountered when policy leadership becomes divorced from authority is another matter. No guidelines are imposed on the effective decision maker by the legitimate authority, nor is the de facto policy leader necessarily responsible to the public. In other words, informal delegation of authority does not necessarily carry with it the concomitant obligation of accountability. Instead of the ideal flow of control from the public to its surrogate to the object of control, the process is reversed. When the leader establishes policy, it is legitimized by the formal authority and subsequently "sold" to the public. It is this informal process which students of educational government have observed in local school districts. This disparity between theory and practice is not limited to school government; similar incongruities between authority and leadership are found in a variety of political subsystems at all levels. Since the conditions that spawn such situations in noneducational subsystems parallel those within local educational governments, the results of the present investigation will benefit the more general study of political institutions. It has been suggested, for instance, that the school board-superintendent relationship is similar to the connection between the city manager and the city council.[11] Other analogous relationships exist between a legislative committee and the principal interests within its scope of authority and between federal regulatory agencies and their "client" industries.

Such deceptively simple comparisons, however, assume that since the death of the separation of education and politics has been declared, the task is to analyze educational decision making with the traditional concepts of political science. Let us examine one example. A key concept of political science is "responsiveness." As Eulau and Prewitt in their exhaustive study of city councils have written:

> *"For, in a democracy, the degree to which the governors are responsive to the preferences of the governed is the* sine qua non *of whether democracy in fact exists."*[12]

Stated more dramatically, Dahl refers to control of leaders (or response *by* leaders) as the "first problem of politics."[13] The relation of rulers to the ruled has provided the central focus of political research since antiquity. The literature of political science abounds with empirical and theoretical formulations of the problem of representation and control.

A flourishing concern is *not* shared by students of the history of educational administration. As Wirt and Kirst convincingly demonstrate in their review of the literature, the conventional wisdom of educational administration is concerned with "centralization, expertise, professionalization, non political control, and efficiency."[14] Indeed, the bulk of the thrust against bureaucracy, including demands for "community participation," is scarcely a decade old. The new demands for responsive schools may be entirely compatible with the ideology of professionalization and expertise. Schumpeter has argued that an independent and politically powerful bureaucracy, rather than being detrimental, is essential to

democracy.[15] However, Dahl is more accurate when he asserts that vigorous
political competition is an essential condition of polyarchy. Since polyarchy,
control of leaders, is a political, representational process, and since political
activity in the narrow sense has traditionally been regarded as evil by theorists and
practitioners of educational administration, it is not surprising that concern for
the responsiveness of schools is recent.

There is a schizophrenic nature to theories of educational administration.
On one hand, there is the traditional deference toward the "will of the people"
that is expected in a larger social milieu that is institutionally democratic. On the
other hand, there is the overpowering force of professionalism, which by its nature
asserts the right of the professional to tell the client the appropriate course of
action. School administrators, like city managers and other bureaucrats, believe
they are professional. They have a technology which enables them to perform
a specified task satisfactorily. Professional relationships involve a substantial
atmosphere of authority, producing inherent conflicting tendencies in a democratic society.[16]

At the risk of oversimplification, the thrust of standard political theory is
that, even though a balance between efficiency and responsiveness must be maintained, the ultimate policy initiative *should* rest with the elected representative
bodies.[17] The failure of democratic institutions to control bureaucratic expertise
has alarmed social critics from Galbraith to Roszak.[18]

Similar concern has only recently come to the attention of educationalists.
Is this because educationalists are evil tyrants? Hardly. The fact is that problems
of responsiveness are more complex, or at least different, in educational decision
making than they are in other arenas. Consider, for example, the following lament:
"I am now convinced that very much of what has happened in American education
since 1900 can be explained on the basis of the extreme vulnerability of our
schools to public criticism and pressure . . . this is an inadequate and inappropriate
basis for establishing sound educational policy."[19] The author is stating an obvious
truth: Participation by laymen in "professional" matters often increases decision
costs and decreases decision efficiency. There is certainly no assumption here that
administration, even indirectly, should be subject to representative constraints.
We are not, of course, suggesting that such views are even an approximation of
unanimity on the part of administrators. What we *are* suggesting is that schools
really *are* different.

Eulau and Prewitt, as we have noted previously, regard the responsive
and non-responsive behavior of city council as central to their explorations.[20] Can
we say the same for school boards? Are city councils an appropriate model upon
which to base an analysis of school governance? Consider the nature of a city
council, a state legislature or any political-representative body. Who are the clients
of the city council? Blau and Scott refer to governing bodies as "commonweal
associations," meaning that the members (citizens) are the prime beneficiaries. It is
within the confines of such mutual benefit associations that several classic concerns
of political science have developed. "The iron law of oligarchy" and "the first

problem of politics are key examples."[21] A distinctive characteristic of a common-weal organization is *that the public at large is the prime beneficiary*. As a corollary to being the prime beneficiary the public is assumed to possess the means of con-trolling the ends served by these institutions.

Political scientists have too readily assumed that schools are common-weal organizations. According to Blau and Scott, they are not. Schools are *service* organizations:

> *A service organization has been defined as one whose prime beneficiary is the part of the public in direct contact with the organization, with whom and on whom its members work – in short, an organization whose basic function is to serve clients. Included in this category are social work agencies, hospitals, schools, legal aid societies, and mental health clinics. The crucial problems of these organizations center around providing professional services. The welfare of the client is presumed to be the chief concern of service organizations.*[22]

Clearly implied is the assumption that the client does not know what will best serve his interest. A basic distinction between a commonweal organization and a service organization concerns the best judge of clients' interest. In a com-monweal organization members or clients are qualified, but in a service organization members are not. Although the governors of a commonweal organization may legitimately submit to the wishes of their constituents, that is, become delegates, professionals are viewed by their peers with disfavor when they thereby become "captives" of the clientele.

It is apparent that schools are not pure service organizations. Schools are expected to provide public "goods," that is, an educated citizenry which provides benefit to the community in addition to the client. The struggle between the professional and lay client, the "deprofessionalization process" as Eulau calls it, extends to nominal commonweal organizations.[23] Thus the struggle over lay control of police departments is an example of efforts to achieve the trappings of a commonweal institution for an organization which is threatened by them.[24]

One might argue that police departments are more suited to lay control than schools are, and that we should not examine the responsiveness of schools, but rather abolish school boards and let the experts educate the youth. Most European countries have operated educational systems on exactly this premise. An apt comparison is the English education system:

> *This insulation [from social pressure] is not a matter of accident. From 1870 to 1902, in England and Wales, each area had its own school board, providing schools and schooling according to the regulations of a Central Education Department but with a considerable amount of freedom. The Education Act of 1902 absolished these school boards, which numbered several thousands, and brought education within the scope*

of the all-purpose local government bodies that have since served as local education authorities. There was a whole complex of reasons for abolishing the school boards – educational, administrative, and legal – but one pronounced notice was the desire to 'insulate' the schools from popular pressure at the local level. Conservative, Labour and Liberal parties alike have consistently held to the view that the control of education and methods of instruction are not matters for popular debate and decision, but should be left in the hands of teachers themselves and of other professional educators.[25]

Let us assume that such a view, although a part of the appeals to abolish school boards, is not conducive to the American culture. This effort appeared in this country at the same time as it did in England, but it failed. The point is that there is no consensus regarding the appropriate role of polyarchy in the governance of education.

The problem is further compounded by the unique clientele of schools, the students. Students are not presumed competent to participate in the larger commonweal until they have achieved an age which normally places them well beyond the domain of public schools. Any dimension of democracy or suffrage routinely eliminates youth as a legitimate component of the public in whose name democracies govern. "But who are the people? . . . After a long period of wavering and uncertainty, our answer . . . is fixed and firm . . . and no one is thought of as excluded from a voice in ruling *except the very young*, the insane and feebleminded, felons, and transients or aliens."[26] Thus the most direct clients of schools, those who are the targets of professional skills, are presumed incompetent. To overstate the case, an organization comparable to the school is the mental hospital. Where are the cries for community control of mental hospitals?

Obviously the clientele of education must be extended to include the parents of those who absorb the services of the school, and optimally, to the entire community, or the notion of a school as a commonweal institution becomes absurd. If we assume that the services of schools have value only to the immediate clients who are incompetent to judge what is best, then the most responsive educational systems will be those unhindered by the intrusion of demands from the community. Such a notion is by no means far-fetched or untried. Hitler, Lenin, or any number of practitioners of totalitarianism, assumed that elections interfered with their more accurate perception of the needs of their clients. Even overtly authoritarian commonweal systems believe they are "acting in the interest of the represented in a manner responsive to them" and perhaps they are.[27] In the case of Lenin, one can argue that although he might not have contested an election successfully, his long range view of Russian society is now a reasonably consensual one.

When the same problem is encountered in educational decision making, the proponents of community control believe that professional assessments of the ends (and frequently the means) of education should be subordinate to the will of "the people" which is transmitted to professionals by a local board with significant authority over curriculum, personnel, and finances. The demands for community control come largely from blacks and liberal intellectuals. Liberal intellectuals assume that community control and innovative education are part of the same reform package. In fact, there is evidence that ghetto clients prefer a more traditional, authoritarian school than students currently experience.[28] Whether "progressive" or "traditional" education is better is not a relevant topic for this book, but we should note that what the public wants from education is somewhat different than what the professionals strive to provide. A redistribution of influence will involve a shift in the method and content of education.

We do not pretend to provide easy solutions to these kinds of problems. We *do* intend to adopt the perspective of political scientists. We assume that school governance, whatever its attendant ancillary and primary functions, is a set of behaviors that should be appropriately examined by the traditional yardsticks of democratic theory. We agree with Bidwell that the division of labor between board and superintendent is a neglected and crucial area of research. We intend to examine "attempts by superintendents or board members to mobilize power resources within the school system or in its environment."[29] However, our concern is equally concentrated upon relationships between the board and the community which it serves because the prescriptions for democratic theory are as salient and critical in that area as in the area of board-superintendent interaction. These relationships will be considered with respect to the selection of school district governors and the linkage mechanisms between them and their constituents.

PLACING THE PROBLEM IN PERSPECTIVE

One of the earliest studies of educational government conducted by social scientists was undertaken by Gross and his colleagues during the mid-1950s.[30] They administered a questionnaire to a selected sample of school superintendents and their school boards in Massachusetts in order to explore their attitudes, perceptions, and role orientations. This investigation represents a milestone in the field of educational research, since it was the first widely disseminated study of educational government which employed concepts and techniques from social science. The weak points of the study include the limited scope of questions to which it was addressed and the restricted, single-state sample which limited the generalizability of its findings. Nevertheless, the insights it provided were substantial, and it bridged the gap between the social sciences and educational inquiry.

Although there is cause for optimism since the political dynamics involved in the control of education have emerged as salient objects of interest for scholars, it is unwarranted to assume that we now "know about" the politics of education in this country. A paradigm into which every school district in America could be placed would immediately make apparent all of the social and political forces which affect the control of public educational institutions. An account of the various relationships among the myriad actors at local, state, and federal levels and an account of the variations in the structural relationships among the formal institutions of government and the informal centers of power are needed to provide such a descriptive framework. Such an undertaking would be not only Herculean, but also would result in a decidedly unparsimonious theory of educational control. Understandably, therefore, those who have attacked questions pertaining to educational government have confined the breadth of their discourse to one or another segment of that whole.

Although this division of labor is a legitimate and probably a necessary way of approaching a more complete understanding of the subject, it does raise an additional, unresolved problem — how do all of the discrete pieces of information and the various subareas of investigation fit together? Unless it is theoretically possible to link the findings of the highest quality of research concerning the political control of education to the product of that control, the classroom student, then the major benefits of the research are lost. And from the standpoint of *educational* scholarship, the research represents little more than an academic exercise.

Each piece of investigative scholarship does not need to trace its findings through the entire system of public education in order to ascertain their effects on classroom behavior. By analogy, it would be unrealistic to demand that scholars who analyze the decision-making process in the U.S. House of Representatives Education and Labor Committee not only explain the forces that affect committee decisions but also explicitly relate thoese decisions to classroom situations, accounting for all of the intervening factors that affect them between the committee room and the school house. Those who read the study of committee decision making and have a scholarly interest in the quality of public education, however, should be equipped to view the findings from a perspective tempered by an understanding of the types of factors that will ultimately have an effect on the translation of committee outputs into school outputs.

Policy Levels

In order to develop such a perspective it is necessary to recognize the various levels at which educational policies are made, to identify the numerous actors and institutions which affect the implementation of such policies, and to apply ourselves to the task of analyzing the political dynamics of these centers of educational power. The conceptualization of the federal, state, district, school, and classroom policy-making levels, as indicated in Figure 1–1, gives a perspective which encompasses the range of conceivable initiators of policy, allows for analysis of intermediate effects, and maintains the integrity of the object level of educational policies — the classroom. Moreover, this conceptualization can serve as a guide for comparative research concerning educational government, since the limits of applicability of any study are readily ascertained. Gross's study, for example, fits into the district level of analysis, since it focused on district school boards and

FIGURE 1-1
Levels of Educational Policy Analysis

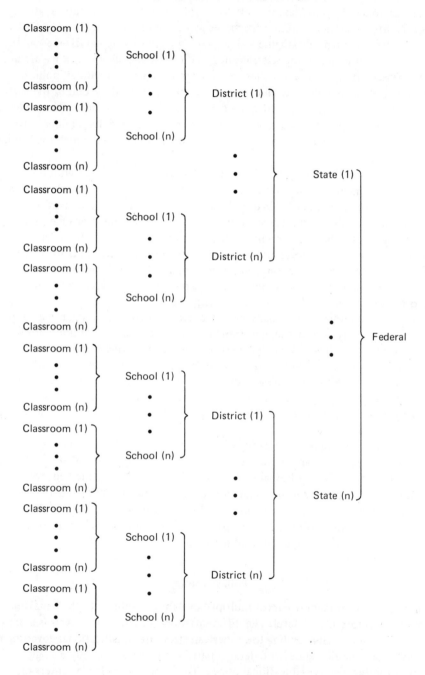

superintendents. Because the study was limited to districts within one state, however, variations in observable behavior owing to the peculiarities of environmental factors unique to Massachusetts cannot be ascertained. Therefore, attempts to generalize to districts within other states would be unwarranted.

Methodologically, Figure 1-1 provides a logic for comparative research. Descriptively, it indicates the relationships of the various policy levels. We are not, however, attempting to present a model of centralized control with all policies originating at the federal level and trickling down through the system to the classroom level, since a variety of educational policies originate at each of the five levels. What we convey in this figure is the number of control points that are operative between the level at which a policy is enunciated and the level at which that policy affects students.

Policies which are felt in local schools may have originated within the federal government. Federal grants for innovative programs, for example, encourage schools to adopt particular kinds of policies in order to share in the distribution of grant moneys. Similarly, federal court school integration decisions have had substantial impact. State governments, too, participate in educational decision making. Although procedures differ from state to state, requirements for teacher certification, textbook selection, and curriculum are often determined by state boards of education. Moreover, between 20 percent and 50 percent of local expenditures are financed by the state legislatures.

Because there are so many policy levels, the first task confronting anyone who plans to study educational government is the establishment of limits to the investigation. It is obvious that some levels of decision making will have to be eliminated from investigation. Our choice was to focus on the level at which most of the decisions with immediate and practical effects on the quality of the educational programs of public schools are made. Despite evidence pointing toward growing state and federal involvement, immediate control over school policies still resides at the district level.

Although we hear increasing demands for decentralization and community control, American schools in contrast with those of other Western nations are decentralized. The traditional pattern of school governance emerged from a variety of diffuse historical trends including a weak state educational department with limited leadership for a very large number of local units. In spite of the decline in the number of districts, this pattern remains intact. We feel justified, therefore, in concentrating upon local school districts.

Policy Actors

Educational government occurs at multiple levels and is subject to the behavior of multiple actors at each level. The differentiation of hierarchical levels is merely the initial step in understanding the American structure of educational government, for no school, district, state, or federal department is subject to only a single source of influence over educational policy. There may be multiple centers of formal authority. At the state level, we find the legislature, the chief executive, the board of education, the superintendent of public instruction, and even the judiciary exerting varying degrees of control over educational policy. At the district level, the local board and the district superintendent are involved in the policy-making process. Within each school there is the principal who must interpret and execute district policy. Finally, at the classroom level, the teacher formulates educational policy within the framework of the guidelines handed down from above.

Although this cursory listing of actors who take part in educational decision making is formidable, it is far from comprehensive. It includes only the more obvious *formal* participants. Many other individuals and organizations exert indirect influence over educational policies at all levels. Teachers' organizations, for instance, have become increasingly militant in recent years, and as a result they have injected new demands and new participants into the educational political arena. Taxpayer organizations have also become more active and more influential during the past decade. When we add some of the more traditional groups and individuals who are interested in educational policies, including PTAs, city and county government officials, schools of education, and local informal power holders, the complexity of educational decision-making analysis becomes apparent.

Two points concerning the school board should be stressed. First, since the schools are intimately related in the popular view with democratic values, the school board serves as an affective symbol representing the popular value of local control of education. Parochialism has historically been as significant in understanding public attitudes toward education as any aspect of the educational culture of the nation, especially in small-town and rural America where the school and the community are integrated socially and culturally.[31] Alford's study of two rural school districts in California and Vidich and Bensman's classic study of a small town in the northeast both attest to this fact.[32] Localism is not confined to rural America. Masotti's case study of a suburban Chicago school district indicates how jealously suburban dwellers will defend the principle of local control.[33] Popular response to court-imposed busing in recent years has underscored this trend across the country. Reflection on the current demands for "neighborhood schools" in some of our larger cities shows that parochialism applies in those surroundings as well.

The importance of this attachment to local control from the standpoint of the present investigation is highlighted when we consider the second point to be made: the school board, whether appointed or elected, is the representative body through which local control is exercised. Although there normally may be widespread apathy concerning the bulk of board decisions or even hostility toward a particular board or board member, the local school board, as an abstract representative institution, typically enjoys a reservoir of latent support. As we shall see, the ability of an incumbent school board to mobilize this potential support has important consequences for the process of decision making within the district.

The local school board was initially conceived of as a representative institution through which the public could govern its schools. As school systems grew and issues became more complex, the resources of the lay school board were insufficient to cope with the variety of problems involved in the overall supervision of district schools. In the late nineteenth century, a new profession was born. The office of school district superintendent, a full-time administrative position, came into being. It was the superintendent's job to perform the day-to-day administrative and supervisory tasks that had become a burden to board members. Theoretically, his function was to implement the policies made by the school board. In practice, however, the superintendent eventually assumed much of the policy-making power of the school board in addition to his purely administrative duties.

Those who have studied the distribution of control over policy making in local educational systems typically place the superintendent in a crucial, perhaps dominant role.[34] Although he (virtually all are male) does not possess the formal authority to set school policy, he usually exercises considerable influence as the chief administrative officer for the district and as its ranking professional. The following observations illustrate the superintendent preponderance as viewed by scholars in recent years:

> *Superintendents have been making more of the major educational decisions year after year in the twentieth century.*[35]

> *School boards chiefly perform the function of* legitimizing *the policies of the school system to the community rather than* representing *the various segments of the community to the school administration, especially with regard to the educational program.*[36]

> *He [the superintendent] emerges as the servant who manipulates his board, selects his master, and educates them to their responsibilities.*[37]

Agreement on dominance by the superintendent may be high among scholars, but the bases upon which the conclusions are drawn suffer from a lack of systematic observation. One of our objectives, therefore, is to assess the extent to which school boards are dominated by their superintendents and to explore the factors which lead to variations.

Leadership in the present context is defined as the state of de facto dominance within a decision-making network of ordered relationships among two or more elements. Leadership pertains to pragmatic dominance, whereas authority relates to formal or de jure dominance. Nevertheless, to say that superintendents appear to be the key local leaders is merely to place educational decision making within the general context of most modern executive-legislative relationships. However, the astonishing power of the executive vis-à-vis congress does not relegate studies of legislative behavior to the role of trivia. Like congress, which rises up to strike strong blows for the separation of powers, school boards send unsuccessful superintendents packing. Alliances and feuds also develop between the superintendent's office and the school board. Finally, the rule of anticipated reactions undoubtedly guides superintendents in their dealings with the board.

Moreover, although the burden of day-to-day policy making has long since passed into the hands of professional educators, boards have traditionally continued to exercise influence in the areas of finances, physical structures, oversight of the superintendent's performance, and episodic crises in controversial areas. A lay board of education also has great symbolic importance. Even if boards never affected policy, the public's belief that they do is a key element in the impression that there is a democratic, representational process. Boards also serve a critical safety-valve function. When the constituency becomes disrupted, its members can seek redress through their representatives, even to the point of turning them out of office. Taking all of these factors into consideration, it is apparent that the study of school district governance must include the authoritative, representative body as well as the chief administrator and key influential.

Not only are these partners consistently the most visible actors in the policy-making process, but either or both of them must also give at least tacit consent to all policies except those decided by public referenda. They are not, however, the only participants, nor always the most important participants in setting educational policy. Wielders of influence and of power, and the range of individuals and organizations interested in educational policy, will vary from district to district and from issue to issue. The extent to which such interested parties are drawn into educational politics will affect the governing process, for as Schattschneider pointed out over a decade ago, "the contagiousness of conflict, the elasticity of its scope, and the fluidity of the involvement of people are the X factors in politics."[38] Accordingly, in our investigation we shall consider the behavior of organized interest groups and the mass public in order to evaluate their roles in educational governance.

Conceptual Levels and Measurement Techniques

Most of the data on which this study is based came from personal interviews conducted with national samples of school board members and superintendents. During the summer of 1968 we interviewed 490 board members and 82 superintendents distributed across 83 school districts. These interviews were supplemented in several ways. First, in order to speak with greater certainty about large city school districts we augmented these base samples with additional, shortened interviews with 91 board members and 12 superintendents located in 13 large city school districts. Second, much additional information was gathered about the political and socioeconomic characteristics of the districts from local sources and government publications. Finally, interviews with a portion of the mass public residing in the districts were utilized for the analysis of mass-elite congruence (Chapter 7). More details about the design and field work are presented in Appendix A.

Eulau, in distinguishing between the subject of inquiry and the object of inquiry, has pointed out that the two need not — and in some instances cannot — exist on the same analytic level.[39] He suggests that when one's object of inquiry is a collective decision-making body, there are irreducible properties of that body which cannot be analyzed merely by focusing upon the behavior of the individuals who compose it *at the individual level.* Although Eulau grants that it is "difficult if not impossible to observe the behavior of the group without observing the behavior of the individuals within the group,"[40] he argues for the employment of procedures which will permit inference from the subject unit (the individual) to the object unit (the collectivity). There are methodological pitfalls which confront the analyst in this procedure, for so little work has been done in this area, and few guidelines are established.[41]

Since most of our data were collected from individual school board members and school superintendents, evaluation of the school boards confronted us with precisely the type of situation that concerned Eulau. Our object of inquiry was a collective decision-making entity, whereas the subjects of inquiry were the individual persons who composed it. We had to transform individual data into board level variables for much of the present study, although in some chapters we use individual-level data where appropriate for purposes of analysis. The data aggregation method varied with the concept being measured. We used three basic techniques. When the individual level data were measured on nominal scales, conversion was done by computing the percent of board members in the different categories within each board. When data were ordinal or interval, one of two procedures was used. If theoretical interest was on a summarizing measure of central tendency, the arithmetic mean of member data was computed for each board. If, however, our interest was on the dispersion or heterogeneity that exists within the school board, then the variance of individual board member data was computed within each district.

One obvious problem that is inherent in such procedures stems from the relatively small, unequal numbers of board members in the various districts. Boards in our sample range in size from three to fifteen members. Although the mathematical properties of the mean render it comparable across categories of unequal size, the same cannot be said of a percentage figure or variance, since each has certain limits on the values it may attain when based on a small number of cases. Neither of the latter statistics is truly continuous or directly comparable for boards of unequal size. We regret this mathematical fact of life, but see no way of overcoming it. We consider it more desirable to use imperfect indicators of interesting concepts than to deny ourselves their use. In this we agree with Tukey, who observed, "Far better an approximate answer to the right question, which is often vague, than an exact answer to the wrong question, which can always be made precise."[42]

Moreover, the board-level measures which we have employed constitute quasi-interval scales. Thus they lend themselves to a wide variety of relatively powerful analytic techniques. The subjective confidence in the findings that emerge from such analyses is affected by measurement imprecision. However, rigorous adherence to statistical and mathematical canons, as it has been argued, occasionally takes a back seat to explanatory richness, if social science is to progress. Furthermore, although transformation of individual data to within group percentages and variance figures does not produce continuous interval scales when the groups are small, the results which occur are monotonic. Labovitz has argued persuasively that the treatment of such scales as if they were continuous interval scales results in minimal distortion and permits greater statistical interpretability.[43] We believe that our aggregating techniques are defensible on the grounds that they hold the promise of providing heuristic insights into political relationships that would otherwise remain obscure.

Our approach to the study materials also departs from some other common approaches since it puts emphasis on structural and institutional factors as the independent and intervening variables in accounting for how school districts are governed. During the course of the interviews we asked a great number of questions which tapped board member and superintendent goals, values, and attitudes. Many of these could be introduced to "explain" how board members interact with the community and the superintendent. For example, the board member's conception of the role of board member might be used to account for levels of opposition to the superintendent. Similarly, expressions of educational philosophy might be employed to account for the level of agreement between board members and constituents.

Certainly such variables might be very instrumental in our analysis. Yet for the most part we have eschewed their use. One reason for this decision is the inability to do everything in one place. Another reason is the danger of developing circular relationships, of relating "attitudes to attitudes" without sufficient attention to the antecedents and the behavioral consequences of attitudes. The most important reason is our conviction, born out of a search of the literature, that institutions and structures are powerful determinants of local elite behavior. Indeed, they may be so powerful that they override personal characteristics. This effect can happen in two ways. First, certain institutions and structures offer different sorts of elite actors. The successful board aspirant in a semirural district in the Plains area is likely to be of a different stripe than his counterpart in a cosmopolitan Eastern city. In the second place, once in office these same institutions and structures constrain the behavior of elite actors. For example, it is unlikely that board members gaining office in at-large elections will have the same constituency in mind as those elected on a ward basis.

It is probable, of course, that the same values and attitudes will be differentially engaged depending upon the institutional and structural matrix; conversely, the latter will have differential consequences depending upon the value and attitudinal configuration of elite actors. Undertaking such a combinatorial approach to the data is very tempting, but in the interest of covering a broad range of substantive questions we have decided against that rich approach.

We are interested in four types of institutions and structures as they impinge on school governance. The specific indicators are spelled out as they are introduced into the analysis. For the present, however, we may indicate their general parameters. The first type consist of properties inherent in locational factors. Our understanding of local politics in general and school politics in particular led us to hypothesize that the level of social complexity embodied in larger, more urban places yields a different set of vectors and constraints than the level found in smaller, less urban locales. We have employed spatial, demographic variables (including region), in the full realization that they are at best summary variables for a host of historical and contemporary forces operative in geographically-bound areas.

A second set of institutional-structural factors is explicitly political. We were drawn initially to these as a result of trying to assess the contemporary consequences of the political reforms which swept public education after the turn of the century and which still have a powerful (though varying) grip on school governance. Based on research in other domains of politics, we also felt that additional political characteristics of school districts would have a bearing on governance. Indeed, such variables as the quantity and quality of competition for office appeared significant enough to require their own explanation.

A third set of institutional-structural factors consists of opinion and behavior extant in the publics embraced by the school districts. In this area we refer to such phenomena as levels of public quiescence, support for district policies, the level and tension of organized group activity, and issue preferences on the part of the public. We believe that such structures of behavior and opinion not only have the capacity to influence directly the conduct of school governance, but also mark the limits within which board members and superintendents can act.

A final set of behavioral structures and patterns are reflected in the actions of boards and superintendents. Although such behaviors may not have quite the regularity and uniformity to merit the designation of "structures," we shall apply that term. We refer primarily to modes of behavior, rather than attitudes, which constitute settings or constraints for other behaviors and value expressions. For example, some superintendents seek more public support than do others. A key question for us is is this behavioral variation relfected in differing levels of opposition to the superintendent on the part of the board?

AN OVERVIEW OF THE BOOK

Our central focus will be on the school board as the authoritative and representative political body in the school system. As the foregoing discussion has suggested, we are interested in three components of school district governance from the lay board's perspective. Simply stated they are: (1) how are the authoritative governors selected? (2) how do the governors relate to those being governed? and (3) how do the governors confront the massive, professional side of district governance as represented in the office of the superintendent? These questions form the basis for the three major parts of the book. We attempt to build upon what we have learned in answering one question as we move on to a consideration of the next. Thus each part stands alone but also provides necessary background for succeeding sections.

Part I — Selection to the Board

In one sense governance begins with the processes by which the governors acquire their positions. Our concerns with selection are two-fold. First, there are widely held criteria about how leaders should be selected. One of our objectives is to see how successfully some of those criteria are met. A second reason for considering the selection process is that the means by which office is attained is hypothesized to have some bearing on the conduct of office. Consequently Part I will also lay the groundwork for later discussion. The major topics taken up include the social and political backgrounds of board members, the conditions which provide for sorting out the few leaders from the many potential ones, the tension level of the electoral process, and the electoral process, and the electoral consequence of the political reforms beginning at the turn of the century.

Part II — Linkages between Boards and Citizens

From the process of recruitment our inquiry extends in the second phase to a consideration of how boards interact with the community. Questions lying at the heart of representative theories of democracy are addressed in this part. We will present three components of analysis: how board members approach the question of political responsiveness, how various publics influence policy through interest groups, and how accurately the preferences and perceptions of constituents are reflected in the values of school boards. The first two questions are highlighted by examining the effects of social complexity, political structures, and public opinion upon the response posture of boards. The final question is illuminated by the presentation of views drawn from rank and file citizens located within several districts.

Part III — Conflict and Cooperation between Boards and Superintendents

In the final portion of the book we will shift from a treatment of how the board interacts with the community to an analysis of how the board confronts the super-intendent. The power which has evolved in the office of the superintendency raises serious questions about the policy-making role of the lay board. Our perspective will be that the superintendent and the board are engaged in a contest for influence. We will take as indicators of the board's assertive role the prevalence of opposition to the superintendent and the likelihood of prevailing against him. We will seek to isolate those factors which heighten board resistance, paying special attention to the social and political features of the district introduced previously. In addition we will assess the effects of superintendent activism and board cohesion. The charac-teristics of the superintendent's opponents will be scrutinized in some detail and the controversial area of race relations will be given special attention within the framework of board-superintendent interaction.

NOTES

1. Michael W. Kirst and Edith K. Mosher, "Politics of Education," *Review of Educational Research*, 39 (December, 1969), pp. 623–640; W.W. Charters, Jr., *A Bibliography of Empirical Studies of School Boards* (Eugene, Oregon: Center for the Advanced Study of Educational Administration, University of Oregon, 1968).

2. See Charles Silberman, *Crisis in the Classroom: The Remaking of American Education* (New York: Random House, 1970); Ivan Illich, *De-Schooling Society* (New York: Harper and Row, 1971); Hyman Rickover, *Education and Freedom* (New York: Dutton, 1959); and Christopher Jencks, *et. al., Inequality: A Reassessment of the Effect of Family and Schooling in America* (New York: Basic Books, 1972).

3. U.S. Bureau of the Census, "Small Area Data Notes," Vol. 8, No. 5 (Washington, D.C., May, 1973).

4. Roscoe C. Martin, "School Government," *Governing Education: A Reader on Politics, Power, and Public School Policy*, ed. Alan Rosenthal (Garden City, N.Y.: Anchor Books, 1969), p. 274.

5. Robert H. Salisbury, "Schools and Politics in the Big City," *Harvard Educational Review*, 37 (Summer, 1967), p. 414.

6. Martin, *op. cit.*, p. 270.

7. Thomas H. Eliot, "Toward an Understanding of Public School Politics," *American Political Science Review*, 52 (December, 1959), p. 1035.

8. *Ibid.*, p. 1036.

9. Lavern L. Cunningham, "Community Power: Implications for Education," *The Politics of Education in the Local Community*, eds. Robert S. Cahill and Stephen P. Hencley (Danville, Ill.: Interstate Printers and Publishers, 1964), p. 33.

10. Among early works dealing with the local level see David W. Minar, *Educational Decision-Making in Suburban Communities*, Cooperative Research Project No. 2440, Research sponsored by the U.S. Office of Education (Evanston, Ill.: Northwestern University Press, 1966); and William Bloomberg, Jr. and Morris Sunshine, *Suburban Power Structures and Public Education* (Syracuse, N.Y.: Syracuse University Press, 1963).

11. Reuben Joseph Snow, "Local Experts: Their Roles as Conflict Managers in Municipal and Educational Government: A Comparative Assessment of the Implications of Social Contexts upon the Roles of City Managers and School Superintendents" (Ph.D. dissertation, Northwestern University, 1966). See also Martin, *op. cit.*, p. 62.

12. Heinz Eulau and Kenneth Prewitt, *Labyrinths of Democracy: Adaptations, Linkages, Representation, and Policies in Urban Politics* (Indianapolis: Bobbs-Merrill, 1973), p. 24.

13. Robert A. Dahl and Charles E. Lindblom, *Politics, Economics, and Welfare* (New York: Harper and Row, 1953), p. 273.

14. Frederick M. Wirt and Michael W. Kirst, *The Political Web of American Schools* (Boston: Little, Brown, 1972), p. 7.

15. Joseph A. Schumpeter, *Capitalism, Socialism, and Democracy* (New York: Harper and Row, 1942), p. 255.

16. Heinz Eulau, "Skill Revolution and Consultative Commonwealth," *American Political Science Review*, 67 (March, 1973), p. 176.

17. James Q. Wilson, "The Bureaucracy Problem," *The Public Interest* (Winter, 1967), pp. 3–9.

18. John K. Galbraith, *The New Industrial State* (New York: New American Library, 1965), and Theodore Roszak, *Where the Wasteland Ends* (New York: Doubleday, 1972).

19. Raymond E. Callahan, *Education and the Cult of Efficiency* (Chicago: University of Chicago Press, 1962).

20. Eulau and Prewitt, *op. cit.*, p. 426.

21. Peter M. Blau and W. Richard Scott, *Formal Organizations* (San Francisco: Chandler, 1962), p. 45.

22. *Ibid.*, p. 51.

23. Eulau, *op. cit.*, p. 178.

24. James Q. Wilson, *Varieties of Police Behavior* (Cambridge: Harvard University Press, 1968), pp. 289–290.

25. George Baron and Asher Tropp, "Teachers in England and America," *Education, Economy, and Society*, eds. A.H. Halsey, Jean Floud, and C. Arnold Anderson (New York: Free Press, 1961), p. 547.

26. Harry K. Givertz, *Democracy and Elitism* (New York: Charter Scribners, 1967), p. 4. (Emphasis added.)

27. Hannah Pitkin, *The Concept of Representation* (Berkeley: University of California Press, 1967), p. 209.

28. Jeffrey A. Roffel, "Responsiveness in Urban Schools: A Study of School System Adaptation to Parental Preferences in an Urban Environment," (Ph.D. dissertation, MIT, 1972).

29. Charles Bidwell, "The School as a Formal Organization," *Handbook of Organizations*, ed. James G. March (Chicago: Rand McNally, 1965), p. 996.

30. Neal Gross, *Who Runs Our Schools?* (New York: Wiley, 1958); and Neal Gross, Ward S. Mason, and Alexander W. McEachern, *Explorations in Role Analysis: Studies of the School Superintendency Role* (New York: Wiley, 1958).

31. Charles E. Bidwell, *op. cit.*, p. 1010.

32. Robert R. Alford, "School District Reorganization and Community Integration," *Harvard Educational Review*, 30 (Fall, 1960), pp. 350–371; Arthur J. Vidich and Joseph Bensman, *Small Town in Mass Society: Class, Power, and Religion in a Rural Community* (Princeton: Princeton University Press, 1958).

33. Louis Masotti, *Education and Politics in Suburbia: The New Trier Experience* (Cleveland: Western Reserve University Press, 1967).

34. Two such scholars are Raymond E. Callahan in "The History of the Fight to Control Policy in Public Education," *Struggle for Power in Education*, ed. Frank W. Lutz and Joseph J. Azzarelli (New York: The Center for Applied Research in Education, Inc., 1966), pp. 16–34, and Norman D. Kerr, "The School

Board as an Agency of Legitimation," *Sociology of Education*, 38 (Fall, 1964), p. 35.

    35. Callahan, *op. cit.*, p. 30.

    36. Kerr, *op. cit.*, p. 35.

    37. Laurence Iannaccone and Frank W. Lutz, *Politics, Power, and Policy: The Governing of Local School Districts* (Columbus, Ohio: Charles F. Merrill, 1970), p. 231.

    38. E. E. Schattschneider, *The Semisovereign People: A Realist's View of Democracy in America* (New York: Holt, Rinehart, and Winston, 1960), p. 3.

    39. Heinz Eulau, *Micro-Macro Political Analysis: Accents of Inquiry* (Chicago: Aldine, 1969), pp. 8–16.

    40. *Ibid.*, p. 6.

    41. Among recent publications which have employed this mode of analysis are Kenneth Prewitt and Heinz Eulau, "Political Matrix and Political Representation: Prolegomenon to a New Departure from an Old Problem," *American Political Science Review*, 63 (June, 1969), pp. 427–441, and Heinz Eulau and Robert Eyestone, "Policy Maps of City Councils and Policy Outcomes: A Developmental Analysis," *American Political Science Review*, 62 (March, 1968), pp. 124–143. The major report of this investigation is Eulau and Prewitt, *Labyrinths of Democracy: Adaptations, Linkages, Representations, and Policies in Urban Politics.*

    42. John W. Tukey, "The Future of Data Analysis," *The Annals of Mathematical Statistics*, 33 (March, 1962), pp. 13–14.

    43. Sanford Labovitz, "The Assignment of Numbers to Rank Order Categories," *American Sociological Review*, 35 (June, 1970), pp. 515–524.

PART I

Selection to

the Board

Chapter 2

Pathways to

the School Board

In this chapter we examine the social and political backgrounds of school board members. The elements of background and the conditions of entry partially explain how people will behave once they are on the board. We are led to suspect, along with Bidwell, that

> To the extent that recruitment patterns affect the orientations of board members and superintendents, the conditions of recruitment to these roles will be important determinants of consensus or conflict between these levels of the school system. In this way they may color the formation of the school system policies and administrative practices.[1]

A look at the pathways to board membership serves a second function. Most people have some notion, however primitive, about the components of leadership selection in a democratic society. Some of these beliefs are so pervasive that they have become national norms. People believe, for example, that the opportunity to seek office should not be restricted unduly, that a choice of candidates is ordinarily preferable to only one, that public attention should be engaged, that elections should be fair, and that the losers should step out in favor of the winners. Such elements lie at the heart of democratic selection procedures.[2]

We shall examine the extent to which some of these criteria are met, especially those dealing with public involvement and meaningful competition, in the next two chapters. One theme that unites all chapters in this part of our study is that the selection of local education leaders scarcely meets the stiff requirements of the democratic ideal.

Our present objective is to describe three sets of conditions which act as qualifiers for school board candidates, in order to illustrate how the selection process operates. The first set involves background or nonproximate conditions which are properties of the individual's life-space. The second set of conditions, which we call proximate conditions, are closer in time and less ascriptive in character. Finally, the events which tip the selected few into candidacy are precipitating conditions.

NONPROXIMATE CONDITIONS

Legal qualifications in the past severely circumscribed the pool of potential school board members. Today, the main restriction requires that the potential candidates be qualified voters in the district in which they reside. This restriction places limitations of age and length of residency on the pool.

Goldhammer noted in 1964 that eleven states had an educational requirement, four demanded that board members be freeholders, and four required that they be either a taxpayer or a parent.[3] Aside from the educational requirements, which are not extreme, the legal qualifications at that time were not severe and have lessened since. The main exception is the disfranchisement of blacks, through either formal or informal means. Since it is necessary to be a qualified voter in order to be a board member, blacks in the past could not run for the board if they were not qualified voters. So swift has been the removal of formal and informal barriers within the past few years, however, that even this restriction no longer poses the serious obstacle for blacks that it once did.

The most obvious and often reported aspect of the winnowing-out process rests in the socioeconomic characteristics of public elites. For school boards the seminal account was rendered by Counts in 1927.[4] More recent surveys show the same bias toward the upper ranges of the socioeconomic continuum. Although to infer attitudes and behaviors from the social origins and positions of public officials is a well-established fallacy, social characteristics are important in at least three aspects. First, the inclusion or exclusion of certain strata has great symbolic value, especially for upwardly aspiring minority groups and for people who want successful persons as their leaders. Second, it is undoubtedly true that some public leaders do serve their class interests; although this behavior is more visible among minority group officials, there is little reason to believe it is more prevalent there. Finally, it seems undeniable that certain perspectives or *Weltanschauung* are inevitably underrepresented on governing bodies by virtue of their status bias. Specific decisions or policies might not be attributable to a middle and upper class ethos, but it does seem likely that the agenda of problems and possible solutions as well as the style of decision making are affected by composition factors.[5] We will have occasion in several chapters to see whether these three perspectives are borne out.

With these considerations in mind we may consider briefly some prominent indicators of social status. Comparisons are drawn with a 1968 cross-section sample of the American public.[6] An added advantage of this latter sample is that it utilizes the same primary sampling units that the school board sample uses. In addition to the comparisons which address the question of selecting the few from the many one may also use Table 2–1 as a source with which to consider the possible political implications of social stratification.

The table shows that when board members are compared with the general public, the members have qualities which traditionally have been more valued and esteemed in American society. Specifically they are more often male, white, middle-aged, much better educated, more prestigiously employed, Protestant, devout, and Republican, and have been residents longer in their communities. School board members also emanated more often from a home where the father was self-employed and better educated than did the general public (not shown).

The path to school board membership shrinks considerably as a result of the screening accomplished by social stratification. Further narrowing occurs as a result of other forces. One of these is the familial context during childhood and adulthood. Educational elites might be expected to come disproportionately from "educational" families. We should, therefore, look at the incidence of educational occupations in the family backgrounds of the board members.

Current board members have a lot of relatives in education; three-fifths have at least one. More than half of the board members have one or both parents or a spouse in education. While the great majority (88 percent) mentioned relatives who were teachers, 14 percent had relatives who were board members, and 10 percent had school administrators among their kin. The conclusion is that the presence of close family members in education, some of them highly placed, predisposes individuals toward an interest in board membership. Certain skills and information acquired from familial exposure probably give these people an advantage in the screening process and perhaps in the ultimate choice by the electorate or the appointing body.

Educational careers are also in evidence among board members. Twenty-one percent have held jobs in education. Of this total, approximately two-thirds served more than two years in the profession; two-fifths held the job in the same community where they later became board members (and another third in the same state); three-fourths were teachers; one-half were with the public school systems below the collegiate level, and nearly two-fifths were from the collegiate community; and one-fourth were currently employed in education. It is difficult to draw precise comparisons with the adult population but it is apparent that the occupational involvement of board members in education far exceeds the involvement of the general public.

Familial background operates in additional ways to predispose and prepare certain individuals for political office. Since the governing of schools is

TABLE 2-1
Social and Economic Comparison between
Board Members and General Public[a]

Characteristics	General Public	Board Members
Sex:		
Males	48%	90%
Females	52	10
Race:		
Whites	89	96
Nonwhites	11	4
Age:		
Under 40	37	24
40–59	39	63
60 and over	23	13
Years Lived in Community:		
0–5	25	2
6–15	22	18
16–35	26	35
36 and over (incl. all life)	26	45
Education:		
Less than 12 grades	41	7
12 grades	32	22
1–4 years college	23	47
Graduate and professional school	4	25
Income:		
Under $7,500	56	10
$7,500–19,999	39	54
$20,000 and over	6	36
Occupation:		
Professional and technical	16	34
Managers, officials, and proprietors	14	32
Farmers	5	13
Clerical and Sales	11	9
Craftsmen and foremen	19	8
Operatives	16	2
Service workers and laborers	11	2
Other	8	—
Home Ownership:		
Yes	66	93
No	34	7
Religious Preference:		
Protestant	74	85
Non-Protestant	26	15
Church Attendance:		
Weekly	38	61
Less than weekly	62	39
Political Party Identification:		
Democratic	46	40
Independent	30	16
Republican	24	44

[a]Percentages should be read down the columns. The percentages for each characteristic within each sample will total 100% except for rounding error.

part of the political process, we might expect board members to spring disproportionately from politicized homes. In absolute terms the numbers who do are
not at all in accord with expectations. Even in recounting the interest of their
fathers in public affairs and politics only one-third labeled their fathers as "very
much interested;" one-fifth put their mothers in that category. In sum the salience
of politics for one's parents does not restrict the pool of eventual board members.

If we compare board members with the mass-public sample, it becomes
clear that board members came at the same rate as the general public from homes
where public affairs assumed a high profile. Adjusting the mass-public sample by
age and socioeconomic status to conform more to the board sample does not
alter these figures significantly. For all of the conventional wisdom about the
political backgrounds of political elites, the wisdom obviously does not apply to
local elites in education.

PROXIMATE CONDITIONS

In this stage a great deal of self-selection takes place. People become involved
differentially in endeavors which convince them and others that they are among
the pool of eligibles. Sometimes this is done through sheer dint of occupational
visibility. The head of the largest bank, the most successful farmer, the prominent
educator, and the leading physician are examples of immediate eligibles. More
often, however, there must be something else accompanying this visibility or acting
in place of it.

Some accomplishments which are not part of one's occupational life
must accompany or replace occupational visibility. To tap the depth and breadth
of these activities we compiled a recent life history for all board members con-
sisting of the number and types of public affairs steps they traversed prior to
board membership. Our approach was straightforward. We asked: "Can you spell
out the steps between your earliest activity in public affairs and your initial
membership on the school board?"

One of the most startling aspects of the replies is the extreme variation
in the number of steps taken, as Table 2-2 shows. Some members land on the board
only after prodigious efforts, whereas others have scarcely participated at all.
Indeed, the 13 percent with no explicit steps provide sharp evidence that prior
activity in public affairs is not a sine qua non to eventual elite status. Our interpretation is that these members were either very occupationally and socially
visible or that they were involved in activity not explicitly in the domain of public
affairs.[7]

Most board members, however, serve apprenticeships in public affairs,
and it is important to know the nature of these apprenticeships. We categorized
the steps employed into three major dimensions: political-governmental, civic-
business, and educational. When one or another mode predominates we say that
the eventual winners have followed a particular stream of traffic. Multiple lanes

TABLE 2-2
Steps Prior to Board Membership

Number of Steps	Percent of Members
0	13%
1	31
2	25
3	15
4	9
5+	8
	101% (*N* = 619)

TABLE 2-3
Steps in Three Modes

Number	Civic- Business	Political- Governmental	Educational
0	53%	64%	66%
1	23	25	23
2+	25	11	11
	101%	100%	100%
	(*N* = 624)	(*N* = 624)	(*N* = 624)

are available for the potential winners to the degree that equity exists. The distributions for each of the three major modes are presented in Table 2-3.

Two key points emerge from these figures. First, there is evidence that no one dimension predominates along the pathways to the board. A candidate is not removed from contention either by ignoring or by stressing a particular dimension. Further evidence for this point may be adduced by examining the intercorrelation among the three pairs of combinations. High positive relationships would indicate that board members needed more than one mode; high negative relationships would suggest that an aspirant must specialize in only one mode; and no relationship would mean that participation in one dimension has no connection with participation in another. The latter result conforms closely to the data, with the *tau-b* correlations as follows: civic-business and educational = − .06; educational and political-governmental = − .08; and political-governmental and civic-business = − .12.

The second important feature of these figures is the civic-business emphasis. Despite strength in all three areas, fewer board members avoided the civic-business domain completely, and more members concentrated heavily in that area. This emphasis is also expressed by taking the total number of *responses* instead of *respondents* as the base of calculation. Out of all steps cited those in civic-business led the way with 44 percent, followed by political-governmental at 29 percent, and educational at 28 percent. Moreover, this margin, with a minor exception, prevails regardless of how many steps are considered. Therefore, regardless of how many steps the board member has taken before board entry, civic-business is most prevalent, and educational and governmental-political are closely matched for runner-up honors.

The senior position of the civic-business references testifies to the important role such organizations and activities play in funneling nascent political leaders into the immediate pool of eligible leaders. As a variety of community studies have shown, such organizations as the Chamber of Commerce, the luncheon-service clubs, and the cultural and welfare fund-raising enterprises are prominent actors in the drama of local politics. Potential political elites often call attention to themselves in such organizations. While most will not go on to hold elective office, a large number will. Boards of education provide an even more congenial destination for such people than city councils or state legislatures offer. A fact well-known to close observers of school politics is that the province of local education is commonly viewed as nonpolitical and as above politics.[8] What could be better preparation for service in a nonpolitical agency of vital importance than proven ability in the voluntary civic-business organizational world?

Although the singular place of the civic-business route is not denied, it should be acknowledged that taken together the educational and governmental-political arenas are more prominent. Clearly the route to board membership is not paved solely with civic-business building materials.

The place of educational affairs as a recruiting ground for board members is further highlighted by responses to a direct question about the board members' participation in education-related activities prior to board membership. Although 55 percent placed themselves in the active category, this amount might be considered a low rather than high proportion. Why are the responsibilities for the education of the young entrusted to people with no previous experience in school affairs?

The apparent paradox of a limited pool and moderate experience in educational activities is easily resolved in the American context. Competence is assumed to be transferable. Even the successful actor, businessman, or athlete with some flair for public contacts is a possibility for political leadership, partly since politics necessarily embraces a wide variety of skills and interests. Consider how much more easily one can generalize from one endeavor of public and civic affairs to education per se. Facilitating this halo effect is the long-standing image of lay control in education. An added fact is that everyone has had at least several years of direct contact with the school system as student, parent, or both. Under these conditions it is not surprising that nearly half of the sample began their board service with little or no apprenticeship in educational affairs.

Of those who participated directly in educational matters the great majority utilized one of three vehicles. Work or leadership in the venerable PTAs

(42 percent) lead the way. PTAs are the organizations most identified with lay participation in the schools. They are visible and penetrable, and typically have good relationships with the administration and the board of education; indeed they are sometimes accused of being coopted by the school authorities. Through a variety of accidental and purposive ways an individual citizen can attain considerable prominence in the local education scene by virtue of PTA participation.

A second leading educational group is that generally called a "Citizens Advisory Committee" (CAC). Some 21 percent of the educationally active board members reported former membership on such a committee. More prestigious than the PTAs, the CACs are usually study, advisory, or promotional committees comprised of people with some visibility and status in the community. People on these committees customarily have worked on a lower-level educational project, although it is not uncommon for a CAC to be dotted with local notables whose main achievements are financial-occupational. Having served on a prestigious CAC, aspiring board candidates have achieved some degree of public visibility; and if the plans and efforts of the committee have reaped success, they are in a position to show past competence.

A final vehicle for educational activities is the service organizations, which are voluntary, interest-specific organizations whose primary focus is not on education. Yet since educational matters permeate so much of a community's life, it is almost inevitable that these organizations devote attention from time to time to the business of local education. Among the most frequently mentioned groups of this type were the luncheon service clubs (Lions, Rotary, Kiwanis, etc.), the Chamber of Commerce, and social work-charity organizations (United Fund, Red Cross, etc.). For the outsider who has neither the inclination nor the opportunity to act through the PTA or the CAC, these service groups provide a respectable, safe way in which to enter the pool of eligibles.

PRECIPITATING CONDITIONS

The next logical step in our reduction process should be to determine how the board members run for office and win. Two factors stand in the way of this immediate step. First, not all boards of education are elective. Within our sample 9 percent of the board members representing 11 percent of all the districts were on appointive boards. Second, 21 percent of the sample is comprised of elective board members who originally obtained their seats by appointment. Altogether three in every ten board members gained office as appointees. The image of open competition as the vehicle for gaining office must be modified substantially.

If appointees do not compete in the electoral marketplace of the board of education, how are they chosen? Nearly three out of every five appointees were active in an education-related committee or group. Although it was not very often a known factor, the appointment sometimes occurred because of the individual's identification with certain strata of the community. Thus one-fifth of those citing a background feature believed that their appointment resulted from a desire that they represent certain interests or groups in the district. A key route for appointees in elective districts is presumably an unsuccessful bid for office in the past. However, only 14 percent were former losers.

The manner in which appointees come to the threshold of board membership is not appreciably different than those that characterize their elected brethren. Obviously the decision to enter the electoral lists and to campaign for office is an important distinction. It is impossible to tell with the available data how important this distinction is and whether it seriously alters the composition of boards. Since the appointees resemble so strongly the initially elected in terms of preboard experiences — and since board members tend to look for compatible replacements — our conclusion is that the composition is not appreciably different than it would be had all board members first joined the board via the election route.

Although speculation is appropriate regarding the selection of appointees, we are more certain about the activating sources for those elected to office. Initially we may set aside those first appointed to elective boards who were subsequently elected to office. The presumption is that the triggering device is primarily board membership. There is little doubt that most appointees are expected to run for office when the term expires unless they were appointed early in a long-term seat. These people receive additional stimuli from their colleagues. Over two-fifths specifically cited encouragement from other board members as a reason for their first running. Once on the board, the psychic and group pressures for running are ordinarily intense.

A total of 69 percent of the *entire* sample originally joined an elective board through elections. Few people enter the electoral lists without the encouragement of significant others. For several of our interviewees, however, this encouragement must have been extremely subtle: 23 percent claimed that no individuals or groups had requested that they run for the board. The wording of this question contributed to this sizeable proportion because it intimated that purposive contacts were at issue. The result was as intended, since we were searching for the array of agents which intentionally propel people into contesting for office. Nevertheless, the fact that nearly a quarter of those first elected were self-starters signifies the relative ease with which the elite circle can be penetrated *given the right sort of proximate facilitators.*

Among those who were sought out by others the range of initiating agents was considerable. Most of the agents could be allocated into five categories as shown in Table 2-4.

An elected governing body can ensure a perpetuation of its style and policies if it hand-picks its successors. Although such designees do not always fulfill the promise of their supporters, and although the lone dissident or two on the board may be most active in encouraging others to run, it seems probable that board members encourage like-minded individuals to join them. Those who are successful will probably prove compatible with the existing board members. Adding to this probability is the socialization of new members into the norms and

TABLE 2-4
Source of Encouragement to Run for Board

Source	*Percentage of Board Members*
Board members	29%
Formal citizens groups	21
Friends and neighbors	21
Professional school personnel	14
Governmental and political figures	13
	98%[a]
	(*N* = 444)

[a]Total percentage less than 100 because some responses did not fit these categories.

folkways of the board. If the new entrants initially consider diverging from their fellow members, such deviancy is quickly attenuated in the socialization process — especially since the new members owe their presence on the board to the instigation of board personnel.

As the figures demonstrate, other board members are the major source of encouragement. How much of this effort was expended by members who later welcomed the victorious candidates as colleagues? The question assumes some importance because it helps answer the question of whether an in-office, continuing elite seeks to fill vacancies or whether those who are leaving the elite must fill the vacancies. The sense of obligation or responsibility the recruited members may feel toward other personnel on the existing board is another point highlighted by the question.

Of all the encouragement sources emanating from board personnel, at least three-fifths definitely came from board members still sitting on the board. Thus the more common form of perpetuation is for board members to solicit candidates who will be serving with them. This behavior tends to place similar minds and allies on the postelection board. To this figure may be added an unknown portion from the ranks of those respondents who cited former board members as the stimulus. Presumably some and probably most of the respondents in this category served at least a year or more with the former members. Estimating conservatively that one-half did meet this condition means that about seven in ten of the board-encouraged candidates later served with one or more of their admirers.

We come finally to those instances when outgoing board members sought to have their place filled by someone of their choice. Approximately 30 percent of all board sources were of this type. One may picture these efforts as designed to pass the mantle of leadership on to able hands. Through their experience and contacts board personnel have undoubtedly developed not only an idea of what the role entails but also some appreciation for who among their fellow citizens might fill the role.

Encouragement from board members need not provide the last push for a person on the precipice of candidacy. From examining the protocols it became clear that arm-twisting and cajoling were also much in evidence. Part of the reason for the latter forms of inducement is that board membership is not often seen as a means to any other political end, as will be demonstrated in the following chapter. Nor is the prospect of improving one's self socially or occupationally a prime force. In addition to wanting congenial, ideologically sound people to serve with them, board members also engage in recruiting simply to develop any respectable candidates at all!

The two next most active sources of encouragement are quite different in terms of their formal properties. Formal citizen groups range from Citizens for Good Schools to the Chamber of Commerce. Occasionally an ad hoc, informal group of citizens provided the stimulus, but usually the source was a formal organization. The opposite of the organized group, but an equally frequent source, includes "friends and neighbors." In a majority of cases these were literally individuals who were identified as friends and neighbors. Also included are occupational associates and family members. Actually the proportions for this source are expressed very conservatively, since well over a quarter of the board members mentioned unspecified individuals termed, "interested people," "they," and "just some people." Chances are that a majority of these individuals would be cast under our friends and neighbors category if the information were more precise. The equal prominence of casual, informal sources with the more formal suggests the almost happenstance character of board recruitment. Systematic recruitment mechanisms such as those exerted by formal, ongoing organizations are not that common.

In addition to board members other school personnel spark candidacies. Most frequently this is the superintendent or a teacher. PTA officials are included in this category because school professionals are not only members of the organization but also they tend to shape the actions of the lay officials. If these sources are added to school board sources, at least two-fifths of the elected board members can be said to have been inspired by representatives of the school system. To a substantial degree the pool of eligibles comes to be those people recognized by the local educational elites as potential board members.

The final specific source of encouragement consists of governmental and political persons other than educational personnel. Foremost among these agents are individuals and organizations connected with the political parties. Not surprisingly these nudges occur most often in districts marked by partisan elections. Despite the decades of efforts by both professional and lay personnel to "take politics out of the school" there are still explicit residues of partisan influences in school politics, as we shall see in the following two chapters.

Two measures, applicable only to elective boards, were constructed which pertain to the degree of closure in school board selection procedures. The first, which we shall call the sponsorship variable, is an index representing the proportion of current board members on each board who were either encouraged to run by members of a previous board, were initially appointed to fill an unexpired term, or both.[9] Table 2-5 shows the distribution of districts according to board sponsorship (the higher the score the greater the sponsorship). Some degree of sponsorship occurs in the vast majority of districts. Thus there is a tendency toward system closure at work throughout the school districts.[10]

Another indicator of closure relates to the absence of competition in board elections. Twenty-three districts (24 percent of all elective districts) experienced no competition in the election preceding our study, whereas 72 (76 percent of all elective districts) had at least one contested seat. Of course the absence of electoral competition does not necessarily mean that selection procedures are controlled; it may merely be an indication of apathy on the part of potential candidates. However, we have evidence that more is reflected by it, since sponsorship is negatively related to the presence of competition in the preceding election ($r = -.40$). Thus districts where the educational elite is most active in its attempts to control board selection procedures also tend to be those districts where fewer challenges to elite control are issued during elections.

This negative relationship between competition and sponsorship can serve as an opening wedge for a consideration of the next phase of office attainment. Aside from the appointive board districts, all districts hold periodic elections. These elections normally constitute the vehicle whereby the citizenry authorizes and legitimizes the choice of who will govern its school districts. How well do the workings of this procedure match the democratic norms popularly subscribed to in this country? Is the rather apolitical, circumscribed, and insulated process which characterizes pathways to the board also characteristic of the electoral stage? Or do elections open up the process, exploit political drives and ambitions, provide discernible choices for the electorate, and involve the public in large-scale terms? And what, if any, is the relationship between pathways to the board and

TABLE 2-5
Distribution of Elective Districts According
to Their Degree of Board Sponsorship

Index	Score	Dists.	%[a]	Cum. %
Low:	0 to 20	9	9.5	9.5
	21 to 40	25	26.3	35.8
	41 to 60	22	23.1	58.9
	61 to 80	13	13.7	72.6
	81 to 100	19	20.0	92.6
High:	101 to 180	7	7.4	100.0
	Total	95	100.0	100.0

[a]Percents and statistics throughout this book are calculated on the basis of fractional cases resulting from the weighting procedures used. The reported frequencies have been rounded to whole integers. Therefore, the discrepancies between frequencies and percentages are due to rounding error.

the electoral climate? It is to a consideration of such questions that we turn in the next chapter, leaving until the end of that chapter an overview of these two chapters taken together.

NOTES

1. Charles E. Bidwell, "The School as a Formal Organization," *Handbook of Organizations*, ed. James G. March (Chicago: Rand McNally, 1965), p. 1001.

2. For a theoretical discussion and an empirical test of such elements see Kenneth Prewitt, "Political Ambition, Volunteerism, and Electoral Accountability," *American Political Science Review*, 64 (March, 1970), pp. 5–17.

3. Keith Goldhammer, *The School Board* (New York: The Center for Applied Research in Education, Inc., 1964), p. 26.

4. George P. Counts, *The Social Composition of Boards of Education* (Chicago: University of Chicago Press, 1927).

5. This is a theme picked by David Minar, "The Community Basis of Conflict in School System Politics," *American Sociological Review*, 31 (December, 1966), pp. 822–835; see also Louis H. Masotti, "Political Integration in Suburban Education Communities," *The New Urbanization*, ed. Scott Greer, *et al.* (New York: St. Martin's, 1968), chapter 14.

6. The sample (N = 1557) was drawn by the Survey Research Center of the University of Michigan for use in its 1968 presidential election study. See Appendix A for more details.

7. Kenneth Prewitt and Heinz Eulau refer to this lack of background as lateral entry. In their study of 88 California Bay Area city councils they concluded that 12 percent of the councilmen were lateral entrants. See Kenneth Prewitt and Heinz Eulau, "Social Bias in Leadership Selection," *Journal of Politics*, 33 (May, 1971), pp. 293–315.

8. Roscoe C. Martin, *Government and the Suburban School* (Syracuse: Syracuse University Press, 1962), makes this point and the accompanying paradoxes.

9. The actual steps in constructing this variable involved our initially computing the proportion of each board that had been appointed to office and the percent that had been encouraged to run. These percentage figures were then added in order to arrive at a summary measure of sponsorship. Since technical considerations necessitated our assigning scores of 1 to boards that actually had zero percent either appointed or encouraged, the minimum value that could result was 2. The theoretical maximum was, of course, 200.

10. This conclusion conforms to the dynamic model of school government outlined in Laurence Iannaccone and Frank W. Lutz, *Politics, Power and Policy* (Columbus, Ohio: Charles E. Merrill, 1970), pp. 86–88.

Chapter 3

The Electoral Climate

Americans elect more of their public officials than do citizens of any other Western nation. The beliefs that the best check on official rectitude and that the best method of translating public preferences into public policy rest in the electoral marketplace are deeply ingrained and seemingly unchallengeable. With the widespread introduction of public education into the country during the nineteenth century, it was perhaps inevitable that the lay governance of such a crucial institution should fall under the sway of the popular election ethic. But as with other electoral arenas, we may also ask of the educational one: how well are some of the traditional expectations met?

It should be reemphasized at the outset that a significant number of board members gained membership without facing any competition. Even if one removes from the computational base the appointive boards, it still leaves 34 percent of all elective board members having secured office either by appointment or without initial electoral opposition.[1] This finding undermines even further the traditional notions about public office attainment discussed in the previous chapter. Capturing a seat on the school board is almost as much a matter of becoming attractively visible as it is of beating competition at the polls. School boards are but an imperfect reflection of the belief that membership results from open competition in free elections.

Of all board members *ultimately* elected to office 81 percent faced competition in their first outing. This figure may appear high or low, depending upon one's criteria of what an accountable political system is supposed to contain. Certainly all major offices in this country now have a higher rate of contesting.

On the other hand, the figures can be interpreted as indicating that in the over-whelming majority of cases elected board members did have to scramble for their first victory.

The built-in edge of incumbency does not prevent those appointed to elective boards from experiencing competition in their first electoral outing. Whereas 83 percent of all those originally *elected* faced competition, the same was true of 73 percent of those originally *appointed*. Without knowing how the full pool of office seekers did over any period of time, we cannot say exactly how much that incumbency was worth. Reconstruction of recent electoral history in the districts covered by this study shows, however, that one-half of the board members were in districts where between 89 and 100 percent of all incumbents were reelected.

For those four-fifths of elective board members who faced opposition in their initial forays, the severity of competition undoubtedly varied a good deal. We have some indication about how stiff the opposition was: out of all those with opposition ($N = 433$), one-third did not face an incumbent. This finding shakes the traditional notion of a healthy, responsible system in which challengers try to unseat incumbents. Particularly in the absence of ongoing cleavages in the form of political parties, the challenge phenomenon would seem to be especially needed. Yet one-third of those with opposition were not trying to unseat anyone, although it is possible that some small portion of them were running against the *records* of persons who just retired or of incumbents whose seats were not presently on the line.

Even the remaining two-thirds must be undervalued to some extent, since candidates running against incumbents in at-large elections would not be in head-to-head competition. If candidates are in an at-large election where there are fewer incumbents running than seats to be filled, then they are not necessarily competing against an incumbent. How much the 66 percent figure should be deflated to reflect actual one-on-one conflict is impossible to estimate precisely with the data at our command. To recapitulate, here are the first-term figures for all elective board members who had experienced an election: 19 percent faced no opposition; 27 percent faced opposition, but no incumbents were involved; 54 percent faced opposition and incumbents were involved.

POLITICAL AMBITIONS

The data regarding sponsorship and competition lead us to suspect that the electoral climate of school district governance is by no means universally heated. Subsequent sections of this chapter will document that suspicion. First, however, it is impor-tant to show that the electoral climate throughout most districts is conditioned by the low ambitions of officeseekers. The nature of political ambitions implies much about the responsiveness and accountability potential of school board members.

The road to school board membership ordinarily terminates at a dead end, as shall be demonstrated shortly. Other pieces of evidence are at hand also. If one peruses the biographies of the nation's more esteemed political positions (Presidency, Congress, Governorships) only rarely will one find a school board background. Less casually, we may refer to Schlesinger's monumental work on the background of contestants for governorship and U.S. senatorship in roughly the first half of the twentieth century. Although school board positions are not listed specifically, there is a category for local elective offices. Significantly, such offices are least used, by far, as the base office for advancement.[2] When we consider that school board positions constitute only a portion of all local elective offices, it is apparent that historically the school board has been infrequently used as a springboard for political advancement.

How does this singular lack of advancement from school board member-ship to other political office fit into our concern about the requirements of a healthy governing system? It is postulated by one school of democratic political theorists that ambition is a requisite for meaningful elections and an accountable political process. Schlesinger stresses ambition as the driving force of politics.[3] It is held that without ambition for reelection and political mobility, the desire of office holders to solve problems, pay attention to their constituents, and in general deport themselves within the norms of democratic leadership will be impaired. Ambitions, in short, determine behavior.

A counterargument, more popular among political reformers than among democratic theorists, is that ambition corrupts office holders and prevents them from discharging their duties free of the idea of personal or group gains. From this view the ambitious politician makes decisions to please present and future electorates; considerations of the "true" public interest goes begging. Researchers observed this reasoning repeatedly in their study of California Bay Area city councilmen.[4] One might call this the civic conscience or civic duty theory, as opposed to the ambition theory.

All the returns are not yet in from this intriguing question. Yet given both the prevailing popular beliefs and the democratic theorists' contention, it seems reasonable to apply the theory of ambitions to school board member selection. Under the logic of ambition theory the school board members should exhibit at least moderate rates of aspiration, if they are to be held accountable. Of course, ambition is affected by one's stage in the natural and political life cycle. If we were trying to account for differential rates of ambition, we would take these and other determinants into consideration. Our primary goal, however, is to observe whether the incidence of ambitious board members is sufficient to support the requirements of accountability and electoral tension.

Two types of ambitions may be noted. First, there are office-bound ambitions. If the aspirations are for a single term the ambitions are discrete; if for more than one term, they are static.[5] The other, more tantalizing type are upward bound or progressive ambitions. Here the office holders are eyeing another position, usually one which by most standards would be considered more prestigious, powerful, or remunerative. The stereotype of the truly ambitious politicians is that they are seeking ever higher office.

We can dispense rather quickly with the office-bound aspirations. When asked whether they desired another term, the board members divided themselves as follows: 32 percent yes; 37 percent not sure, maybe, have to wait and see, etc.; 31 percent no. Not surprisingly, there is a small negative relationship between intentions to seek reelection and years of service, *tau-b* = −.05. That it is not stronger may be attributed to the fact that some "old timers" have become so accustomed to being on the board that they find it difficult to imagine their lives without it. Since only 15 percent of the first term members definitely declined intention of seeking another term, the prevalence of discrete ambitions is meager.

Using office-bound ambitions as the criteria, school board members receive perhaps a passing grade. When one-third frankly admit to wanting another term in the interview situation, it must be counted as indicating a sizable pro-portion which have their eyes cocked in the direction of constituent monitoring. By the same token the fact that one-third definitely do not want another term reflects a combination of personal and occupational reasons which might be expected in a lay board of this type. At the same time it should be noted that this figure is far higher than what one would observe among Congress and most state legislatures. Exactly what one is to make of the middle third who have not made up their minds is unclear. It is among them that the theory of ambition would seem to suffer most in its application. They may swing one way or the other, depending in part perhaps on feedback from the electorate.

Although board members do reasonably well in terms of office-bound ambitions, the same cannot be said for upward-bound aspirations. It is with respect to such ambitions that we might expect board members to be most responsive to the public, dramatic in their behavior, and innovative in their policies. But precious few respondents expressed any interest in other offices. Eighty-one percent flatly ruled out any interest in such positions; a bare 12 percent acknowl-edged aspirations; and another 7 percent said maybe they would be interested. Even by the most generous definitions only 19 percent of the sample could be said to have notions of moving on. It is assuredly difficult to say what proportion of a governing body should be upwardly mobile in order to classify it as ambitious, but these meager proportions show that on the average most boards are bereft of ambitious types. The criterion of ambition for an accountable and lively electoral process is, therefore, not met. Were Americans to rely upon the upward ambitions of their school board officials as a means of ensuring responsive governance, they would have a very slender reed upon which to rely.

If it is true that most board members are not ambitious, it is equally true that high aspirations do not abound among the ambitious. Illustratively, 44 percent of the self-confessed ambitious had their sights set tentatively on nothing higher than another local or county position. Whether such offices merit the description of representing upward mobility is questionable. In terms of local conditions, some would and some would not. In terms of national norms, seeking such positions would ordinarily be considered lateral movement. From the viewpoint of constituencies, such movement would usually represent no large change in composition.

Forty-two percent of the ambitious designated positions which, by most accounts, would exhibit upward movement. The bulk of these consisted of state government positions, with a handful of Congressional and other federal designations. Another 4 percent of the ambitious mentioned political party work of some sort; strictly speaking, these are not government positions. Finally 9 percent are included in a miscellaneous category, the varied contents of which proved resistant to any of the other classifications.

Overall, about two-fifths of the ambitious had concrete notions of moving upward. Even this proportion must be tempered by the realization that the certain as well as the uncertain were asked which specific offices they had in mind. Additionally this two-fifths represents only 6 percent of all elective board members. One would be reluctant to pin hopes of ambition as a guarantee of accountability on such a small base, especially because there is a concentration of the upwardly ambitious among a relatively small number of boards ($N = 27$).

The generally modest levels of office-bound ambitions and the uniformly low levels of upward-bound ambitions must be borne in mind in evaluating many of the results from our study. Constraints which bind elected officials at higher levels simply do not apply to the majority of school district governors. It is unlikely that the electorate will be attended to in the same fashion as when the arena is filled with the politically ambitious. It is also unlikely that the electoral climate will be vigorous because the personal stakes are so low.[6]

ISSUE DIFFERENCES AND COMPETITION

Basic to the vigor of a system of electoral accountability is the range of issue differences between contestants for public office. For meaningful competition to exist, voters must be presented with a choice of real alternatives, articulated by candidates or parties which define issues in such a way that the voter has a clear feeling that one course of action will produce more desirable consequences than another. It is not necessary that voters be familiar with the intricacies of policy alternatives. What *is* necessary is that the options available provide a clear image of seriously varying policy alternatives. How much difference between alternatives can be tolerated before the limits of societal consensus are reached is a subject of considerable debate among scholars and laymen. Some argue that both major parties are mere cheerleaders for the middle class, while others argue that their alternative programs provide genuine choice. Still others argue that consensus about ends, with disagreement limited to means, is the genius of American politics.

Since a majority of school board elections do not involve party selection procedures, cohesive and ideological positions cannot always be expected. Yet, at a minimum, it is reasonable to expect that the linkage accountability process is strengthened when candidates differ on substantive issues of educational policy. If the choice is merely between two candidates promising to "provide the best education for the least money," then something is lost in the translating of constituent expectations into board behavior.

When laid against the ideal norm, the performance of school board candidates falls far short, as would probably be the case for most local offices. In response to a question which asked them if their ". . . ideas about schools were different from those of some other candidates" only 58 percent replied in the affirmative. Certainly it is possible that some of these successful candidates may have forgotten any such differences, but the contrary hypothesis of retrospective inventing of differences is equally plausible. It is also possible that had we been able to interview losing candidates that they would have reported more differences. Still, it seems unlikely that the true figure is significantly higher than the one reported here. Even though the electorate might perceive the situation differently, again it is unlikely that the proportions believing there were issue differences would be higher than this reported figure.

A conjecture based on earlier discussion is that issue differences would be most intense when incumbents were involved, since challengers are presumably convinced that they would be better board members than the current ones. Some of these ways undoubtedly involve style and personality modes, rather than substantive policy matters. Still there should be more direct challenge on issue dimensions than when incumbents are not present, because contestants are less likely to be running *against* something. The results shown in Table 3-1 bear out these conjectures. Clearly, the absence of incumbents depresses the likelihood that issue differences will be recognized. Correspondingly, the presence of incumbents enhances the likelihood. Thus the criteria of policy differences among contestants for office is most nearly met when challengers are in confrontation with office holders.

What are these differences all about? Do they hinge on narrow specific issues or do they concern matters of broad policy consideration? Are they focussed on board behavior and conduct or on more substantive issues and programs? In replying to a question about the nature of the differences the respondents gave a

TABLE 3-1
Differences with Other Candidates

	Opposition Included	
	Incumbents	*No Incumbents*
Yes	66%	42%
No	34	58
	100%	100%
	(*N* = 282)	(*N* = 145)

bewildering variety of answers, citing over 80 distinct differences between the candidate and the opposition. We have grouped this unwieldy number under four major rubrics:

A. Board Roles – the board's internal relationships and style of operation; relationships between superintendent and board; board's posture toward community; board composition.
B. Educational Program and Personnel – the curriculum; student problems; quality and handling of instructional staff.
C. Physical and Fiscal Problems – quality and quantity of physical plants; consolidation and reorganization; expenditure and finance structure.
D. Civil Rights and Civil Liberties – racial integration and bias; religious issues; radical teaching (left or right).

Sizable proportions of the board members cited differences in each area, as these figures show.[7]

Board Roles	38%
Educational Program and Personnel	33%
Physical and Fiscal Problems	27%
Civil Rights and Civil Liberties	22%

From an educational point of view what is most striking about these results is that the educational program and personnel category is no larger than it is. After all, that is primarily what schooling is supposed to be all about. It is decisions and policies in this area which have the most direct, observable impact on the students. Nevertheless, only a third of the candidates having differences with their opponents saw them in what is the heart of the educational process. Even this fraction represents some inflation over what is ordinarily meant by the term educational program, for the category includes some reference to teachers who have but little to do with the educational program per se. For example, the problems of teacher organization, militancy, and sanctioning mechanisms are included here. Such problems are undoubtedly related to aspects of teacher performance, and hence the educational life of the school; but they are not as directly relevant as questions of teacher quality and hiring standards.

From a political point of view, however, the predominance of the other three categories is not surprising. Whereas the components of the educational program curriculum, student problems, instructional methods, and differential emphases tend to be hidden, the components of publicly-viewed board behavior, money and plant problems, and controversies over civil rights cannot be hidden. These are manifestly observable phenomena which have the capacity to touch extremely sensitive chords in the community. Examples of board role issues are seen in the comments by candidates who differed with their opponents on how the board should "handle" the superintendent, and how the board was "treating" the public. Publicity in either of these areas tends to generate a considerable amount of heat among both elites and mass publics.

Even more to the point are differences in the area of fiscal problems. Citizens are unusually alert to money issues, and the course of bond referenda and tax proposal outcomes in recent years shows an increasing reluctance on their part to tax themselves. Finally, the civil rights issues — embracing emotion-laden questions of integration, busing, teacher assignments, and the like — have been among the most visible and talked about issues in school districts during the 1960s. Given the reasonable practice of candidates to deal with visible, comprehensible, and symbolically important matters, it is not surprising to see these three domains collectively swamp the educational program domain.

We saw previously that the presence of incumbents makes a difference in whether disputes between candidates will emerge. Extending that line of reasoning, we ask whether the presence of incumbents makes a difference in the kinds of issues raised. The figures in Table 3–2 suggest a modest but intriguing consequence. When incumbents are present, the board's record is on the line and is more likely to be capitalized upon, especially by challengers. Thus in the classic sense of a policy-making body putting up its essential functions and roles to the electorate, the issues are best drawn when incumbents are being challenged.

Moving to the other three domains the pattern shifts, a shift represented by comparing percentages as well as by the eventual change in signs among the *tau-b* correlations. The absence of incumbents means that substantive issues get more play. Without a representative of the standing board, the differences crop up in less personalized and board-specific domains. Whether this raises the level of

TABLE 3–2
Effect of Incumbent Presence on Issues Raised

Issue Difference Involved	Opposition Included		
	Incumbents	Nonincumbents	tau-b
Board Role			
Yes	41%	28%	
No	59	72	
			.11
Physical and Fiscal			
Yes	28	25	
No	72	75	
			.03
Civil Rights and Liberties			
Yes	20	30	
No	80	70	
			-.10
Educational Program and Personnel			
Yes	30	41	
No	70	59	
			-.11

public debate is uncertain. True, it facilitates the emergence of specific, concrete problems of direct policy concern. On the other hand, in addition to the policy importance of board roles there are great symbolic implications. Legitimate and pressing questions in a representative system include what sort of makeup the governing board shall have, how it shall relate to its constituents, and how it shall monitor the professionals. Although the differential effects are not large, it is clear that such questions are more prevalent when incumbents are defending their records, and other specific issues are more common when the incumbents are not present.

PUBLIC INVOLVEMENT AND COMPETITION

A basic notion of popular participation in the selection of who governs is that some portions of the populace should become mobilized in an attempt to decide the victors. Mobilization means going beyond the sheer act of voting; it means making efforts to persuade others that your candidate has virtues. People who engage in such activities are sometimes called opinion leaders, activists, gladiators, cadres, or the politicized. It would be unreasonable to demand that all of the public become so involved, but the idea of a responsible electoral system is robbed of much of its vitality if the public becomes involved in only a passive, spectator fashion. From a different basis, it would be argued that most elections should witness such engagement.

Judging by the celebrated cases of hotly-contested school district balloting one would conclude that overt public involvement in board elections is the rule rather than the exception. Especially in cases of recall elections, or of movements to reconstitute the board with new personnel, activity does flourish. Both formal and informal groups spread the word through the media and by word of mouth. Are these spectacular instances simply exaggerations of what occurs at a more subdued level in most board campaigns? Or are they the exception rather than the rule?

It seems pointless to inquire about manifest signs of support for candidates when no individual or group encouraged candidacy. We therefore eliminate from consideration those members who said no one prevailed upon them to run in their first election. Again, it is sound testimony to the penetrability of office-holding that 23 percent could cite no group or individual that encouraged them. Under typologies developed by students of political recruitment, we would label such people "self-starters." Although self-starters among our respondents may have eventually mobilized formal public support, all the circumstantial evidence indicates that this happened infrequently. Self-starters typically come from areas where organizational life is low and competition for office anemic.

The 77 percent who did report urgings from their fellow citizens were asked: "Did they publicly support your candidacy or was it completely informal?" We took an "informal" response to mean that the election was low key, that committees and organizations did not try to mobilize the vote, and that candidate differences on issues and policies were ordinarily spelled out less explicitly. "Public support" denotes the opposite of these characteristics. Approximately one-half (48 percent) of those receiving some support reported public, organized manifestations. If our reasoning is correct, a very substantial proportion of board members claim office in settings of low electoral temperature. By this standard the requirement that the public be involved through manifest, organized forms of campaign behavior is honored by its absence as much as its presence. Accepting the assumption that those members not encouraged to run by others had even lower rates of formal support, the total proportion without public backing is lower still.

We observed earlier that the presence of opposition and the presence of incumbents within the opposition are linked to various other circumstances of election to office. The figures in Table 3–3 show that the relationship applies to the existence of public support. We will not try to make the argument that the presence of opposition and the composition of the opposition necessarily cause greater manifestation of public support. Nevertheless, it is undeniable that the elements covary to some extent. And controls for region and metropolitanism alter the vitality of the relationships only in non-Standard Metropolitan Statistical Areas (SMSAs) and in the Midwest.[8] Moreover, the association has a face validity. Without opposition there is less need for any manifest signs of support. When the opposition consists of nonincumbents there is more of a challenge context, so that the marshalling of forces is greater than when no contest was present. But the final situation, when incumbents are defending their seats, presents the strongest obstacle to gaining office. It is here that greater efforts are needed, given the advantage of incumbency.

Candidates with formal support also differ more with their opponents. Whereas 64 percent of those with formal backing disagreed with their opponents, the same was true of 48 percent of those without such support. Again the patterns hold by region and metropolitan status. Very much of a piece with these findings is one showing that even before the campaign started, those with eventual public

TABLE 3–3
Relationship of Opposition and Public Support

Public Support for Candidacy	Opposition Included		No opposition
	Incumbents	Non-incumbents	
Yes	56%	43%	34%
No	44	57	66
	100%	100%	100%
	(*N* = 215)	(*N* = 127)	(*N* = 80)

support desired changes in some "policies or practices" within the district. Thus, 56 percent of those desiring change later commanded public support, compared with 42 percent of those satisfied with the status quo.[9] The engagement of the public in formal campaign activities is heightened when combative, change-oriented properties are most in evidence.

COMPETITION AND PREENTRY STEPS

We noted in Chapter 2 that three main sets of activities led to board membership: civic, political, and educational. We will now view our data to determine whether people emphasizing any one of these sets of activities more closely approximate the standards which conform to a responsible leadership selection process. If this is the case, then strong arguments can be advanced for attempting to create political environments which facilitate office attainment of persons with certain preboard backgrounds.

We took information relating to our respondents' backgrounds and allocated the data into our three categories of activities. Our task was to see whether the respondents could be typed according to their modal, dominant types of steps. For a number of respondents this was simple because they reported no specific steps. We call them nonactives. A number of others reported only one, again presenting no problems. Nor was there difficulty if two or more steps in the same area were cited. It was the multiple mentions across different domains which created assignment difficulties. When one domain outnumbered the other(s), the person was put in the dominant area. When multiple mentions were evenly distributed across two or three areas, allocation was made to a new category which we label diffuse actives. The results of the assignment process are presented in Table 3-4. These percentages are for all board members; since elective board members comprise 91 percent of the total sample, the distribution for them is quite similar.[10] The distribution reflects in part our earlier findings about the prominence of civic endeavors. Possibly that prominence is now exaggerated. Although non-actives and diffuse actives anchor the listing, there is no *necessary* dimensionality implied.

Before considering how these modal types are related to seat acquisition, one place correlate should be noted. The most striking feature of the nonactives is that they come disproportionately from nonmetropolitan areas. Whereas 25 percent of the members in these less urbanized areas had no "formal preparation," the same is true of only 12 percent in the medium sized SMSAs, and 8 percent in large SMSAs. Members in the smaller areas do not have the depth and breadth of presumably relevant experiences characteristic of the other settings. The inequity also means that some of the findings could be contaminated if they reflect type of place more than type of preentry emphasis. There are two reasons why this is not a significant problem. First, the nonactives comprise only 17 percent of the sample and only one of the five modal types which we are considering. The other

TABLE 3-4
Modal Types of
Attaining Board Membership

Modal Type	Percentage of Boards
Nonactives	17%
Civic Notables	32
Educational Dilettantes	16
Politicos	20
Diffuse Actives	16
	101%

types do not differ substantially by place characteristics. Second, we are not so much concerned with establishing the cause of behavior as with the connections between various types of behaviors. We reason that it is the patterning of inter-connections which helps us isolate those strains more nearly approaching the accountable model.[11]

Table 3-5 presents the rank orders for the five different patterns. The percentage differences upon which these rank orders are based vary from substantial to weak, but the overall pattern is quite suggestive.

The nonactives and civic notables fare least well on the average, since their scores are lowest or among the lowest of the six criteria employed. Nonactives fit an appealing image of the amateur coming in to uplift a school board or to do his civic duty despite lack of prior public affairs experience. But the circumstances surrounding their arrival show that they tend to fall somewhat short of the other types in meeting our criteria. These differences should not be exaggerated, however. They are not always the lowest performers; nor are there always wide gulfs between them and the other types.

Indeed, the civic notables do less well in meeting the suggested criteria. Judging from the words of the early and latter-day good government spokesmen, the civic notables come closest to their ideas of what a board member should be. They have demonstrated their capacity to do good works for the community by their civic endeavors. As a corollary they will almost inevitably have sufficiently high social status to be admired and respected. Perhaps most important of all, they are free of political party taint. They realize the great importance of public education for the community and place it above any "political" considerations.

Although the civic notables in our sample meet these requirements, they do less well when measured in terms of an accountable and responsible selection system. Civic notables were least often originally elected to a board, least often engaged public support when campaigning, and least often ran in slate or parti-san districts. They were equally low with the nonactives in desiring changes in district policies, were next to lowest in differing with other candidates, and were

TABLE 3–5
Differential Preparation for Board and Election Ambience

		Modal Types		
	Politicos	Diffuse Actives	Education Dilettantes	Nonactives	Civic Notables
			Rank Order[a]		
Originally Elected to Board[b]	1	2	4	3	5
Having Public Support in Campaign[c]	2	3	1	4	5
Runnining in Slate or Party District[c]	1	2	3	4	5
Desiring Changes in District[d]	1	2	3	4.5	4.5
Having Different Ideas than Other Candidates[c]	1	2	3	5	4
Differences over Board Roles[c]	1	3	2	4	5

[a]The lower the number the higher the percentage represented in the cell.
[b]Based on entire sample.
[c]Based on all those having run for office.
[d]Based on those initially running for office.

least likely to differ over board roles. Given certain preferences about school district politics these performances might be reassuring. But they hardly seem to satisfy requirements for contested elections, issue differences, challenging the status quo, and looking back over one's shoulder at the mood of the constituency. Of all those board members with prior public affairs experience the civic notables are the blandest and gained office in the least competitive fashion.

Perhaps the second choice of the early reformers and contemporary professional educators would be community activists in education. Such people typically receive their major cues from the professionals. The education dilettantes tend to occupy intermediate positions on most of the measures. Only with respect to manifest public support do they outperform the other types. They also have to contend with more initial-election opposition than do the other types (not shown). These factors suggest that the education dilettantes have to try harder to gain office. This is partly a function of their slightly greater incidence in large urban areas, where competition is a little more severe. On most of the other dimensions they lie approximately midway between the nonactives and civic notables on the one side and the politocos and diffuse actives on the other.

If there is a single type of preboard preparation which the opponents of "education-as-politics" fear, and proponents favor, it is preparation associated with government and politics, especially if partisan colors have been involved. Opponents hold that the introduction of politics demeans and damages the cause of education in general and the selection process in particular. Proponents argue that the politicos are simply making explicit the political nature of the school system and perhaps introducing new and needed dimensions.

Since politicos are found more often in partisan districts — 42 percent versus 26 percent for all elective board members — we should expect them to register comparatively better accounts than do other types. This flows from the fact that partisan (and slate) districts tended to meet several of the criteria in better fashion than did the autonomous districts. Verification of this better performance is found in Table 3–5. With the exception of manifest public support the politicos lead in every category, with the margin (in percentage terms) being very visible when compared with the nonactives, civic notables, and education dilettantes. Differences with the latter three are especially marked with respect to desiring changes and having campaign differences with the opposition and being in a slate or partisan district. No one can charge that the politicos glide into office in a placid fashion.

Our final category is that of the diffuse actives. Since they combine two or more different emphases of the other types (except, of course, the nonactives), it is not surprising that they also do relatively well on most of the criteria. Contributing to their performance is that fact that three-fifths of them had a political component in their eclecticism. Only the pure politicos do better across the entire range of behaviors than do these diffuse participants. One lesson to be drawn from this is that a multiplicity of preboard activities does not lead to an amalgamated state where the individual backs off from situations likely to contain conflict and differences. If anything the opposite is true because, except for the politicos, the diffuse actives score highest on desiring district policy changes, having contrary ideas to their opponents, and wanting other public offices.

We began Chapter 2 by looking at the background characteristics of school board members. It is hardly surprising, since most governing bodies exhibit similar characteristics, to note the dominant WASPish element among board members. Nor do we find it unusual that school board members tend to come from families with educational experience and to have community activist backgrounds.

The more novel aspects, from the point of view of democratic lay control of education, appear when we consider more subtle restrictions upon board membership. Clearly emerging is the self-perpetuation process operating among school boards. Approximately one-half of the members first gained office either through appointment or after being inspired to seek office by school board members. This finding suggests in unequivocal nature the existence of an educational elite which is consciously self-perpetuating. We are not so simplistic as to assume that there is a definable "public" which is being underrepresented on school boards. We also recognize the legitimate interest a governing body has in the quality of its makeup. It is also true that candidates for the school board are often hard to come by. However, we do suggest that the self-perpetuating nature of school boards is subversive of the notion of lay control. If one of the surest avenues to school board membership is through members of the existing board, then one can hardly expect boards to cherish unorthodoxy or to break with tradition.

Perhaps the orthodoxy of boards helps to explain and is explained by the relatively noncombative nature of recruitment to the board, as illustrated in the present chapter. An unusually small number of elections involve intense public participation. Similarly, the ideological or policy difference components of election campaigns are slight. Only a fraction of the board members differed with their opponents over the educational program of the district. The image of the responsible assertion of lay control over education is clearly shaken. What is so astonishing about the low-keyed nature of the recruitment process is that it occurs when the educational system is swept up in a turmoil of controversy.

Our findings suggest that the early educational reformers, those who wanted to keep politics and education separate, succeeded all too well. Ironically, efforts to separate education from politics exaggerate the conditions described above. The more "political" the recruitment process is, the more likely the existence of genuine competition. It is not necessary that the politics be partisan; but the existence of controversy, the desire for change, the restlessness with the status quo which is the very heart of the electoral process are enhanced when the road to the board is marked with "political" signposts.

This latter theme, barely documented in the foregoing materials of this chapter, clearly warrants more detailed attention. For it is in the nature of the structural parameters surrounding school board elections that we will find at least part of the answer to why the school board electoral process so often fails to measure up to the standards of democratic leadership selection.

NOTES

1. Excluded from the base for computing this percentage are those respondents ($N = 22$) who had been appointed to elective boards but had not yet filled out their terms.

2. Joseph Schlesinger, *Ambition and Politics: Political Careers in the United States* (Chicago: Rand McNally, 1966), p. 73.

3. *Ibid.*, chapter 1.

4. See especially Kenneth Prewitt, "Political Ambitions, Volunteerism, and Electoral Accountability," *American Political Science Review*, 64 (March, 1970), pp. 5–17; and Gordon S. Black, "A Theory of Political Ambition: Career Choices and the Role of Structural Incentives," *American Political Science Review*, 66 (March, 1972), pp. 144–59.

5. Schlesinger, *op. cit.*, p. 10.

6. Unfortunately, our number of upwardly aspiring board members is too small to even permit an empirical test of the relationships between ambition and attendance to the electorate, responsiveness, campaign industriousness, and the like.

7. Percentages total more than 100 percent due to differences being cited in more than one area by some of the respondents.

8. The four regions used here and in subsequent reference are the Northeast, Midwest, South, and West. These correspond to Census Bureau classifications, although we use "Midwest" instead of "North Central." The metropolitan measure is derived from the Census Bureau's Standard Metropolitan Statistical Areas (SMSAs) classification. School districts are categorized by those in the thirteen largest SMSAs, those in other SMSAs, and those outside SMSAs.

9. With controls this relationship is shown to hold only in the twelve largest SMSAs and in the Northeast and Western regions.

10. The reason why 17 percent are classified as nonactive whereas 13 percent were previously classified as having taken no steps prior to board membership is that a few of the "one-step" respondents gave such vague, ambiguous, or miscellaneous descriptions that they could not be classified in any of the activity areas.

11. Even with these arguments in mind it is still noteworthy that the major differences to be presented tend to hold within each SMSA type and within each of the four regions. In several instances where these controls are used the number of cases per cell becomes quite small.

Chapter 4

Electoral Structure:

The Legacy of Reform

Prior to the reforms of the turn of the century, school board members frequently were supported by political parties and were elected on a ward basis. In some urban areas, there were between 30 and 50 boards totalling hundreds of members elected from districts. These men won their seats through hotly fought election battles. The fact that these contests were partisan and on a decentralized basis contributed to the success of lower middle class aspirants.[1]

In the wake of the massive big-city political reform movements sparked by the press and by the Progressives, the electoral structure of school districts also faced changes. The reformers were convinced that partisanship was a condition devoutly to be avoided. Politics and politicians were anathema to them. The reformers suggested the institution of smaller boards, longer terms of office, at-large elections, de jure nonpartisanship, and appointive boards as mechanisms which would eliminate the influence of party politicians. Furthermore, such reforms would increase the influence of the ascendant business-professional elites and the middle classes in general and would stamp the school boards with the mark of respectability. Although the key objectives of the reformers were in the big cities, their programs applied eventually to school districts in general.[2]

It is by now a common assumption that municipal reform in many respects succeeded magnificiently in quelling the impact of party organizations. Not that politics were eliminated; the old machines were displaced by the politics of middle class, "good government" organizations and the politics of the bureaucracy. Whatever the salutary consequences of municipal reform were, they did not include increasing (or perhaps even maintaining) the certainty of opposition at election time, the prominence of issues in election, and the engagement of the public in events surrounding elections.[3]

Our specific interest lies in the effects on competition of two key reform institutions: nonpartisanship and at-large elections. As with the municipal reform movement, these were the central pillars of electoral reform on the educational front. The ideology upon which they rested was essentially the same as it is now. Elimination of the partisan election mitigated the pernicious influence of the party apparatus, but also made participation and choice making more difficult for the poorer, less-informed citizenry. Creation of at-large elections eliminated the problems of localism and the hegemony of the ward bosses. Such changes made the board member beholden to a wider constituency, enhanced the strength of the articulate middle classes, and weakened the "closed circle" basis of ward politics.

Despite the onrushing tide of reformism, many places managed to resist these two fundamental changes; less frequently others tried them but found them wanting; and other districts, yet unborn at the time of the great reform movement, did not incorporate them. As a result, the districts under study here include both de jure partisan and nonpartisan types, those with ward and those with at-large elections. For our purposes, ward-based elections shall also include a smattering of school districts which have ward-type residential requirements for the candidates but which ballot on an at-large basis. Similarly, partisan districts include those which have legally partisan elections and about half again that number which have more or less regularized slate competition. Altogether, some 73 percent of the districts have pure, at-large elections and 59 percent have neither party nor slate competition. Our primary task in this chapter is to assess the impact of these two structural variables on both the *quantity and quality* of electoral competition. Another task is to explore the connection between levels of competition and another key reform, the strong superintendency.

THE QUANTITY OF ELECTORAL COMPETITION

There are many ways to classify the quantitative competitiveness of any electoral unit. One can look, for example, at the absolute frequency of contested seats, the size of winning margins, how often seats change hands, the duration of one-party control in partisan units, the convergence of one unit's behavior with that of other units, and long-term versus short-term cycles. Our measures are limited by the amount of electoral data that it was possible to obtain from the districts. Especially in smaller areas the historical records of school elections are fragmentary. We are also constrained from making some of the usual sorts of analysis because partisan elections obtain in only a minority of the districts. Thus we cannot talk about party shifts nor can we divide up districts in terms of which party is usually dominant.

With these limitations in mind it is still possible to derive several measures denoting levels of competition from both the historical records and from the personal interviews. The first is simply the presence or absence of opposition in either the last primary or general election preceding our interviewing in the spring of 1968. Utilizing only one electoral period distorts to some extent the recent electoral profile of the district, but using the last round of elections means that "time" is more or less held constant. Since most of our other measures tap the district's electoral histories over divergent periods of time, it seems wise to have one which is definitely timebound. The analytic results obtained by using this measure are quite similar to those obtained by using a measure with a longer time frame. It is a tribute to the noncompetitiveness of school board elections that in one-fourth of the districts the officeseekers had no opposition in the last election.

The second measure of competition intensity looks at the rate of turnover in office. One way of assessing turnover is to determine the mean length of service on a board. It stands to reason that the longer board members serve the less turnover there is. Note that this measure says nothing about the presence of competition nor the size of winning margins. On the other hand, to the extent that competitiveness embodies a changing of the guard the mean length of tenure is a perfectly suitable indicator. Across the districts the mean number of years on the board is 5.1. This measure will be scored in the same direction as the others if we reverse the scoring; thus the higher the score the more competitive the district. For the sake of consistent terminology let us call this measure "turnover rate."

The third indicator of competitiveness is the rate of defeated incumbents. By any account one of the clearest expressions of competition is the degree to which incumbents are forced out of office, or alternatively, the degree to which incumbents are reelected in the face of opposition. Although it is well-established that incumbents have a tremendous advantage in most American elections and usually do succeed themselves when trying for reelection, the threat of defeat and the desire to win are presumed to affect the behavior of incumbents. Moreover, rates of removal vary over time and typically peak in periods of stress. It is, at the last remove, a way in which the electorate indicates the ultimate in dissatisfaction.

In trying to develop a forced turnover measure for the school districts we were plagued not only by the unevenness of the available data but also by the unevenness of terms of office and frequency of elections. Our solution was to employ the best estimates possible for each district, without going so far back in time as to make the cross-district comparisons suspect. No more than four elections for any district, therefore, were used in computing the incumbent defeat rate.

It is an astounding fact that in 43 percent of the districts no incumbents had been forced out of office in the recent past. At the other extreme, in only 6 percent of the districts had all incumbents trying for reelection been defeated. Of course part of the reason for these figures is that incumbents often do not choose to run again. Some portion of them may be discouraged because of the prospect of defeat, others because they have now "performed their civic duty." Overall, the average rate of incumbent removal was 34 percent.

In assessing the electoral impact of nonpartisan and at-large elections we used control factors to account for differences between the districts which might be underlying any apparent connection between the political forms and competition levels. Election frequency, whether there are district referenda coterminous with board elections, and whether there are state and/or national elections coterminous with board elections were three political structure variables held constant. Another broad set of important factors may be summed up as socioeconomic complexity, which embraces such concepts as population size, degree of urbanism, cultural diversity, organizational scale, and community interdependencies.[5] It is generally held that greater socioeconomic complexity is associated with a richer, more organized form of political life. We have introduced directly into the regression analysis the size of the adult population in each school district.

Size alone will not define the larger environment, particularly for small to medium size places. Illustratively, a district with 15,000 inhabitants is embedded in a different environment depending upon whether it comprises the school district for an incorporated town far away from a large city or whether it serves a suburban area adjacent to a teeming central city. We have, therefore, conducted our analysis at three levels: for all districts, for districts within Standard Metropolitan Statistical Areas, and for districts outside of such areas. There is also a prominent thesis that school board competition varies with the socioeconomic status of the districts. That thesis will be entertained subsequently.

In general, the consequences of nonpartisanship and at-large elections on the quantitative intensity of competition are negative (Table 4-1). But this generalization needs qualification, as we shall see. Disregarding whether the district is inside or outside of a metropolitan area the relationships are all negative, with every regression coefficient except one above - .20. Considering that population size as well as a number of other political variables are involved in the regression equations, these results demonstrate a discernible and certainly statistically significant impact from the two reform institutions.[6]

The simplicity of this generalization dissolves when we divide the districts according to their metropolitan status. Let us initially consider the operation of nonpartisanship. As far as the sheer presence of competition is concerned, the generalization holds; there is scarcely any difference by location of district. However, nonpartisanship works in a different fashion with respect to office turnover and incumbent defeats. In the metro districts the effects are large and negative. By contrast they are small and even positive in the nonmetro districts. To the extent that office turnover and incumbent defeats signify an attentive, responsive electorate, and a generally healthy, competitive system the presence of nonpartisanship marginally abets the process in nonmetro districts, while seriously undermining it in the metro areas.

Accounting for these differential effects is no simple task. The major clues seem to lie in the striking differences between the political culture of relatively isolated rural and small town politics versus that of the cosmopolitan and more diverse metropolitan areas. The nonmetro areas are more likely to be bounded,

TABLE 4-1
Quantitative Competition in School Board Elections

	Partisan/Nonpartisan		Ward/At-large	
	Simple r	*Beta*	*Simple r*	*Beta*
Presence of Competition				
Total	-.22	-.32[a]	-.16	-.27
Metro	-.17	-.26	-.19	-.28
Nonmetro	-.22	-.29	-.21	-.30
Office Turnover				
Total	-.08	-.07	-.18	-.21
Metro	-.27	-.30	-.05	-.13
Nonmetro	.09	.16	-.28	-.31
Incumbent Defeats				
Total	-.17	-.27	-.17	-.23
Metro	-.30	-.44	-.25	-.35
Nonmetro	.06	.11	-.10	-.08

[a]In addition to taking into account the other variables in the column headings, these partial beta coefficients also take into account the effects of district population, election frequency, whether there are school referenda coterminous with board elections and whether state and/or federal elections coincide with board elections.

to have their own distinctive ways of doing things, and to have a more pervasive political culture marking the entire area. If this is true, then a procedural difference such as partisan versus nonpartisan elections may account for relatively small differences in such matters as incumbent defeats in office. The culture of small town politics overrides particular political institutions. Not so in the more complex, amorphous metropolitan areas where distinctive independent political cultures are more difficult to maintain.

Both the heterogeneity of the central cities and the lack of autonomy among the satellite communities make districts in the metro areas more vulnerable to the particular effects of nonpartisanship versus partisanship. In the absence of a "community ideology," which occurs more often in the nonmetro areas, the metro districts may succumb more readily to the debilitating effects of nonpartisanship. That this is true for office turnover and incumbent defeats but not for the sheer presence of competition suggests a threshold effect: nonpartisanship discourages contesting across all types of districts, but crosses the threshold of affecting changes in office only in the metro areas.

An example of a specific process which dampens the effects of reform versus nonreform practices in nonmetro areas lies in use of office sponsorship, which is discussed in Chapter 3. One would expect districts with greater sponsorship to have less intense rates of competition. This is true for both metro and nonmetro districts, but the effects are much sharper in the latter case. In addition, sponsorship is more common in these nonmetro districts. The greater incidence plus a more pronounced impact helps sponsorship override the impact which nonpartisanship and at-large elections might have. It is not just that the incidence of office sponsorship is lower in metro districts; it is that (aside from outright appointments) sponsorship is less effectively brought off in the metro districts. It is one thing to manage board succession in the intimate confines of the less complex environment of the nonmetro districts; it is quite another in the metro districts, with their more variegated atmosphere and much greater monitoring by interest groups.

At-large elections depress the levels of competition, regardless of which measure is used, in the districts as a whole and in both metro and nonmetro areas. It is not a uniform picture because the consequences are the same in both areas with respect to the presence of competition, more severe for the nonmetro areas on office turnover, and more severe for metro areas on the occurrence of incumbent defeats. Still, the most important message is the standard negative result, ranging from the weak to the very substantial. At-large elections appear to scare potential candidates away from competing for office. Prospective officeholders are less sure of their goals and strategies when operating outside their home area. They may be intimidated by the candidacies of local notables, whereas the potential aspirants in the ward system will compare themselves with local fellows who do not appear to be giants. It may be easier for people to encourage potential candidates in the more familiar confines of the ward than in the more inclusive ones of the entire district.

Circulation in office and turning incumbents out of office are also discouraged by at-large systems, probably for reasons of propinquity, visibility, and feelings of direct accountability. At-large officeholders are accountable to everyone in general yet no one in particular. Ward officeholders have a specific constituency which has the capability of holding a specific person accountable. It becomes easier to "turn the rascals out" because of the overlapping concentration of interests and votes. Similarly, ward-based incumbents may be discouraged from running again because they realize there is an area-bound constituency. Board members in at-large districts may be conscious of specific group reprisals or monitoring, but they also know that such feelings may be lost in the common balloting. The reformers' aims of reducing dependency on ward bosses and of removing the territorial-based interests probably succeeded only too well. To the extent that they wished this innovation to drive down competition and ensure longevity in office they also succeeded.

As noted before, district population is used in our analysis as a summary variable denoting the scale and complexity of socio-political life within the school district. Since we are also examining all relationships by whether the district lies within or outside a metropolitan area, we have a general check on whether the effects of the two reform processes are simply standing in place of socioeconomic complexity. While used in this sense as a control variable, it is also worthwhile to see to what extent population size, as a summary variable, contributes to levels of competition in school board elections.[7] In this fashion we can gain some appreciation for the relative contribution of reform practices to variation in competition.

Although the picture is checkered, it is rather startling to observe that the two explicitly political variables usually emerge from the regression equations as strong or stronger than district size. This is invariably the case if only the metropolitan districts are being considered. In addition, population does not necessarily work in the direction one might expect. True, the larger the population the more sheer competition there is, though even here both the simple and partial coefficients are much smaller than those for the two political variables. For office turnover and incumbent defeats the relationships are slightly on the negative side. Hence the relative importance of the two political variables is by no means negligible.

Conspicuously absent from our analysis of reform impact on school board competition has been the element of socioeconomic status. In an important article Minar presented evidence for Chicago suburban elementary districts which showed that competition for school board seats varied inversely with the status of the districts, as measured by education, income and occupation.[8] Competition was assessed in terms of the total percent of votes cast for losing candidates as a proportion of all votes cast. (Minar also showed that turnout varied inversely with status.) Moreover, status was the single most important predictor of electoral conflict. Minar concluded that status was so important because it signified the presence of conflict management skills in the districts — skills which could be used to control the course of politics, primarily through the extensive use of nominating caucuses.

These findings are particularly challenging because they run against much of the grain of the literature in community politics, a grain which describes higher levels of conflict and immobilization as socioeconomic status rises (except perhaps at the very top of the status hierarchy.)[9] While Minar's findings are timebound and, much more significantly, placebound, the prominence and acceptance of the results by the scholarly community demands that we take the basic hypothesis into consideration in our own work.

The question we must ask is whether the moderate to strong effects of reform practices are actually disguising the role of social status. Two measures of district socioeconomic status are used here: 1) median years of education of persons twenty-five years and older; and 2) median family income. These figures are based on 1960 census data. Where the school districts perfectly or approximately coincide with other civil units used in census reports (such as cities or counties) the application of census data to school districts presented no problem. In other cases it was impossible to determine with much precision the overlay of district on census units. As a result we can report with reasonable assurance on two-thirds of the total supplementary sample (weighted $N = 109$, raw $N = 70$). These are the districts which coincide with counties and separate cities. Extrapolations for other districts suggest that the results for this large subset would not change appreciably if the whole set were included.

The regressions reported above were recalculated with the inclusion of the status variables, each one included separately in order to minimize the known high intercorrelation of the two. The results do not support a strong role for social status. In the first place the simple, zero order correlations between the status variables and the competition variables are exceedingly meager. For education the figures never rise above .15, even with a physical control by SMSA vs. non-SMSA. For income the figures are slightly stronger, but even here the highest is .25. Moreover, the signs are not always in the direction predicted by Minar's model. And when the beta coefficients were calculated for the status variables, their weak strength declined even further. Income again produces the highest figure, .20. By contrast the average betas for the two reform variables is .32. One question is, therefore, answered: social status variables have but a minor impact on the quantitative aspects of school board competition.

There is, however, a corollary question — does the inclusion of income and education in the analysis weaken (or strengthen) the impact of reform institutions? The best way to answer this question is to compare the regression coefficients for the reform variables before and after the status variables are entered into the equations. When this is done, it is apparent that socioeconomic status has only a minimal effect on the strength of the reform institutions. Indeed, in many instances the inclusion of status enhances the contribution of the reform variables. That is, holding constant the district's socioeconomic status often strengthens the explanatory power of election forms vis à vis the quantitative side of electoral competition.

Given such a sharp disjuncture between our findings and those of Minar and others who have worked with districts similar to his, how are the differences to be resolved? Two sources for the discrepancy may be suggested. One source is on the dependent variable, that is, the measure of electoral conflict. Minar used only one indicator — the percent tallied by the losing opponents. Although we have used more indicators, and hence have more fixes on competition, we were not able to use that same measure. Thus the different results could spring from these differences in indicators.

It seems more likely, however, that the dissimilarity comes from other sources, those concerning the independent variable and the nature of the samples. There was little variance in the districts studied by Minar. (One of the weaknesses of much of the literature in school district politics is its localistic nature.) The districts were all elementary, relatively small, in the Chicago area, nonpartisan in formal terms, and apparently used at-large elections. Only on the socioeconomic dimension were there graphic differences. On the other hand, our sample runs the full range of meaningful distinctions, including those just listed. In addition, the very fact that these districts include high school makes a profound difference, inasmuch as high school inclusive districts almost by definition are less homogeneous than elementary districts.

In sum, the suburban elementary districts provide a perfect opportunity for socioeconomic variables to work their effects, whereas our national sample of districts allows other factors, such as reform versus nonreform institutions, to have an impact. The earlier findings, then, are perfectly appropriate for the districts covered, but their generalizability is distinctly limited. Correspondingly, the place of social status variables in affecting school board competition should be sharply revised downward, and the place of electoral forms and practices revised upward.

THE QUALITY OF COMPETITION

Contesting for office, turnover rates, and the ousting of incumbents illustrate the quantitative side of school board elections, but they tell little about the nature of the competition. We do not know, for example, the prominence of policy differences in the elections, the types of issues raised, the sorts of appeals made to the electorate, the heat of the campaign, and so forth. The absence of this side of electoral politics characterizes most studies of competition outside the realm of the individual case study. In general, we know much more about the outcomes than the processes of competition.

A thorough understanding of the qualitative dimension of school board competition requires more information than we were able to gather. Nevertheless, substantial inroads can be made on the topic. Three major strands adumbrated in the previous chapter will be followed. First, there is the question of whether aspiring board members have alternative policies in mind for the school district. Do they have any ideas about changes which might be in order? One can imagine situations in which no policy changes are needed in an absolute sense. Yet the very essence of political choice lies in the notion of alternative policy preferences. Furthermore, the troubled substantive history of even the calmer school districts in the past decade suggests that alternatives might have at least occurred to board aspirants, if only to counterpoint the prevailing ones. It is a commentary on the status quo orientation of board members that the mean rate of desired changes across districts was 47 percent.

A second index of electoral ambience carries further into the heart of the election campaign. Potential board members may have ideas for change but are unopposed at election time or are appointed to office. As we saw, one-third of our sample entered elective boards in one or the other fashion. Even when there is opposition, there may be no recognized disagreement on the substantive issues. In principle, however, if there are multiple candidates for the same position, the criteria of meaningful choice demands that they differ on some issues. Yet across districts an average of only 56 percent of the board members affirmed that their ". . . ideas about schools were different from those of some other candidates."

Issue differences have a wide range. We may capitalize upon this range to develop a third indicator of qualitative competition, one of particular importance to students of political representation. We established in Chapter 3 that a majority of issue differences pivot on such traditional matters as finances, instructional staff, the educational program, and issues of civil rights. One broad issue domain, however, focuses on the *conduct* of the board rather than its product or substantive decisions. We are referring to such topics as the composition of the board; how its members relate to one another; the degree to which the board is responsive to the community; and its relationships to the bureaucracy. These aspects of board behavior have great symbolic as well as practical importance. This issue domain is contrasted with the others by its concern with the *process* of governing whereas the others are concerned with the *substance* of governance. Alternatively, since it embraces most of the major conceptions of representational government, one might call it the representation issue domain.

A number of interesting aspects of school board elections accompany the occurrence of this issue. Analysis of the various issue domains revealed that when process questions arose they tended to preempt or neutralize other kinds of issues, whereas other issues were more often found clustering together. Process issues also arose more frequently when incumbents were challenged (see Chapter 3), suggesting that a direct confrontation with the board was more likely when representational roles were at issue. Finally, it is instructive to observe that the more often process issues emerged the more often incumbents were defeated. Therefore, it seems wise to include the incidence of process issues as a third index of the quality of competition. Across all districts the prevalence of this type of issue averaged 36 percent.

Nonpartisanship and at-large elections have a debilitating effect on the qualitative intensity of competition, both in metro and nonmetro areas (Table 4-2). It is nevertheless apparent that there are differential effects within metro versus nonmetro districts according to the type of qualitative competition. Thus the two reform practices have a much greater effect in the metro districts with respect to the desire for policy changes and the incidence of explicit differences with opponents. Indeed, on the latter there is virtually no impact in nonmetro areas. On the other hand, the likelihood of conflict on representational roles is depressed much more in the nonmetro districts with reform institutions. A general way to assess the different patterns is to say that nonpartisanship and at-large balloting have a greater impact on the metro districts in terms of whether differences will emerge at all; but in terms of the specific domain of process or representational roles, the two reforms have more consequence on the nonmetro districts.

Why do nonpartisanship and at-large elections generally discourage a desire for policy changes, issue differences with opponents, and specific differences on the representational roles of the board? Stated more normatively, why do these two institutions drive down the quality of competition, reducing the presence of those elements which comprise the essence of democratic elections? In the instance of nonpartisan versus partisan elections, the answer seems to lie in the patterning of regularized competition for office. Once it is established that two parties (or slates) will compete more or less regularly for office, and since the public and officeseekers are accustomed to the idea that parties and slates are supposed to offer alternatives, then it follows that the candidates will be encouraged and perhaps forced into considering policy alternatives, challenging their opposition, and cutting to the heart of much politics — representational roles.

By contrast, nonpartisanship does not have this forcing effect. Candidates

TABLE 4-2
The Quality of Competition in School Board Elections

	Partisan/Nonpartisan		Ward/At-large	
	Simple r	*Beta*	*Simple r*	*Beta*
Desire for Policy Changes				
Total	-.37	-.36[a]	-.33	-.36
Metro	-.42	-.55	-.42	-.50
Nonmetro	-.26	-.15	-.31	-.17
Issue Differences with Opponents				
Total	-.25	-.24	-.11	-.06
Metro	-.34	-.35	-.13	-.12
Nonmetro	-.13	-.01	-.16	-.03
Differences on Board Roles				
Total	-.20	-.28	-.19	-.25
Metro	-.09	-.33	-.02	-.22
Nonmetro	-.30	-.48	-.31	-.34

[a]See note to Table 4-1.

may and often do choose to heat up the campaign in nonpartisan elections, but this happens much more erratically and idiosyncratically, and it is not institutionalized. That the nonmetro districts are less swayed by partisanship at the gross level of policy change preferences and issue differences is sound testimony to the smothering effects that small town and rural political cultures may have on any sort of formal political arrangements.

Turning to the impact of at-large versus ward based elections, the reasoning is of a different order. What seems to happen is that particularistic versus generalistic interests emerge when smaller constituencies are involved. In the at-large situation candidates are busy trying not to antagonize anyone, since they must receive general support over the district as a whole. Ordinarily the heterogeneity of interests across a whole district is greater than within a single ward or other electoral unit. Seeing the big picture, candidates in at-large districts come more easily to the conclusion that drastic policy changes might upset the whole delicate balance in a district.

Candidates in ward-type districts, on the other hand, are less constrained. They are dealing with a more homogeneous constituency and can develop a sense of what is best for and what appeals to that particular constituency, unencumbered by concern with the reactions of voters in all the other wards. Similarly, the geographical and psychological proximity between candidate and voter in the wards, plus the overwhelming fact of separate constituencies, facilitates a concentration on representation issues.

Although the absolute values of the coefficients pointing to the effects of nonpartisanship and at-large elections are by no means negligible, they acquire more luster when laid alongside those generated by the summary variable, district population. Looking first at the overall picture, there is only one instance in which population size appears to make a substantially greater difference than either of the political practices. This case involves the minimal effects of at-large elections on issue differences with opponents. Otherwise the apparent contribution of population size, and what that entails, lies in the same range as that for the reform institutions.

Without going into the matter in detail, it is nevertheless obvious that population size affects the metro districts much more so than the nonmetro ones. In fact, the signs are not always in the same direction. Another interesting aspect about the population factor is that while it acts to increase the level of desire for policy changes and of issue differences (at least for the metro districts), it actually depresses the likelihood of conflict about representational roles. And this is true for both metro and nonmetro districts. We suspect that the reason for this is that the pressing substantive issues assume front stage prominence in the larger districts. There is a general correlation between district size and the frequency of substantive issues such as finances, integration, physical plant problems, and teacher negotiations. These manifest, often spirited issues serve to usurp the place which the process issues might play. It is as though the larger districts cannot afford the luxury of fighting about representational roles. Less beset by monumental problems, the smaller districts — other things being equal — have more opportunity for pushing forward the process issues. In addition, the smaller districts almost inevitably will have more primary ties, friends and neighbors, politics, and enduring political memories, all of which would foster more emphasis on the process and style of board behavior rather than on substantive outcomes.

As with the quantitative side of competition, we should examine the role of social status in affecting the quality of competition. In this instance the literature of educational politics provides a less certain guide than it did in the case of quantitative competition. Nevertheless, if we take Minar's findings as a source,[10] it would follow that social status should be negatively associated with the incidence and severity of policy differences in school board elections. Since higher status districts can manage the level of conflict as expressed in nomination procedures and in voting behavior, then they should also be better able to suppress the heat of the contest itself. On the other hand, if one accepts the Crain and Rosenthal argument about higher status leading to greater opposition and open conflict,[11] then it should follow that higher status districts will have more *signs* of qualitative competition.

Working again with the subset of districts for which we have reliable education and income statistics, we repeated the analysis and included the two status indicators. At the overall level the results lend little support to either argument. The zero order correlations for the districts as a whole in no instance, exceeded .19; nor were they always in the same direction. Broken down into metro and nonmetro districts, the results showed that both education and income had greater impact in the nonmetro districts, and that these were primarily negative relationships. Findings in the metro districts were essentially unchanged. Thus in nonmetro areas higher status seemed to be associated with less conflict, thereby supporting the general model proposed by Minar.

When the full set of other variables was taken into account, however, this picture changed dramatically. The two indicators still had virtually no impact in the metro districts. In the nonmetro districts, though, the relationship became positive rather than negative and also increased in its magnitude. Now the Crain-Rosenthal thesis is supported. We do not intend to resolve the conflicting models. Explaining why the effects are strong in the nonmetro areas but trivial in the metro areas is an especially difficult task. On balance, however, it is apparent that status has more bearing on the conduct of the campaign for office than on the electoral outcome of the campaign — but only in the less complex world of the nonmetropolitan school districts.

The other side of the coin leads to the question: does controlling for the effects of income and education seriously alter the apparent contribution of the two reform institutions to the quality of the contest? For the most part, the answer is in the negative. Under certain conditions the values of their respective beta coefficients decline; but under other circumstances they increase. With virtually no exceptions the interpretation arrived at previously still stands: nonpartisanship and at-large elections depress the exposition of differences among candidates for the school board. Considering the number of other factors which are being taken into account in an analysis of this sort, the staying power of these two single electoral arrangements is impressive indeed.

COMPETITION AND THE SUPERINTENDENCY

In addition to the electoral changes implemented toward the turn of the century, a second major dimension of school reform lay in the centralization of school administration and the companion rise in the status and power of a central superintendent. Especially in the larger municipalities the education system was likely to be a helter skelter of separate or partially independent districts, presided over by lay boards and a variety of administrators. Reform was designed to establish political and fiscal independence for the educational system. Reform also called for central boards and a major administrative figure in the form of a superintendent. Rather than have a number of jurisdictions with complete or at least partial autonomy — and resultant lack of uniformity, diseconomies of small scale, and vulnerability to local interests — it was successfully argued that consolidation should occur. Under reform, the definition of board roles versus superintendent roles were spelled out very explicitly, and to the increasing professional advantage of the superintendent. Questions of curriculum, text, teachers, personnel practices, and fiscal management came under the purview and control of the superintendent. Boards were to be more advisory than anything else. Although the reform movement hit the cities the hardest — where decentralized systems abounded — the logic also applied to other places and to systems yet to come into existence. It is the emphasis placed on the superintendency which draws our interest.

School governance has never completely fallen under the sway of the superintendent's office, but there is no question that the first half of the twentieth century saw enormous gains of power for the office. Our interest lies less in evaluating the desirability of strong versus weak superintendents than it does in observing the effects of the strong superintendency on school board competition. Although the reformers probably did not visualize it, enhancing the office of the superintendent to at least parity with the school board contained not only the seeds of board-superintendent conflict, but also the potential for periodic school district crises. If the superintendent becomes the focal point of educational governance, then anything extraordinary involving the superintendent will probably have repercussions on the board and the district as a whole. Falling under this rubric is the problem of managerial (superintendent) succession which afflicts school boards from time to time. Indeed, Zald has stated that lay boards and boards of directors are most likely to mobilize power when picking executive successors.[12]

The fact that the superintendency has become a focal point of school governance along with the board of education suggests that the fate of the two are not independent of each other. It is apparent even to the most casual observer that the superintendent often becomes the centerpiece in school district controversies. Board members come to be identified with either supporting him or opposing him. Aspirants to the board are often characterized according to whether they approve or disapprove of the current administration of the school district. And it is not uncommon for both superintendents and whole boards to be either roundly condemned or supported by various segments of the public which perceive the board and superintendent as having a united stand.

We may begin with a very simple hypothesis: the longer the superintendent has been in office the fewer the signs of intense competition and electorate dissatisfaction.[13] This hypothesis stems from the foregoing thesis that the superintendent is perhaps *the* central figure in local educational governance. His continued presence in office signifies that all is relatively well in the district primarily because he is, after all, subject to outright removal and pointed suggestions about "moving on." Nor are ambitious superintendents necessarily content to stay in one place. Finally, of course, superintendents do retire and they do die. Regardless of the basis for length of tenure, however, the hypothesis is that (on the average) longer tenure is associated with electoral quietude.

We might note, first of all, that superintendents tend to outlast board members. Whereas the average length of service for the superintendents in our sample was 8.2 years, the corresponding average for board members was 5.1 years. In one very real sense, then, superintendents have a distinct advantage of experience in district politics. There is little question that they trade on this superior experience in their relationships with the board.

While the average tenure is much greater for superintendents than board

members, the variance is also. Whereas the standard deviation for superintendents
is 7.4, it is but 2.4 for board members. What this means, of course, is that at a
given point in time some districts have had their superintendents for a great number
of years whereas others have recently acquired one. Board members, on the other
hand, more often have a moderate amount of experience, with proportionately
fewer of them at either extreme of long or short service.

    Turning now to indicators of electoral heat, it is manifest that length of
time in the superintendency is related to electoral quietude. As Table 4-3 shows,
in all districts tenure is negatively related to the presence of competition, the rate
of turnover, and incumbent defeats. This negative association occurs at the zero
order level as well as when other factors are held constant. Taking districts as
a whole, the hypothesis is supported, although the relationship for the sheer
presence of competition is modest.

TABLE 4-3
Superintendency Tenure and Quantitative
Competition in School Board Elections

	Total		*Metro*		*Nonmetro*	
	Simple r	*Beta*	*Simple r*	*Beta*	*Simple r*	*Beta*
Presence of Competition	-.18	-.13[a]	.14	.05	-.33	-.35
Office Turnover	-.26	-.23	-.12	-.16	-.35	-.29
Incumbent Defeats	-.23	-.23	-.37	-.42	-.08	-.09

[a]These partial beta coefficients take into account the effects of partisan versus nonpartisan
elections, ward versus at-large system, election frequency, coterminous school referenda and
state/federal elections, and district population.

    When the districts are divided according to their metropolitan status,
the pattern holds with only one exception. In the metropolitan districts superintendent longevity is not associated with competition. Otherwise, the negative
relationships persist. Nonmetro districts are particularly sensitive to how long the
superintendent has been on hand with respect to competition and office turnover, whereas the metro districts are especially affected in terms of incumbents
being forced out of office. Since incumbent defeats represent the most severe form
of electoral sanctions, it might be concluded that the fate of metro school board
personnel is the most closely linked to superintendent tenure. Perhaps the trauma
associated with short-lived superintendents in these large places creates more
political ripples and grievances than in the smaller places. In the latter, superintendent tenure scarcely affects forced turnover but definitely affects absolute
competition and overall turnover. These smaller, less complex districts seem to
ride out short tenures without the drastic effects of "turning the rascals out,"
but more board members seem to hitch their own board careers to the superintendent's career. There may be a tendency for board members to time their
departures with that of the superintendents.

It has been implied that the departure of a superintendent creates a crisis for the school board. Although departure could mean retirement or death in office, we will restrict the term to those instances in which the superintendent moved to another position. Retirement in office is usually announced well ahead of time; no acrimony is involved, and the board feels like neither victim nor victimizer. Departures tend to be more abrupt, there may be conflict in the district, and the board may feel as though the departing superintendent is leaving them holding the bag or, conversely, the board may have encouraged the superintendent to leave.

Granting that a departure is probably more traumatic than a retirement, there are two different types of leave-taking. Voluntary departures are presumably more amicable and do not necessarily imply rancor or conflict between board and superintendent. Such departures often involve occupationally or geographically mobile superintendents. Involuntary departures, however, involve quite a different set of circumstances. The board has given a clear signal to the superintendent, either by outright refusal to renew a contract or by making life so difficult that the superintendent has no choice. Inevitably, these situations will have involved school-community tensions, often with the sides being divided for and against the superintendent and possibly his faction on the board.

If the above scenarios are realistic, we should be able to find visible traces of them in the relationship between the type of superintendent departure and the nature of competition for school board positions. Specifically, the quantity and quality of competition should vary, depending upon whether the departure was voluntary or involuntary. Districts were classified according to whether the last departure decision was freely made or forced. Posts vacated by retirement or death were set aside, although in practice the results obtained for the voluntary departures strongly resembled those for retirement and death. Two-thirds of the departures had been either voluntary or involuntary, voluntary farewells outnumbering involuntary ones by a ratio of three to two.

Unfortunately for analytic purposes, these departures range in time from one year to over a dozen in the past. In some instances this means going back to a period antedating the electoral data available for the districts. This problem has been handled in two ways, by logic and by a time control. As for logic, we have reasoned that the conditions which are associated with the two types of departures do not simply disappear overnight. For example, even though an involuntary departure might have occurred several years in the past, we suspect that there are still residues in the electoral history and board member experiences of the district. The second way of coping with the problem is to look only at departures which occurred in the immediate past. We have settled on five years as a reasonable time because it yields enough cases for analysis and because it covers a period during which a majority of members on boards with superintendent departures first entered office.

The guiding hypothesis is that involuntary departures are accompanied by more electoral heat than are voluntary ones. We may return to some of our earlier measures (in slightly different form) to assess the validity of this hypothesis.

Table 4-4 presents the results for all departures and for departures within the past five years. Without exception the direction of the findings falls in line with the hypothesis. Involuntary departures are accompanied by more sheer competition and by higher office turnover. In terms of the electoral experiences of the present board members, those serving in districts with involuntary departures more often had a desire for policy change, they engaged in specific issue differences with their opponents, and these differences more often took the form of conflict about the board's political roles. Moreover, most of these differences are within the range of statistical significance at the .05 level, using the chi square test. Zeroing in on mobility within the last five years sharpens the overall results, attesting to the better time fit between electoral histories and superintendent departures. Again, even though the N's are now quite small, the relationships are clearly not of a chance magnitude.[14]

TABLE 4-4
Last Superintendent Departure and Competitive
Aspects of School Board Elections

		Total		Last Five Years	
		Voluntary	*Involuntary*	*Voluntary*	*Involuntary*
Raw	*N =*	*(32)*[a]	*(19)*	*(20)*	*(9)*
Competition in Last Election					
	No	26%	17%	36%	00%
	Yes	74	83	64	100
Office Turnover					
	Low[b]	55	40	81	00
	High	45	60	19	100
Desire for Policy Changes					
	Low	63	41	69	16
	High	37	59	31	84
Issue Differences with Opponents					
	Low	64	26	71	15
	High	36	74	29	85
Differences on Board Roles					
	Low	49	32	57	21
	High	51	68	43	79

[a]The N's for this table are unweighted.
[b]On this and the remaining variables the distributions have been dichotomized as nearly as possible at the midpoint.

Perhaps the finding with the most theoretical interest involves differences on the process roles of the board. It will be recalled that this measure denotes whether there was a campaign difference about the board's relationships with the community, how the board handled the school bureaucracy, and the board's internal composition and conduct. These are often issues which inevitably involve a definition of what the board should do, and what the administration should do. An obvious case concerns the oversight function of the board. But the interview protocols indicate that the other subissues also either directly or indirectly draw in the administration. For example, the charge that the board is not responsive to the people or that it favors one segment of the community over another directly involves the superintendent because he is often the sponsor and certainly the executor of such policies. What these data show is that such controversies arise much more frequently when the superintendent has been asked (or will be asked) to leave. He becomes the victim, target, or sometimes the scapegoat of such controversies, although he may have inspired such action through his behavior.

Taking into account the findings related to time in office and type of departure leaves little doubt that the superintendency has assumed the focal point which the early reformers so earnestly desired. This conclusion has usually been reached in terms of decision-making studies and the development and application of educational programs. What we have shown here is that the electoral climate of a school district is inextricably intertwined with the career of the superintendent. How long a superintendent has been on hand is a good index of the electoral quietude of the district. Whether he leaves voluntarily or involuntarily not only says something about the quantitative side of competition but also about the qualitative dimension, which is perhaps more significant.

This chapter, as well as the preceding two, has revealed the handiwork of the reformers and the consequences of an avowedly apolitical approach to educational governance. The leadership selection aspect of governance can be characterized as politically tepid on the whole. Yet almost without exception the manifestly political backgrounds and structures work at least partially to overcome the existing legacy. It may be that the populace acts as though it prefers the tepid to the intense, the issue-less to the issue-filled, low competition and nonconfrontation to regularized opposition, and the status quo to the prospect of change. But the prescribed norms of democratic leadership selection run in the contrary direction. These norms tend to be most frequently violated under the institutions of reform and the ethos of educational purity.

NOTES

1. Joseph M. Cronin, "The Board of Education in the Great Cities, 1890–1964," (Ph.D. dissertation, Stanford University, 1965); and his *The Control of Urban Schools: Perspective on the Power of Educational Reformers* (New York: Free Press, 1973).

2. Documentation and a lively discussion are provided by Leigh Stelzer, "The Receptivity of School Board Members: A Study of the Requisites of Representation" (Ph.D. dissertation, University of Michigan, 1971), chapter 2.

3. A good interpretive summary is Edward C. Banfield and James Q. Wilson, *City Politics* (Cambridge: Harvard University Press and M.I.T. Press, 1963). For a historical case study see Jean Stinchcombe, *Reform and Reaction: City Politics in Toledo* (Belmont, Calif.: Wadsworth, 1969). A recent quantitative study of municipal voting turnout shows that "reformed" cities have lower voting turnout. See Robert R. Alford and Eugene C. Lee, "Voting Turnout in American Cities," *American Political Science Review*, 62 (September, 1968), pp. 796–813.

4. Stelzer, *loc cit.*

5. On this point see Jeffrey K. Hadden and Edgar F. Borgatta, *American Cities: Their Social Characteristics* (Chicago: Rand McNally, 1965).

6. In order to have enough boards from very large cities for analytical purposes, it was necessary to oversample from the large city stratum. This addition meant reweighting the rest of the districts. Thus our raw N is 75, but the computational, weighted N is 166. This reweighting is applied throughout this chapter. See Appendix A for more details.

7. District population has a modest relationship to the two reform measures being studied here: .23 with nonpartisanship and .19 with at-large elections. Holding metropolitan status constant raises the relationship slightly in each instance.

8. David W. Minar, "The Community Basis of Conflict in School System Politics," *American Sociological Review*, 31 (December, 1966), pp. 822–34. Among works building on this seminal effort are William L. Boyd, "Community Status and Conflict in Suburban School Politics;" and David O'Shea, "The Structuring of Political Processes in Suburban School District Government," (unpublished papers presented at the annual meetings of the American Educational Research Association, Chicago, 1972).

9. For the full development of this idea see Robert L. Crain and Donald B. Rosenthal, "Community Status as a Dimension of Local Decision-Making," *American Sociological Review*, 32 (December, 1967), pp. 970–84.

10. Minar, *loc cit.*

11. Crain and Rosenthal, *loc cit.*

12. For a persuasive argument on this score see Mayer Zald, "The Power and Functions of Boards of Directors: A Theoretical Synthesis," *American Journal of Sociology*, LXXV (July, 1969), pp. 97–111.

13. It should be stressed that we are not arguing that superintendent longevity or nondeparture "causes" other elements of the district's politics to remain more stable, nor that the flow is the other way around, which is our private hypothesis. Rather, we wish to test whether the two are driven to affect one another. The extent to which they are highlights the superintendency as a critical element in the electoral politics of school districts.

14. Similar results were found in a study of 117 school districts in four southern California counties. See John C. Walden, "School Board Changes and

Superintendent Turnover," *Administrator's Notebook*, XV (January, 1967). Because of the ten-year basis used in that study, Walden was able to establish that involuntary departures were much more common when school board incumbents had been ousted in previous elections.

PART II

Linkages between

Boards and Citizens

Chapter 5

Political Responsiveness

and the District Environment*

For all its historical and contemporary currency the concept of representation is one of the thorniest found in the political arena. Scholarship in the area has yielded delimiting but not definitive descriptions. As Eulau says, ". . . we can finally say with some confidence what representation is not. But in spite of many centuries of theoretical effort, we cannot say what representation is."[1] Most work has cast representation in terms of a one-to-one relationship: the representative and the represented. However, following the recent conceptualizations of Hannah Pitkin, Prewitt and Eulau have urged moving to a plane of systematic, collective relationships, where a viable theory of representation ". . . must be constructed out of an understanding of representation as a relationship between two collectives — the representative assembly and the represented citizenry."[2]

Such a shift from individuals to collectives has many implications. At the theoretical level it means we are more interested in how and with what consequences representative *bodies* define and play their fiduciary roles. By the same token we become as concerned with collectivities of constituents and their interests as with autonomous citizens. At the methodological level we are obliged to consider decision-making bodies rather than the individuals comprising these bodies.

Our point of departure for looking at the representational functions of school boards is the concept of responsiveness or receptivity. Pitkin's bedrock characterization of representation refers to "acting in the interest of the represented in a manner responsive to them."[3] Establishing criteria for evaluating the

*This is a revised version of an article first appearing in the *Midwest Journal of Political Science*, 15 (May, 1971), pp. 290–321.

"interest" portion of this definition is difficult; doing the same for the "responsive" half of the statement is more tractable, however, and this is the area we wish
to explore. Responsiveness will be taken to mean acting on the basis of *expressed*
preferences by constituents. Thus two conditions must be met: 1) there must be
expressions, and 2) they must be taken into account.

Following Prewitt and Eulau in their study of city councils,[4] we are first
concerned with the degree to which school boards are responsive to organized
views in the public, versus the extent to which boards act on the basis of other
sources or their own self-defined images about the needs of the represented.
Board members were asked: "Do representatives of community groups or organizations ever contact you personally to seek your support for their position?"
Three-fifths of the sample replied affirmatively. In a succeeding open-ended
question we attempted to assess the board member's valence regarding such
persuasion attempts. The grounds for this effort were that if all such attempts
were viewed negatively, then the representative was not acting in a responsive
manner. If positively, then the assumption is that the board member is being
responsive to one or more organized views in the public. While the vast majority
of those who had been approached claimed to approve such expressions without
qualifications, 19 percent did not. The qualifications specified that the spokesmen
behave constructively and orderly or that the expression be transmitted directly
through the board as a whole, rather than through them personally. Thus we are
left with 49 percent of the board members professing an unqualified style of
group responsiveness.

We transformed these individual data into board level data by summing
the responses within each board, and then assigning the board a value equal to the
proportion of board members taking a positive stance toward group demands.
Across all boards the mean is 48 percent; the range is from 00 percent to 100
percent; and the standard deviation is 27.

Demands, requests, information, and cues flow into a representative
assembly from the constituency in a variety of ways; they flow from groups, or
from individuals. This observation led us to look for responsiveness of a less
structured fashion. The school board members were asked, ". . . what sources of
information about the attitudes of people in this district are useful to you?"
The word "useful" is crucial because it implies that the board member feels
positively about the sources of information. Taking only the initial replies, it is
fascinating to observe their individual versus group character. The split is almost
even, with 52 percent referring to "people," "individuals," or the "grapevine,"
and with the balance referring to specific groups, to specific role occupants, or to
demand-making situations. There is a quality of casual behavior inherent in
answers of the first type whereas more purposiveness characterizes those of the
second. Neither involves manifest persuasion attempts by those being represented,
but it is assumed that information is relayed with some preference loading. It should
be stressed that the undifferentiated references to individuals undoubtedly included group spokesmen, but the board members did not perceive them as such.

Just as we referred earlier to a group responsiveness style, it seems appropriate to label this style individualized responsiveness. At the board level the mean percentage of individualized responsiveness is 54 percent, the range is 00 percent to 100 percent, and the standard deviation is 28. There is a moderately strong negative association between the two styles at the board level ($r = -.39$). A given board could score equally high or low on the two measures, and the fact that the correlation is only moderately negative demonstrates that the two measures are not simply reverse images. Nevertheless, there is a clear lack of affinity between the two which obviously suggests that responsiveness is a multifaceted process even within the narrow confines of our own conceptualizations.

It is of interest to note that neither of these styles is connected with the representational roles set forth by Edmund Burke: trustee versus delegate self-conceptions.[5] A board's level of trustee orientation bears a weak positive relationship to group responsiveness ($r = .15$) and a weak negative one to individualized receptivity ($r = -.15$). Thus, the classic roles tell us little about these particular behavioral manifestations of representation.[6] The task of representation by school board members has become increasingly complicated in contemporary times. In addition to the sheer increase in the size of constituencies as the population grows, there is the additional growth inspired by large-scale school district consolidation. From 1941 to 1972 the number of independent school districts declined by nearly 80 percent.[7] With this shrinkage of districts came greater geographical and population heterodoxy even among the smaller districts, which have been the main targets of consolidation. Perhaps even more significantly, the assignment of public education has changed drastically from the founding days of the nation. The demands on the school system range far and wide, and it is a rare board that can blithely proceed with a program unchallenged by the changing values and aspirations of modern society. Thus, either the simple translation of relatively homogeneous preferences into school policy or the relatively simple range of interests which board members need to consider has been substantially modified.

The representation responsibilities of boards have been modified because of the demand for efficiency and the increasing complexity of educational policy. In the early years of the public school system, the authority to manage schools was in the hands of school boards. Boards had leaders, raised money, selected texts, and even interviewed prospective students.[8] However, in the middle of the nineteenth century, schools rapidly became compulsory and free. Simultaneously, the country leaped with enthusiasm into the Industrial Revolution, with its accompanying population explosion and urbanization. As schools grew in complexity it became apparent that lay boards did not have time or inclination to continue management. Various schemes (including the currently popular "community school" — the division of large cities into small districts, each with its own board) were tried; but finally the boards gave up. In the latter half of the nineteenth century boards began to hire professional administrators who slowly and inexorably began to assume not only administrative but also policy-making authority,[9] thereby placing one additional level of communication between the public and the content of educational policy.

While not gainsaying the broad social and educational trends affecting

all school districts, it is quite apparent that the composition of constituencies
varies dramatically as one moves across a socio-cultural map of the nation. Some
civil units have much more social, economic, ethnic, and political complexity than
others do, whether they are school districts or municipalities. Our own sample, for
example, ranges all the way from a rural, sparsely settled, homogeneous school
district with less than 1,000 inhabitants to one teeming with over 8,000,000
residents of varied hues and beliefs.

We have used three different but partially interrelated measures to describe
the social and cultural pluralism extant in the school district's population: *Metropolitanism* divides the school districts between those not located in Standard
Metropolitan Statistical Areas (SMSAs) and those located within one; *district
population* is the total adult population within the school boundaries; and *percent
urban* is the percentage of pupils residing in urban places, as estimated by district
officials.

Although these three measures are related to each other, the associations
are not as high as one might suspect: metropolitanism and percent urban = .45;
metropolitanism and population = .24; and population and percent urban = .23. By
no means do the measures speak for each other. One reason they are not more
closely allied is that metropolitan areas (i.e., SMSAs) contain many small to
medium-sized school districts; these are sometimes no larger than those found in
nonmetropolitan areas. A second factor is that school districts often include
sizable but varying proportions of students from fringe and rural areas. The
presence of these students is not directly related to population and metropolitanism per se.

The bearing of these three complexity measures on the two forms of
responsiveness is shown in Table 5-1. The articulation between complexity and
group responsiveness is of the sort one would predict, given a group life interpretation of constituency-school board politics. Regardless of the measure used,
the more complex the school district is, the more responsive the board is to group
demands. Pluralism and complexity enhance rather than impede responsiveness. In
this sense our findings are in full accord with those reported for California Bay
Area city councils.[10]

TABLE 5-1
Social Complexity and School Board Responsiveness

Complexity Indicators	Group Responsiveness		Individualized Responsiveness	
	Simple r	Partial r	Simple r	Partial r
Metropolitanism	.57	.45[a]	-.55	-.48
Percent Urban	.43	.22	-.28	-.03
District Population	.25	.11	-.20	-.08

[a]All partials are second order, controlling for the effects of the two remaining variables listed.

The contribution of the three measures to group responsiveness, however, is disparate. Emerging as the most powerful predictor is metropolitanism, i.e., whether the school district is within or without an SMSA. A virtue of the Census Bureau's classification scheme is that SMSAs include not only central cities of 50,000 or more but also the remaining part of the county plus contiguous counties adjudged to be socially and economically integrated with the central city. For school districts this means that even some relatively small districts are in the orbit of the metropolis. They absorb and are affected by the modes of group life found in the larger environment. Illustratively, two districts of equal size will encounter distinctly different levels of group politics if one is a Southern rural county district and the other is a Chicago suburb. Metropolitanism seems to capture political life styles much more readily than sheer population or urbanism does.

So far the findings support the proposition that responsiveness to the constituency rises in direct proportion to the socio-political complexity of the school district. If we shift to the second column of Table 5-1, however, it is clear that another sort of responsiveness is inversely related to complexity. The very conditions which lead boards to responsiveness to group demands are those which *lessen* responsiveness to individualized sources of preferences and cues. Hence, the apparent irony of the complexity-responsiveness nexus revealed by considering group life is abolished, and the traditional notions of greater responsiveness prevailing in less pluralistic environments is reinstated.

Metropolitanism stands out again as the most significant of the three complexity variables. The ambience of nonmetro districts is conducive to the sort of informal, almost casual inputs of information characteristic of our images of hinterland America. Board members run into their constituents in a variety of informal settings. They see them in such roles as fellow merchant, farmer, luncheon club or church member, former high school classmate, relative, friend, casual acquaintance, or perhaps only as some resident with whom they pass the time of day. The focus of the communication may or may not be restricted to school district business. In any event board members are unlikely to read the encounter as one in which a formal group organization is seeking support for a position. To what extent responsiveness in the group context signifies more "real" responsiveness than it does in the scenario just outlined is a most difficult question. We shall return to that question in the conclusion.

DISTRICT HARMONY AND RESPONSIVENESS

Some school districts seem to cope with their problems over long stretches of time with a minimum of strife. Others seem to be caught in perpetual conflict. It is the latter which make their way into the mass media. When their proportions become large there is a tendency to presume that all districts are exploding in turmoil. What may best characterize school district phenomena of this type is a model of episodic crises.[11] Most districts experience crises and unrest at one time or another;

the difference is that some are marked by frequently recurring episodes whereas others enjoy rather long periods of calm between crises.

The question of district harmony or consensus has interesting implications for school board responsiveness, Can we expect boards to be more or less responsive under conditions of tension? In terms of representational theory, it is important to know whether responsiveness waxes or wanes in response to varying levels of district harmony. As we shall see, the answers depend in part on how one conceptualizes responsiveness.

To gauge the level of district harmony we employ two sets of relationships, one between citizens and boards and the other between citizens alone. The first deals with the public support rendered the school board, and the second considers the tension level within the district over matters of educational policy. Although it would be quite helpful to have the reports of residents themselves, the perceptions held by board members about these matters can be used as surrogates and, of course, have unique significance in their own right.[12] The two sets of relationships are:

> *Mass Support:* A cumulative index score for each board built from responses to three questions, one dealing with the degree to which the board takes unpopular stands, a second indicating the prevalence of board critics in the district, and a third describing the amount of congruence between the board's ideas of appropriate board behavior versus the public's ideas. The range of this index is .20 to 2.80; the mean is 1.71; and the standard deviation is .66.[13]

> *District Consensus:* Based on answers to a single question asking the board members if there is ". . . any tension or conflict among people in the district on questions having to do with school policies." Boards are arrayed according to the percentage of members replying negatively. The range of scores is from 00 percent to 100 percent; the mean is 44 percent; and the standard deviation is 28.

An immediate point to make about these two indicators is their strong affinity for each other, $r = .74$. As citizen support for the board increases, inter-citizen agreement also increases, according to board members' perceptions at any rate. On reflection this symmetry is not at all unreasonable. Over the long run there should be a reciprocal relationship between the district's support levels and its internal dissension. When board support begins to falter, it is manifested in policy conflict among the laity. If the board has presented a unanimous front, the opponents express their displeasure by criticizing the board. The policy supporters uphold the board, and the battle lines are defined. Alternatively, a split board will engender similar splits among the constituency with an overall decline in board support levels. Of course the process may begin at the mass level. Educational policy splits among the citizenry would seem to lead inevitably to an overall lowering of support for the incumbent board. Regardless of the genesis, mass support and district consensus undoubtedly feed on each other. Methodologically, the high intercorrelation of the two variables means that great care must be exercised when they are employed in multivariate analysis.

Both mass support and district consensus show a strong negative relationship to group responsiveness at the zero-order level (Table 5-2). However, support appears to be far stronger than district consensus. Is it a contradiction to say that the more supportive the district is then the less responsive the board? Not if responsiveness is defined as a state in which the representatives pay attention to and are affected by group demands among the represented. Imagine a board beset by scandal or fiscal chaos. As board support dwindles, a corresponding increase in group demands sets in. Although all board members will not be responsive to these pressures, it is probable that a majority will. Conversely, picture a board that has just executed a series of magnificent *coups*. As support waxes, there is less need for group pressures, and so group responsiveness falls off.

TABLE 5-2
District Harmony and School Board Responsiveness

District Harmony	Group Responsiveness		Individualized Responsiveness	
	Simple r	Partial r	Simple r	Partial r
Mass Support	−.59	−.36[a]	.42	.33
District Consensus	−.51	−.13	.28	−.05

[a]These are first-order partials, controlling for the effects of the other variable listed.

One might suspect that the observed relationships are a function of social complexity. Both support and consensus vary inversely with metropolitanism ($r = -.57$ and $-.45$, respectively), the social complexity indicator of greatest power in accounting for responsiveness. Yet with metropolitanism held constant both indicators continue to have a noticeable affect on group responsiveness: $-.35$ for district consensus and $-.39$ for mass support. The relationships are maintained at an even higher level using the other indicators of complexity. The conclusion is, therefore, that district harmony has a distinctive independent effect on group responsiveness.

Turning to district harmony and individualized responsiveness (Table 5-2, col. 2), we find a set of findings at odds with those for group responsiveness. Now the relationships are positive instead of negative, although they are also of lesser magnitude. The common finding with group responsiveness is that mass support is again the stronger of the two harmony variables. As in the case of group responsiveness, the extraordinarily greater power of mass support does not simply reflect the hidden influence of social complexity. Controlling for metropolitanism does depress the original relationship somewhat ($r = .15$), but controlling for population size and percent urbanism has much less effect ($r = .38$ and $.36$, respectively).[14]

Why should support for the board be linked positively to individualized responsiveness whereas it is negatively so for group responsiveness? The answer would seem to lie in the nature of the transactional process occuring under each circumstance. As stated earlier, individualized transactions are not necessarily marked by pressures, demands, and threats. They do consist of cues, and one may legitimately assume that these cues usually have affective content. These cues may simply consist of feedback for the board, signals that their actions are being kindly or poorly received; or they may consist of expressions of preferences on pending policies that are not seen by the boards or their constituents as strong pressures and demands. Even when the cues consist of outright pressures, the settings of the transactions may be such that the petitioner does not see the outcome as zero-sum. Overall, boards relying on unattached individuals for cues are not in a state of siege.

These various conditions do not suggest a pattern in which a board is simply ignoring the public and acting in terms of a self-defined image of what is best for the school district. Rather, they suggest a far subtler, less strident mode of responsiveness. It follows that if neither the represented nor the representatives see their transaction as pitched battles between citizens and boards or between citizen group and citizen group, then the behavior of the board will be looked on with more favor than it is when group tensions and demands are high. Compromises and losses are inevitable in the latter case. It also follows that the fabric of interpersonal ties that attend individualized responsiveness tends to soften the impact of board behavior when it does run counter to segments of the constituency. The result again would be less diminution of board support than it would if articulate, public group demands are rejected or compromised by the board. Group members and identifiers would not have the intervening factor of personal relationships with or knowledge of board members by which they might understand or at least sympathize with the board's ultimate posture. Finally, the existence of individualized contacts and — perhaps more crucial — the *belief* that such contacts are possible seems to be a stronger generator of support when compared to districts where one can have a say only through organized publics.

THE ELECTORAL PROCESS AND RESPONSIVENESS

Up to this point we have seen that social complexity and mass support for the board are strongly related to the style of responsiveness. It would be a mistake to label these variables as nonpolitical. Certainly the levels of mass support for particular political institutions and actors is a key political variable, as the systems-oriented scholars have repeatedly affirmed. Social complexity also may be thought of as a political variable since the style and scope of political life are typically different in more complex environments.[15]

Two types of electoral factors will be considered. On the one hand there are a number of legal and structural constraints governing the selection and election of school board personnel. A second set of electoral factors concerns the structuring of office competition and office retention. These factors are, for the most part, not part of the legal framework. We will look at school board elections in the same fashion that one might examine elections for city councils or state legislatures. Elections are viewed as the ultimate sanction and check on the behavior of representatives. It will be of more than passing interest to see if the structuring of competition is reflected in the responsiveness of boards.

These electoral factors have been alluded to in previous chapters. A synoptic description follows. Legal constraints consist of whether the boards are appointed (scored 0) or elected (scored 1); whether elections have a ward (0) or at-large (1) basis; whether the term of office is 2–3 years (0), 4 years (1), or 5–6 years (2); and the presence of coterminous referenda — whether the votes on bond proposals, tax millages, etc., are held separately (0) from board elections or coterminously (1). The four competition structure variables include whether elections are nonpartisan (0) or partisan or slate (1); the proportion of office sponsorship (see Chapter 3); the absence (0) or presence (1) of electoral opposition in the last primary or general election preceding the date of the study; and the proportion of forced turnovers of incumbents in immediately previous elections.

We turn first to the official mode of gaining board position, i.e., by appointment or election. One reason for discussing this feature initially is that the remaining variables deal only with elected boards. There is a good deal of mythology about the responsiveness of appointed versus elected officials in public life. The common view is that elected officials are more responsive because they know that they can be sanctioned by defeat at the polls. A minority view is that appointees can at least be more eclectic in their responsiveness since they are not under the constant threat of the electorate. One of the extolled virtues of the public education system in the United States is local control via predominantly elected boards. But are these boards more responsive than appointed ones? Since we are working with a handful of appointed boards (raw $N = 13$), our conclusion must be tentative.

On balance, however, the results lend only partial support to the virtuous image of elected boards. Compared with appointed boards the elected ones are somewhat less responsive to group pressures, but somewhat more responsive to individuals. The association is focused sharply by using the asymmetric measure, Somers's d (Table 5-3).[16] Inferentially, elected boards are more sensitive to individual voters because of the potential sanctions. Conversely, appointed boards, keyed perhaps to larger segments of the district's political profile, can afford to pay more attention to group interests.

These relationships are of a magnitude to suggest that the method of gaining office has at least some effect on responsiveness.[17] There is, however, the suspicion that other factors lie behind the apparent connection. For example, appointed boards occur more often in larger districts. On the other hand, they are more common in the South, and are found as often outside as within SMSAs.

After controlling one at a time for the variables previously introduced into

TABLE 5-3

**Relationship between Appointed Boards versus
Elected Boards and Board Responsiveness**

		Appointed		*Elected*
Group Responsiveness		Raw N = 13 Wt. N = 19		Raw N = 75 Wt. N = 166
Low (1)		18%		32%
(2)		09		24
(3)		37		22
High (4)		35		22
	Total	99%		100%

tau-b = −.15

Somers's *d* = −.33[a]

Individualized Responsiveness				
Low (1)		43%		23%
(2)		29		26
(3)		28		24
High (4)		00		27
	Total	100%		100%

tau-b = .19

Somers's *d* = .44

[a]Somers's *d* is an asymmetric measure of association for ordinal variables. In the present instance the responsiveness scores are the dependent variables. Both the *tau-b* and Somers's *d* coefficients have been calculated on the basis of uncollapsed responsiveness scores. The corresponding Pearsonian coefficients are r = −.19 and .23 for group and individualized responsiveness, respectively.

the analysis it became apparent that the modest association between being appointed or being elected and responsiveness had great persistence. The method of office attainment is thus an intervening or conditioning variable residing between environmental complexity and public support on the one side, and responsiveness on the other side. Indeed, we shall see that several of the electoral variables seem to operate in this fashion. The process at work can be demonstrated by reexamining the basic metropolitanism-responsiveness correlations according to two categories — appointed and elected boards (Table 5-4). Since they make up such a large part of the sample, it is not surprising that the relationship for elected boards scarcely differs from that for all boards. Without doubt the relationship for group responsiveness is heightened among appointed boards; and that for individualized responsiveness is depressed among appointed boards. For each type the condition of being appointed exerts a salutary effect on the metropolitanism-responsiveness nexus, in the one case raising a positive correlation and in the other lowering a negative one.

Serving on an appointed board seems to heighten the propensity of

TABLE 5-4
Metropolitanism-Responsiveness Correlations

	Group Responsiveness	Individualized Responsiveness
	r	*r*
Metropolitanism — All Boards	.56	−.55
Metropolitanism — Appointed Boards	.71	−.25
Metropolitanism — Elected Boards	.55	−.57

responsiveness, given social complexity variations. Why this occurs is not easily answered, and we will not concern ourselves in detail with answers. It is sufficient to suggest that the workaday political lives of both elected and appointed board members are marked by similar concerns, interests, and motivations. As we have seen, the fear of electoral sanctions is not particularly grave for elected board members. Appointed boards may, in fact, overcompensate in their responsive behavior in the absence of being officially "the people's choice." Finally, whether the board of education is elected or appointed is probably an unknown fact for many of the constituents and an irrelevant fact in a tactical sense for others.

Our findings — tentative due to the small number of appointed boards with which to work — cast serious doubt on the facile assumption that the form of election produces the substance of representation. Admittedly we have tapped but one aspect of representation, albeit two conceptualizations of this aspect have been advanced. As students of the executive and bureaucracy have long contended, there is no reason for supposing that appointed officials are not governed by at least some of the same constraints of representative democracy as those that govern elected officials. At the level of national politics, for example, departmental and agency officialdom is characterized by varying modes and levels of responsiveness. The key question is whether responsiveness varies among officials with similar constituencies depending upon how they attained office.

For school board members the answer to the question is not encouraging for those placing their bets on elected boards as being more responsive. At best, elected boards exhibit more receptivity only in the individualized mode. At worst, elected boards depress the linkage between structural conditions promoting either group or individualized receptivity. Obviously the fact that appointed boards are determined by elected officials is a complicating, qualifying condition to this conclusion. As typically posed, however, the issue simply involves the virtues of appointed versus elected governing bodies.

Our treatment of the other electoral variables will be brief. At the absolute level the remaining three legal parameters have a very modest connection with either type of response style, with no correlation higher than $r = .25$. There is some slight evidence that the legal constraints abetting one type of responsiveness serve to depress the other type. This evidence is clearest with respect to the venerable debate topic of ward versus at-large elections. Controlling for metropolitanism and board support, at-large elections slightly depress group responsiveness ($r = -.15$), but slightly improve individualized responsiveness ($r = .09$). Overall, though, the direct effects of legal parameters approach triviality.

As we noted in previous chapters, the competitive milieu of school board elections is not fierce. It should also be noted that on half of the boards no more than 25 percent of the incumbents were definitely committed to seeking another term. Inferentially, the force of competition, the threat of defeat, and the desire to remain in office are of little moment for school boards in keeping them responsive to their publics.

Still, school boards do vary extensively in their competition structure, and we should observe the consequences of these variations on responsiveness. The classic argument, of course, is that the more structured and intense the competition the greater is the responsiveness. The presumption is that less responsive boards, or particular members, will be ousted because they are not responsive. This presumption is at the heart of the theory that free, competitive elections invoke responsiveness.

Nevertheless, competition characteristics have only a tenuous tie with responsiveness. With metropolitanism and mass support held constant, the strongest relationships are the positive ones involving forced turnover ($r = .12$ for each type of responsiveness). Nor are the results consistent, since those boards with contested seats in the last election were *less* responsive than those with contests ($r = -.10$ and $-.11$ for group and individualized receptivity, respectively).[18] The key to responsiveness appears to lie outside the structure of competition.

Taken as a whole, the seven electoral measures fail to make as strong a contribution to responsiveness as do the three social complexity and two district harmony variables. Altogether the twelve variables account for 49 percent of the variance in group responsiveness and 40 percent in the individualized style. Using step-wise regression, metropolitanism and mass support alone account for 40 percent of the variance in the group mode and 35 percent of the variance in the individualized mode. Clearly the addition of the electoral dimensions will not markedly improve our *statistical* explanations. Even if the electoral measures are forced into the regression equation first, they account for no more than 12 percent of the variance in group responsiveness, and 18 percent for individualized responsiveness.[19]

The Mediating Function of Electoral Processes

The foregoing account scarcely supports the proposition that electoral characteristics have much to do with a key element of school district politics. Does this mean that the heralded importance of electoral variations as determinants of representational democracy is, in reality, a fraud? While some might agree on other grounds, we believe that within the confines of our responsiveness dimensions there are grounds for asserting that electoral properties do make a difference.[20]

In the first place the contribution of the electoral variables refuses to disappear even in the regression analysis, especially in the case of individualized response style. This staying power is more noteworthy when it is recognized that the complexity measures in particular summarize a wide gamut of socioeconomic-political processes which are cumulative in nature. These processes are reflective of more momentous aspects of political life than, say, whether the school board is nonpartisan or partisan.

There is another manner in which the effects of electoral processes may be observed. If we grant that such overarching elements as social complexity and mass support are the major determinants of response style, then we may look for differential patterns as the electoral environment varies. We may expect electoral processes to serve as a mediating or interpreting device in the articulation between complexity-mass support and responsiveness. This view is similar to the familiar argument that electoral institutions and outcomes filter or regulate the connections between mass beliefs and broad societal forces on the one hand, and the behavior of elites on the other.

Our procedure separates out subcategories of the electoral variables and holds them physically constant while observing the association between metro-politanism and responsiveness. We do not present the results for the district harmony-responsiveness nexus, but they yielded directly comparable results. First the legal and then the competition structure variables will be treated. The results are given in Table 5–5. Each of the three legal properties has an effect on the metropolitanism-individualized responsiveness association. The initial negative connection is exacerbated among at-large districts, those where coterminous school referenda are held, and those where term of office is shorter. In the case of the electoral units the social and geographical distance between individual board members and their constituents is widened. Given a greater geographical and population base, the board members are less able to engage in the face-to-face, personal transactions accompanying individualized responsiveness, or if they do, they do not find such contacts very helpful in the task of serving as the people's representatives.

The effects of school district referenda coinciding with school board elections are more difficult to explain. Since they usually involve money, these referenda command as much or more interest from the voters and generate a plethora of demand-making encounters. Our guess is that coterminous referenda add more complexity to that already occasioned by the components of the metropolitan culture. In general, it would seem that the less noise and multiple stimuli there are in the environment the more easily individual preferences can be successfully communicated to boards. The periodic convergence of board elections and referenda may simply augment the dissociation between social complexity and individualized responsiveness by injecting a recurrent choice-making process which ordinarily divides the school district severely. We are not completely pleased with this explanation, partly because it is not counterbalanced by movements in the group responsiveness dimension.

Long terms of office nearly vanquish the negative association between

TABLE 5-5
Relationship between Environmental Complexity
(Metropolitanism) and Responsiveness,
by Electoral Factors

	Group Responsiveness	Individualized Responsiveness	Proportion of Sample
	r	*r*	
All Boards	.55	-.57	100%
Election Area			
At-large	.56	-.64	73%
Wards[a]	.57	-.44	27%
Coterminous Referenda			
Yes	.56	-.78	44%
No	.54	-.44	56%
Length of Term in Years			
2-3	.46	-.68	32%
4	.55	-.75	43%
5-6	.64	-.13	24%
Electoral Opposition			
No	.01	-.66	23%
Yes	.65	-.48	77%
Forced Turnover			
No[b]	.40	-.74	47%
Yes	.68	-.42	53%
Office Sponsorship			
High	.42	-.70	51%
Low	.67	-.42	49%
Partisanship			
No	.52	-.66	59%
Yes[c]	.57	-.44	41%

[a]Includes school districts electing from subdistricts and those with subdistrict residence requirements.
[b]Includes 3% where forced turnover ranged from 1-10%.
[c]Partisan includes districts with legally partisan elections and those where slates are active.

social complexity and individualized responsiveness. Traditional theories of accountability would hold just the opposite view, that long terms would further depress an already negative picture. This would follow from the insecurity of shorter terms and the resulting rationale of frequent contacts with the constituency in order to remain in office. What actually seems to happen is that a longer term enables board members to override the compelling force of social complexity, possibly because they are more recognizable and approachable by unattached individuals, regardless of the social complexity at hand.

It is also significant that term of office is the sole one of the three legal variables which also has a bearing on the complexity-*group* responsiveness linkage. Again the effect is heightened responsiveness, and there is an orderly rise in the correlations from shorter to longer terms. Repeated exposure is probably one explanation for the phenomena. Another is that boards with longer tenure conceivably feel freer to be responsive to various sorts of groups because there is a longer period of time in which bad group experiences and outcomes can be tempered. Threats of immediate retaliation against the board members by potentially dissatisfied group claimants are discounted more than when all or half of the board members are up for immediate reelection. What we are suggesting is that if social complexity is a powerful incentive for group responsiveness, the leisureliness of longer terms accentuates this incentive.

Turning to the impact of the competition structure, we see that the effects are more severe and consistent than those for the legal parameters. Our rationale for introducing these variables is predicated upon forces of competition acting at the interface between social complexity and responsiveness. Most theories of representation and electoral behavior hold that as competition becomes more severe, the responsiveness of the representatives increases. The articulation between the preferences of the represented and the representatives, however, does not necessarily rise. Quite the opposite: as competition decreases, the probabilities of symmetry between constituents and elites would seem to rise. What we are saying is that more competition reflects greater diversity of views, that these views are more likely to be transmitted to elites, and that the elites will be more responsive in the sense of acting on the basis of the views. All of this would constrain the overarching connection between metropolitanism and responsiveness. In effect we are hypothesizing that, given this strong connection, there are additional effects contingent upon the competition structure.

Foremost among the contingencies are the simple matters of electoral opposition and forced turnovers. The lack of opposition in the previous election completely destroys the association between metropolitanism and group responsiveness and exaggerates the negative one with individualized responsiveness. Similarly, the lower the rate of incumbents forced out of office over the past several elections the lower is the responsiveness in each dimension.

Despite our earlier evidence showing the relatively low intensity found in office-seeking and retention, it is nevertheless patent that competition acts as a strong mediating force between the environment and a school board's receptivity to constituents' claims and cues. Those who hold that competition increases responsiveness would be vindicated by these findings even though the relationship is not a simple, direct one. What seems to happen is that competitiveness does bring the boards into more contact with the public and presumably results in their viewing public cues and demands in a more favorable light. Whether this stems from greater initiation on the part of the constituency or the board is difficult to determine, although both sources are probably involved.

Board sponsorship also has a pronounced effect on the linkage between social complexity and response style. When incumbent boards are more successful in bringing ostensibly like-minded colleagues onto the board, the basic linkage is moved in favor of less responsiveness for both the group and individual categories. Boards less successful on this score show the opposite pattern. One can imagine the contrasting situations. Board members who were sponsored feel a greater insularity from the public since they have been virtually anointed by the board in being. Their electoral victory probably came more easily for them than for the rank outsiders who were not anointed. This sense of privilege leads to greater protection from forces in the environment, with less vulnerability to the components operative in more complex socio-political environments. Feeling somewhat less a part of a self-sustaining and anointed dynasty, the boards with fewer sponsored members are, in turn, more susceptible to forces increasing their responsiveness.

The final variable, presence or absence of partisanship, is the weakest of the competition structure factors. The correlations for group responsiveness are barely affected, although the movement is in the direction hypothesized if one postulated a model of competing interest aggregations located at the interface between complexity and receptivity. But the effects are more noticeable for individualized responsiveness, with the presence of partisanship lowering the overall negative complexity-responsiveness association. The argument seems fairly straightforward. In the absence of a more competitive structure (i.e., partisanship) a primary influence such as complexity works its will more readily upon boards.

The upshot of the analysis is that electoral characteristics of the school district do leave an imprint on the responsiveness of school boards. Appreciation for the magnitude of the differences created can be gained by squaring the simple correlations in Table 5–5 to obtain measures of explained variance. But the imprint occurs because these characteristics provide differential settings within which the strong elements of socio-political complexity (and mass support) operate. It seems probable, therefore, that tinkering with the legal framework and fostering more competition for office would sooner or later affect the response linkage between constituents and school boards. At the theoretical level, our simple model of environmental pluralism and mass support as prime determinants of responsiveness must be modified. Not that they no longer successfully predict response style; rather that the degree of success is systematically affected by electoral variations.

Our findings have disclosed two contrasting styles of school board representation, one which responds to formal groups while the other responds to unattached individuals. While our research does support the paradox of diminished responsiveness to groups as the complexity of the represented unit decreases and the level of public support increases, we found that these factors do not, in fact, necessarily reduce responsiveness on the part of the local officials. It is the agents being responded to that differ. Thus, we found that the less complex the district, and the higher the mass support, the more likelihood there was of finding a school board responsive to individualized preferences.

The two dimensions of representation have implications for controversies about the territorial scope of school districts.[21] To solve the racial and social ills of urban education, it is proposed that control be radically decentralized in the central cities. To solve the economic ills of urban education, the proposed salvation lies in some form of "Metro" government or "Metro" school districts. If our findings can be extrapolated to large-scale movements in either direction, the gains and losses in terms of representation become apparent. With decentralization, public support and individualized responsiveness would increase — goals which urban minorities are espousing. With "Metro," support would diminish but group responsiveness would climb. As our analysis suggests, these movements would be tempered according to the particular electoral milieu in which they transpire. Such are the dilemmas of representative democracy.

NOTES

1. Heinz Eulau, "Changing Views of Representation," *Contemporary Political Science: Toward Empirical Theory*, ed. Ithiel de Sola Pool (New York: McGraw Hill, 1967), p. 54.

2. Kenneth Prewitt and Heinz Eulau, "Political Matrix and Political Representation: Prolegomenon to a New Departure from an Old Problem," *American Political Science Review*, 63 (July, 1969), p. 428. Our own thinking and analysis have been heavily influenced by this article. See Hannah Fenichel Pitkin, *The Concept of Representation* (Berkeley and Los Angeles: University of California Press, 1967).

3. Pitkin, *op. cit.*, p. 209.

4. Prewitt and Eulau, *op. cit.*, pp. 427–441.

5. Boards were arranged on a trustee dimension after summing individual responses to two questions asking respondents whether and why they felt board members should "do what people want" or "follow their own judgment." See Chapter 6 for a discussion of Burke's view of representational roles.

6. As in Chapter 4, this chapter utilizes the data set with an oversample from the large city stratum; this means reweighting the rest of the districts for most analyses in the present chapter. Our raw N is 88, which produces a weighted N of 185. Differences between these numbers and those used in the previous chapter (see Note 6) are due to our having used only *elective* districts in that chapter.

7. U.S. Bureau of the Census, "Small-Area Data Notes," Vol. 8, No. 5 (Washington, D.C., May, 1973), p. 1.

8. Raymond E. Callahan and H. Warren Button, "Historical Change of the Role of the Man in the Organization: 1865–1950," *Behavioral Science and Educational Administration Yearbook, Part II*, ed. Daniel E. Griffiths (Chicago: University of Chicago Press, 1964).

9. H. Thomas James, *et. al.*, *Determinants of Educational Expenditures in Large Cities of the United States* (Stanford, California: School of Education, Stanford University, 1963).

10. Prewitt and Eulau, *op. cit.*, p. 431.

11. See Laurence Iannaccone, *Politics in Education* (New York: The Center for Applied Research in Education, 1967), and Alan K. Campbell, "Who Governs the Schools?" *Saturday Review*, 64 (December 21, 1968), pp. 50–52.

12. The use of elite perceptions to categorize constituency characteristics is a common procedure. Strictly speaking, however, one can only say that these are imputations about the purported phenomena. To be conservative one should interpret the following analysis in that view.

13. In building this index each board member was first given a score from 0.0 to 3.0 depending upon the number of his three responses indicative of public support for the board. A mean for each board was developed by summing individual scores and dividing the total by the number of board members.

14. An examination of the partial betas (slopes) indicates that the relationship between mass support and individualized responsiveness is partly spurious, due to the fact that metropolitanism is related both to individualized responsiveness and to mass support. This spurious effect is much less when population or urbanism are considered.

15. Useful discussions of the electoral aspects of school district politics are found in David W. Minar, "The Community Basis of Conflict in School System Politics," *American Sociological Review*, 31 (December, 1966), pp. 822–835, and Robert Salisbury, "Schools and Politics in the Big Cities," *Harvard Educational Review*, 37 (Summer, 1967), pp. 408–424.

16. See Robert Somers, "A New Asymmetric Measure of Association for Ordinal Variables," *American Sociological Review*, 27 (December, 1962), pp. 799–811.

17. For another type of comparison between appointed and elected boards, see Robert L. Crain, *The Politics of School Desegregation* (Chicago: Aldine, 1968), pp. 190–194; 322–324.

18. The strength of metropolitanism and mass support are not similarly affected in the reverse situation. Controlling for the five strongest electoral variables simultaneously, the coefficients are .52 and −.51 between metropolitanism and group and individualized responsiveness, respectively. Corresponding coefficients for mass support are −.52 and .31 for group and individualized responsiveness, respectively.

19. The various electoral measures were also subjected to factor analysis and the major factors were then used instead of the separate indicators in the regression equations. Both the theoretical and statistical results were less satisfying than those obtained by using the indicators singly.

20. For three recent, innovative efforts showing the effects of electoral factors on state and local policy outcomes see Ira Sharkansky and Richard I. Hofferbert, "Dimensions of State Politics, Economics, and Public Policy," *American Political Science Review*, 63 (September, 1969), pp. 867–879; Charles F. Cnudde and Donald J. McCrone, "Party Competition and Welfare Policies in the American States," *American Political Science Review*, 63 (September, 1969), pp. 858–866; and James W. Clark, "Environment, Process, and Policy: A Reconsideration," *American Political Science Review*, 63 (September, 1969), pp. 1172–1182.

21. Robert Bendiner discusses current proposals and experiences in his *The Politics of Schools* (New York: Harper and Row, 1969), Chapters 11–14. See also Cronin, *The Control of Urban Schools*, Chapter 7.

Chapter 6

Participation in

Governance through Interest Groups*

In the preceding chapter we defined two types of publics to which board members respond — the formal and organized versus the informal and unorganized. In this chapter we take the organized side of the public as our point of departure. Whether the boards are responsive to groups is not the key question here, although it remains important. Rather, we will concentrate on the level and variety of group activity, the consequences of activity, and the correlates of differential activity and consequences.

Emerging from the behavioral revolution of the years following World War II after years of neglect, interest groups threatened to assume the role of a "first cause" of public policy. A veritable flood of case studies appeared, dealing with either a single group or a single issue and paying either tacit or overt homage to the patron saints of the "group approach," Bentley and Truman.[1] The difficulty with such studies is that most of them *began* with the assumption that interest groups were powerful (otherwise why would we study them). Further, no matter how laudable the case study method may be, it is extraordinarily difficult to reach valid generalizations from studies of single issues or single groups.

Whatever the validity of case studies, they were soon challenged by a new group of research efforts, relying more on comparative and systematic observations.[2] While no useful purpose is served by an enumeration of the specific findings of this research, there was a theme common to it: interest groups are far less influential than the case studies lead us to suspect. Thus, we have come full circle.

*This is a revised version of a chapter which first appeared in *People and Politics in Urban Society*, ed. Harlan Hahn (Beverly Hills: Sage, 1972), pp. 201–30.

Where interest groups were once thought to be the basic catalyst for the formation of public policy, they are now described as only one of a number of competitors for power and frequently the least effective combatants.

In spite of the vast amount of ink spilled on the subject of interest groups, we have not made much progress. The fault lies not so much with theory as with data. It is very difficult to measure the contribution that interest groups make to the formation of public policy and the resolution of policy disputes. Other political variables are more readily quantified, e.g., financial resources, malapportionment, party competition, etc. It is significant that the major efforts in developing systematic, empirical descriptions of the formation of public policy at the state level make no mention of interest groups.[3] Their exclusion is clearly the result of the fact that nobody has developed an inexpensive and reliable method of measuring interest group strength. For instance, both Zeigler and Froman used the assessment of political scientists as an indication of interest group strength, hardly the sort of measure in which much confidence would be placed.[4] In fact, the only effort — that of Francis — to develop a measure of the activity of interest groups in state politics (group competition rather than group effectiveness) is at odds with the conclusions reached by Zeigler.[5]

The conditions leading to the formation of interest groups have recently been subjected to critical assessment. The traditional position, as enunciated by Truman, is described by Salisbury as the "proliferation" hypothesis.[6] Briefly stated, the argument is that social differentiation leads to specialization. Specialization, especially economic specialization, leads to a diversity of values and — under some not clearly specified conditions — to formal organizations. To specify the conditions under which specialization results in the formation of formal organizations, Truman suggests that the distribution of an established equilibrium by disruptive factors (e.g., changes in the business cycle, technological innovation) leads disadvantaged groups to seek a restoration of balance by political activity.

Recently, Olson and Salisbury have challenged Truman's assertions by use of an exchange theory of the origin of groups.[7] They argue that entrepreneurs offer benefits (only some of which are political) to potential members in exchange for membership. Entrepreneurial activity is the first visible evidence of group formation. In essence Olson and Salisbury look at formal organizations as business enterprises and focus upon the key role of the organizer. In so doing they have added an important dimension to Truman's offerings, for it is apparent from the case material they present that individual entrepreneurs play a significant role in group formation.

Yet they have not rejected either the proliferation or disturbed equilibrium hypothesis. It is clear, even in the Olson-Salisbury argument, that groups originate in response to unsatisfied demands on the part of potential group members. Although unsatisfied demands may be insufficient to stimulate group activity, they are functions of environmental change (proliferation) and unresponsive political systems (inability to restore equilibrium). Demands lie at the heart of interest group formation, even though groups ordinarily need an individual leader (entrepreneur) to channel unsatisfied demands.

We assert that there is still merit in "traditional" group theory. One purpose of this chapter is to see what use can be made of such theories, if we do not rely (as Truman, Olson, and Salisbury have done) on case histories of particular kinds of organizations.

With regard to the consequences of group activity, less serious theorizing has been done. As noted previously, most of the debate has centered around the empirical question of how much influence a particular group can achieve. We wish to address ourselves both to this kind of question and also to the more fundamental problem of the effect of formal organization upon other components of the political system. The question is, thus, one of both uncovering the influential groups in educational decision making and assessing the overall impact of group activity upon the decision-making process.

INTEREST GROUPS IN SCHOOL DISTRICTS

The record of interest groups in education is sporadic and incomplete. Although Gross's study of Massachusetts suggested that interest groups were sometimes able to divide boards of education and weaken financial support,[8] Smoley's study of Baltimore school administration revealed that even in a large city interest groups are uninvolved:

> *Of the 2389 issues considered by the Board of School Commissioners, only 207 included participation by outside groups – less than 19 percent! Furthermore, much of the participation which did take place contained no hint of attempted influence, but was action in the performance of official functions to provide service to the Baltimore school system.[9]*

Similarly, the intensive studies of New York City by Rogers and by Gittell suggest the frustration and lack of influence felt by most interest groups.[10]

Most of the scholarship involving interest groups and local education is of the case study variety. Valuable as such studies may be, they do not lend themselves to easy generalization. In this chapter we sacrifice the depth of the case study for the breadth of sample survey. We will proceed along two tracks, addressing ourselves to the twin questions of the antecedents and the consequences of group activity.

The basic variable with which we will deal is interest group *intensity:* the extent to which interest groups come to the attention of school boards. Intensity is purely an assessment of the quantity of interaction. By itself it does not measure the degree to which organizations play a significant role in the informational, cue-taking, system of school boards. Our measure of interest group intensity is constructed from eight open-ended questions in the interview schedule dealing with the activities of organized groups (Table 6-1).

The range for this measure is .20 to 11.14; the mean is 3.92 and the standard deviation is 2.74. Table 6-2 shows how intensity is distributed over the boards in the sample.[11] What is most striking about the distribution is the skewness

TABLE 6-1
Organizational Activities

Organizations	Maximum Coded Responses
Organizations most interested in the board	3
Organizations from which the board seeks support	2
Organizations working for passage of financial referenda	3
Organizations working for defeat of financial referenda	2
Organizations critical of the board	2
Organizations attempting to influence teacher behavior	3
Organizations which defend teachers when attacked	2
Organizations which attack teachers	2
Total Maximum Possible:	19

TABLE 6-2
Distribution of Organizational Intensity by Boards

Range of Mentions	Number of Boards	Percentage of Boards
< 1	7	6.3%
1-2	23	21.7%
2-3	20	18.7%
3-4	15	13.6%
4-5	11	9.9%
5-6	8	7.9%
6-7	7	6.8%
7-8	2	1.6%
8-9	7	6.3%
9-10	3	2.6%
10-11	4	3.3%
> 11	1	1.2%
Total	108[a]	99.9%

[a]This N exceeds the actual weighted N of 106 due to rounding of noninteger weighted Ns to whole numbers.

toward the lower end of the range, despite the presence of some boards in the very high ranges. If one is to judge by these figures, there are large numbers of districts with relatively impotent *formal* spokesmen for interest groups. We stress *formal* because it seems highly probable that organized interests are sometimes represented informally and that boards do not necessarily perceive such action as interest group activity.

The Distribution of Group Activity

At this point in the development of the measure of group intensity, no categorization by kind of group was attempted. However, it is instructive to note the major categories of groups that come to the attention of boards. Later we will return to this classification to ascertain whether particular kinds of groups are associated with particular kinds of antecedent societal conditions and policy outcomes. The most frequently mentioned groups are, as we would expect, those most intimately concerned with education, PTAs and teachers (Table 6-3). However, it is somewhat surprising that PTAs so decidedly outrank teachers organizations, whose members have a more immediate interest in board policy, for example, salaries. Yet we should recall that teachers organizations have been less than militant in most areas. Although some of the larger cities contain quite active teachers organizations, in general they have not assumed a very political role. From the point of view of school boards, PTAs are a more potent force. Not only do PTAs consist largely of parents, they are also often laced with and frequently dominated by key administrators and teachers.[12]

Of the remaining groups the more ideologically oriented ones take a back seat to those of an "establishment" tinge. Left-wing, right-wing, and taxpayer groups are those which assail the board from an ideological perspective. Of these, left-wing organizations (ACLU, NAACP, etc.) do much more lobbying than right-

TABLE 6-3
Organizations Mentioned by Board Members

Type of Organization	Mean Percent Mentions by Board Members[a]	Percent Range by Board[b]
PTA	60	0–100
Teachers	32	0–100
Left-wing, Civil Rights	29	0–100
Service Clubs	21	0–100
Business and Professional	17	0–100
Taxpayers	16	0–100
Right-wing	13	0–100
League of Women Voters	14	0–100
Religious	11	0–60
Citizens Advisory Committee	11	0–80
Political	5	0–50
Neighborhood	5	0–57
Labor	3	0–40

[a]This is the mean for all individuals in the sample, rather than a grand mean of board means.
[b]E.g., the mean range of PTA mentions varies from 0% – where no member of a board mentioned PTA in response to any of the questions – to 100%, where all members of the board mentioned PTA at least once.

wing (veterans, John Birch Society, etc.) and the heralded taxpayer organizations. Still, if we take the less militant organizations such as service clubs (Kiwanis, school boosters, etc.), League of Women Voters, citizens advisory committees, and the like, their impact (combined with the dominance of PTAs) tends to create the impression that the organizational climate in which school board decisions occur is more oriented toward the status quo. The extent to which broader questions of educational policy are raised is probably dependent upon the activities of the left-wing, civil rights, right-wing, and taxpayer organizations, whose relatively high ranking might tend to balance the numerical dominance of the status quo organizations.

Social Complexity and Organizational Intensity

In searching for the antecedents of organizational intensity in educational politics, we can fall back comfortably upon theories of group activity and look first at some indicators of social complexity. Wirth's classic essay on the urban mode of life sums up such assumptions: "Being reduced to a stage of virtual impotence as an individual, the urbanite is bound to exert himself by joining with others of similar interests into organized groups to obtain his ends."[13] To measure social complexity we will use two of the same indicators referred to in Chapter 5: metropolitanism and district population.

The association between social complexity and organizational intensity is clearly in the direction that one would have predicted (Table 6-4). Both metropolitanism and district population continue to make substantial contributions to the association with the other variable in the equation controlled, as demonstrated by the sizable beta weights.[14] Taken together, nearly half the variance in organizational intensity is accounted for by these two indicators of complexity. Clearly dominant, however, is metropolitanism, i.e., whether the school district is within or outside an SMSA. In later portions of the chapter when complexity is entered into the equation with other categories of variables, metropolitanism will serve as the single indicator. Recall that SMSAs include not only central cities of 50,000 or more but also the remaining part of the county plus contiguous counties adjudged to be socially and economically integrated with the central city. For school districts this means that even some relatively small districts are within the

TABLE 6-4
Relationship between Social Complexity
and Organizational Intensity

Complexity Indicators

	Simple r	Beta
Metropolitanism	.60	.44
District population	.55	.35
R^2	.47	

orbit of the metropolis. They absorb and are affected by the modes of group life found in the larger environment.

Mass Support, Complexity, and Interest Groups

Almost on a par with social complexity as an explanation of group activity is the notion of pressure groups originating to cope with alterations in the social and economic status of people with shared attitudes. Urbanization, contributing to the creation of discontinuity of established patterns of interaction, is an example of the conditions which *lead to* such alterations in status. School districts are particularly suitable for inquiry, for the late 1960s were undoubtedly times of high tension in school district politics. Still, one would expect to find a considerable range of tension across school districts. Some districts experience recurring crisis while others are blessed with rather long periods of calm. Following the dictates of group theory, we expect that those districts with the highest tension will experience the highest levels of group activity. Conversely, those with the highest levels of harmony should be relatively free of the demands of organizations. To assess the level of harmony in school districts we return to our tripartite measure of mass support used in Chapter 6.

Mass support has a strong negative association with organizational intensity ($r = -.75$). As the population becomes more supportive of the policies of the board, organized group activity diminishes. Groups clearly thrive in an atmosphere of conflict between the governed and the governors. It is probable that, once the level of public support has deteriorated to a level sufficient to generate fairly intense group activity, organizations exacerbate the loss of confidence in the board. Declining support and organizational activity undoubtedly feed off of each other. At an earlier point we included a measure of district consensus in the regression equation. Because the measure of district consensus proved to be so weak a predictor compared with mass support, it was excluded from further consideration. However, it is instructive to reveal the results of this effort in order to shed some light upon the interaction between mass support and organizational intensity. The beta between mass support and organizational intensity, with the latter dependent, is .70. If we reverse these positions, making mass support dependent, the beta declines to .49. It is possible to argue, then, that both variables are dependent upon each other but that (given the magnitude of the betas) the stronger "causal" link is from mass support to organizational intensity.[15]

To return to the argument of disturbance in equilibrium, we suggest that as public confidence in board policy declines, the decline in confidence is articulated and given explicit focus by interest groups. They pinpoint, according to their own objectives and interests, the specific aspects of discontent to which they will address their efforts. It is probable, therefore, that decline in mass support becomes less generalized as group intensity increases. The interactive effect is for organizational intensity to direct the generalized discontent toward the board, and back to the publics that they serve.

A natural suspicion is that the strong association between mass support and organizational intensity is a function of social complexity. We could assume that complexity and support vary inversely, given the strong association of both variables with organizational intensity and common sense description of urban life. Using metropolitanism as the measure of complexity, we find that both complexity and mass support retain their strong association with organizational intensity (Table 6–5). Of the two, mass support emerges as the best predictor, suffering less of a loss between the simple correlation and multiple regression. Since neither of the single relationships between mass support, metropolitanism, and intensity is seriously disturbed by the regression analysis, it is clear that each has a unique contribution to make to organizational intensity. The use of partial correlations rather than betas reveals a similar pattern.

TABLE 6–5
Effects of Mass Support and Metropolitanism
on Organizational Intensity

	Simple r	*Beta*
Mass Support	−.75	−.58
Metropolitanism	.60	.30
R^2	.63	

THE ROLE OF ELECTORAL FACTORS

Up to this point we have seen striking evidence in support of the importance of broad range socio-political factors upon group intensity. The next portion of the analysis uses as independent variables factors which are part of the more immediate political environment in which interest groups operate: the structure of electoral competition in the district. Heeding the advice of those who assess the impact of political institutions upon public policy, we are led to examine the relation between interest group activity and characteristics of the electoral system. One of the most frequently asserted dicta of group research, for instance, bears upon the link between interest groups and political parties. It is claimed that interest groups thrive in political systems with weak political parties. We will test this assertion along with those dealing with the importance of competition for office positions. The measures of competition for school board positions include de jure partisan (and slate) versus nonpartisan elections; the proportion of present board members who were either appointed to office, were encouraged to run by members of the previous board, or both; the absence or presence of contested seats in the last primary or general election for school board prior to the beginning of the study; and forced turnover — the proportion of incumbents defeated in immediately previous elections. A party-strength measure was constructed from individual responses in which each party was rated as strong (coded 1), not so strong (coded 2), and weak (coded 3). Measures of strength for each party were first constructed. The percentage of respondents in each category was multiplied by the coded value of that category. The resulting products were summed for each board, and that sum was subtracted from 300. The result was divided by two in order to give a possible range of 0 to 100 for each party. The combined party strength measure was built by adding the squared values of each party and dividing by 200 in order to maintain a 0–100 range.

Electoral variables fall well below social complexity and district harmony as predictors of organizational intensity. Overall, 10 percent of the variance in the dependent variable is accounted for by the electoral variables, most of which can be accounted for by the presence of electoral opposition. Electoral opposition is the only variable which presents a respectable beta (.26), although there is a slight negative association between office sponsorship and organizational intensity (-.09). Further, one worries that both electoral opposition and organizational intensity are dependent upon social complexity and district harmony. Districts beset with a massive decay of support (predominantly metropolitan), in addition to generating interest group activity, could also generate opposition in school board elections. In fact, controlling for metropolitanism and mass support actually reversed the sign of the beta (-.13), indicating that once the effect of the confounding variables is accounted for then the more opposition one finds, the *less* group activity will accompany it! In any case, no electoral variable approaches the explanatory power of complexity and mass support. It is especially noteworthy to observe that measures of partisanship do so poorly. The existence of partisan or nonpartisan elections, or whether there are strong political parties does not influence the activities of interest groups.

The final set of variables used to account for organizational intensity consists of legal parameters which may constrain or channel the activities of organized groups. Students of interest groups have argued that the formal structure of government, rather than simply being a neutral framework, is one of the factors with which groups must reckon. For instance, the American federal system gave black organizations an opportunity to circumvent the hostility of Southern legislatures by turning to Congress and the courts. In educational politics the efforts of good government forces to make the governance of schools uniform have not succeeded in erasing a variety of institutional frameworks. Among those to be considered are whether ward or at-large elections are held; term of office; and whether coterminous referenda are held simultaneously with school board elections.

Such variables do very little by themselves. About 10 percent of the variance in organizational intensity is accounted for. Nonetheless, the controlled relationships do suggest that legal constraints are associated with organizational intensity in a manner compatible with common sense. For example, there is a positive association between the existence of coterminous referenda and organizational intensity (beta = .25). It is likely that, when all school-related elections are held simultaneously, the climate of the elections is more heated than when elections are spread over a longer period of time. Such an explanation is especially probable during periods of taxpayer revolt. In such relatively controversial settings, more visibility would accrue to interest groups. Similarly, the modest association between ward elections and organizational intensity (.10) indicates that, since such elections insure a heterogeneous representation on the board, they attract a wider range of group activities.

Political Factors as Intervening Variables

Although the explained variance is trivial, should such variables be ignored? It is perhaps unfair to argue solely on the basis of amount of variance explained. It is true that when electoral variables and legal constraints are placed into a stepwise regression equation with mass support and metropolitanism, the electoral and legal variables do very poorly. Electoral variables and legal constraints enter the equation last and have very small betas.

Granting that the broader variables of metropolitanism and mass support attain more overarching importance, it is possible that we will find the electoral and legal variables acting as mediating devices in the same manner that they did in our earlier analysis of individual and group responsiveness in Chapter 5. We separated the electoral and legal variables and observed the association between mass support and organizational intensity for each. Because mass support is also strongly associated with metropolitanism, results with the latter variable controlled allow us to assess the separate contribution of mass support under each physical control. Our interpretation will depend upon comparing the beta weights.

Turning first to legal constraints, we found that each has some effect upon the articulation between mass support and organizational intensity. The initial negative association between mass support and organizational intensity is depressed in at-large electoral districts (-.42), those with shorter terms of office (-.49) and those that have no coterminous referenda (-.49). The case of electoral units is perhaps an instance of a widening distance between organized groups and elected representatives, although it makes some intuitive sense to argue that larger geographical units should increase the number of possible groups. What appears to happen, however, is that smaller units aggravate the negative association between mass support and organizational intensity possibly because ward elections provide a clearer focus for grievances that are more likely to be neighborhood linked.

The effects of the competition structure reveals some apparent contradictions. On the one hand, the effect of mass support is strengthened when boards are elected on a partisan basis (-.72). On the other hand, the original association is also heightened when party strength is low (-.72). Our explanation for this contradiction is that party organizations may or may not have anything to do with school board politics. In strong party areas, it is possible that little interaction occurs between parties and the educational system. Yet there is clearly no such problem when we consider whether or not the board has partisan elections. When parties do enter the educational process, interest group activity is enhanced. Rather than operating in competition, interest groups and parties exist side by side. Here is evidence that one or the other of these two forms of political organization need not dominate the political articulation process, as has been occasionally assumed by political scientists. What is more probable is that partisan elections place the school board squarely within the general political process, thus making the school board the target of the pressures which exist within the general political process.

Of the remaining variables, electoral opposition makes very little difference in the original association once metropolitanism is controlled, but both forced turnover and office sponsorship have consistent effects. When forced turnover is low and office sponsorship high, the correlation between mass support and organizational intensity is depressed (–.44 and –.34, respectively). Competition acts as a mediating force in both cases, suggesting that competitiveness brings boards and interest groups into closer contact. Consider, for example, the effect of office sponsorship. When incumbent board members can perpetuate their influence by bringing like-minded colleagues to the board, the interest group-mass support connection tapers off considerably. Boards in these circumstances appear somewhat akin to closed corporations, insulating themselves from the hue and cry of interest group politics. In such cases, popular uprisings or expressions of discontent would come more slowly to the attention of the board through interest group representations.

Although the differences in the basic correlations introduced by holding physically constant the electoral factors are not massive, they point toward a re-conceptualization of how electoral matters figure in school district governance.

A simple model of association between less overtly political variables and organizational intensity is not adequate, for it is apparent that the electoral variables work in conjunction with mass support and metropolitanism to produce distinct patterns of interest group activity. This analysis suggests that the appropriate treatment of these variables should not stop after they have lost in the competition with broader, more societally based variables; rather we should consider them as interacting with such broader variables in a systematic fashion. In general the overall negative association between mass support and organizational intensity rises among the more competitive school districts and those in which the legal parameters facilitate segmentation and differentiation.

SPECIFIC TYPES OF ORGANIZATIONAL INTENSITY

Organizational intensity has thus far been treated without regard for particular varieties of groups. Now we will examine the corollaries of specific organizational types. It is reasonable to assume — given the different ideologies and memberships of the various organizations — that the two major determinants (metropolitanism and mass support) will have markedly different impacts upon distinctive organizations. It is of course true that organization tends to produce counterorganization so that where the right-wing flourishes we might expect a countermovement. We should not necessarily expect, however, that the existence of one kind of organization will automatically be associated with the existence of another, especially when such organizations do not have competing goals.

In Table 6-6 a correlation matrix for the organizations under analysis is presented. It can be seen that there is considerable variation in the tendency of organizations to cluster together. For instance, the most pervasive organization, PTA, is associated with the existence of five of thirteen groups (teachers, League of Women Voters, left-wing, taxpayers, and right-wing), none of which bears any consistent ideological relation to the PTA. Yet the highest correlations exist between ideologically opposed groups, the right- and left-wing organizations. Equally high is the correlation between right-wing and tax groups. The highest correlations are reserved for the groups with the strongest ideological commitment, whatever the nature of that commitment.

By way of illustrating this idea, examine the paired correlations involving clubs, which consist of Kiwanis, Rotary, etc., and also the various local "boosters" clubs. In this case, all but two of the associations are negative. The service clubs are essentially nonideological, even more so than most of the groups which come to the attention of the school board.

Similar to service organizations are the citizen advisory committees created by the board to improve public relations, assist in passing bond issues, and the like. The activity level of this kind of group has no appreciable correlation with that of any other organization, suggesting an essentially nonthreatening posture. Religious organizations, neighborhood groups, and labor organizations also exist in relative isolation. We speculate that the more a group is caught up in a policy struggle, the more association there will be with other types of groups. Nevertheless, Table 6-6 suggests that different kinds of organizations thrive in different kinds of environments.

Let us examine Table 6-7 to determine how the environment affects particular kinds of groups. Organizations listed above the dotted line are more affected by metropolitanism, those below more by mass support. Turning to metropolitanism, we see that this variable is the best predictor of the activities of left-wing and civil right groups but does little to predict the activities of right-wing groups. Mass support, in contrast, does more to predict the activities of right-wing groups, with metropolitanism taking a markedly inferior position. Left groups are less dependent upon widespread hostility whereas the complexity of the environment is of little value in understanding the strength of right-wing organizations. In a similar vein, mass support has a strong negative association with taxpayers associations, another conservative group, and metropolitanism has a trivial impact. It would seem that right-wing organizations seize the initiative in periods of unrest more quickly, and do so whether or not the complexity of the community is generally conducive to organizational activity.

It should be noted that the predictions for all ideological groups — irrespective of the direction of the ideology — are stronger than those for other kinds of organizations. Political organizations also show a strong pattern.

TABLE 6-6
Intercorrelations of Organizational Intensity Among Specific Types of Organizations

Type of Organization	PTA	Teachers	League of Women Voters	Left-wing, Civil Rights	Tax-payers	Right-wing	Religious	Citizen Advisory Committee	Political	Business-Professional	Service Clubs	Neighborhood	Labor
PTA													
Teachers	.32												
League of Women Voters	.31	.22											
Left-wing, Civil Rights	.25	.42	.43										
Taxpayers	.23	.28	.22	.37									
Right-wing	.26	.41	.21	.51	.50								
Religious	.05	-.00	.06	.16	.04	.21							
Citizen Advisory Committee	.12	.04	.04	.17	.10	.16	.11						
Political	.10	.14	.27	.26	.39	.24	-.02	-.00					
Business-Professional	.10	.30	.26	.34	.40	.27	.02	.03	.12				
Service Clubs	.16	-.10	.06	-.39	-.19	-.27	-.23	-.24	-.14	-.08			
Neighborhood	-.06	.10	.07	.30	.03	.15	.00	-.10	-.01	.26	-.24		
Labor	.11	.08	.12	.19	.03	.12	.05	.16	.04	.18	-.01	.26	

TABLE 6-7
Sources of Organizational Intensity:
Metropolitanism and Mass Support

Type of Organization	Simple r	Beta[a]	R²
Left-wing, Civil Rights			
Metropolitanism	.63	.46	
Mass Support	-.58	-.34	.48
Teachers			
Metropolitanism	.51	.34	
Mass Support	-.50	-.32	.34
Business and Professional			
Metropolitanism	.38	.30	
Mass Support	.31	-.15	.16
League of Women Voters			
Metropolitanism	.29	.29	
Mass Support	-.15	_b	.08
PTA			
Metropolitanism	.23	.20	
Mass Support	-.16	-.05	.06
Right-wing			
Mass Support	-.52	-.45	
Metropolitanism	.38	.14	.29
Taxpayers			
Mass Support	-.45	-.42	
Metropolitanism	.28	.05	.20
Service Clubs			
Mass Support	.33	.23	
Metropolitanism	-.31	-.19	.13
Neighborhood			
Mass Support	-.32	-.25	
Metropolitanism	.27	.14	.12
Political			
Mass Support	-.33	-.33	
Metropolitanism	.18	_b	.10
Citizens Advisory Committee			
Mass Support	-.25	-.19	
Metropolitanism	.22	.12	.07
Religious			
Mass Support	-.17	-.11	
Metropolitanism	.17	.11	.04
Labor			
Mass Support	-.18	-.19	
Metropolitanism	.08	-.02	.03

[a]Betas for "Metropolitanism" are with "Mass Support" controlled, and vice versa.

[b]If the tolerance level is very small, the second variable is virtually a combination of the variable(s) already in the equation. Inclusion of such a variable is very often the result of random error in measurement and is difficult to interpret in a meaningful way. Stepwise regression does not allow such variables to enter the equation.

The more political or ideological the organization is, the greater the response is to a decline in mass support. There is also a healthy relation between mass support and teacher organizations, but it is probable that in this case the organizational response is more defensive. As mass support declines, public acquiescence to school board policy declines, stimulating teachers organizations into a more active role.

Mass support appears to be least determinative when the organizations are supportive, e.g., PTA and League of Women Voters. In fact, when we examine the role of service organizations we notice that the association between mass support and intensity is positive, which is the single exception to the rule. The *more* supportive the public is, the greater is the activity of service organizations. As we noted, service organization activity is negatively associated with the existence of other organizations. Here we find they are also a clear exception. Their role is one of local booster, and they thrive when the public is in a mood to boost. In a sense, the positive relationship between service organizations and mass support is an extension of the low negative association for PTAs. Both organizations differ fundamentally from the ideologically and politically combative organizations.

A similar point can be made by examining the R^2 values for the various kinds of organizations. R^2 for ideologically oriented groups tends to be higher than for such groups as PTAs, League of Women Voters, and the like. The more a group is an agent for the maintenance of things as they are, the less we can explain about this occurrence. It is also instructive that R^2 for any single type of organization is considerably lower than the .63 found for the overall measure of organizational intensity, using the same two predictor variables, which suggests a strong threshold effect. The likelihood of a district generating intensity across a *variety* of interest groups increases greatly according to both social complexity and mass support whereas the likelihood of intensity for a given type of organization is customarily only modestly affected. Thus whereas two districts of varying complexity and mass support may both have the same level of intensity by one type of group, they are unlikely to have the same level of intensity when various types of organizations are considered. There is a more clearly defined threshold of circumstances and preconditions for the overall level of group life.

Some Consequences of Organizational Intensity: Issue Arousal

If we view interest groups as bargaining agents in the allocation of public resources, then we need to know what difference they make in the way school districts conduct their business.[16] We earlier made the point that interest groups thrive when mass support for the school board is low. Does it follow that group activity contributes to the heightened tension which accompanies a decline in public confidence? To put the question into another perspective, imagine a school district suffering a decline in public support. Even though interest groups will probably become active in this district, does their activity translate the loss of confidence into observable phenomena? If not, it would make little difference to the school board if mass support is low, since the board would have little evidence of the state of public opinion.

The interview schedule contains some questions designed to tap the degree of "issue arousal" and "issue disposal" within the district. Our question deals with the extent to which interest groups contribute to a tense atmosphere within the district, in contrast to the main question of the previous sections that considered the conditions which contribute to organizational intensity.

We have selected the following items as measures of issue arousal.

Financial Defeats: Whether a district has seen a bond issue or tax referendum go down to defeat in the last three years.

Racial Problems: The percentage of board members who say the district faces racial problems.

Financial Problems: The percentage of board members who say the district has trouble in achieving an adequate level of financing. There is only a moderate (.36) correlation between this item and financial defeats, suggesting that close but successful financial elections still make board members think in terms of troublesome situations.

Teacher Criticism: The percentage of board members who indicate that teachers' classroom performance has come under attack.

Firing of Teachers: The percentage of board members who are aware of tenured teachers being dismissed because of their classroom behavior.

Superintendent Turnover: Whether the superintendent left his position involuntarily in the past three years.

The items give a fairly broad range of issues, dealing with finances, teacher behavior, racial tension, and school management. Some (e.g., financial defeats) are clearly "outputs," since they provide tangible evidence of the state of tension in the district. The others refer more to a general level of tension. Even though the items have a different portent, it was deemed advisable to construct a composite index of issue arousal in order to sketch in the general role of interest groups in this phenomenon.[17] The resulting index ranges from 0 to 100 with a mean of 40.0 and a standard deviation of 23.0. The composite index reflects the essence of the individual items, as is indicated by the following item-index correlation:

Racial problems	.69	Teacher criticism	.56
Financial problems	.68	Superintendent turnover	.52
Financial defeats	.65	Teacher firings	.46

The occurrence or outcomes of these six issues become the dependent variables in our attempt to isolate the effects of organizational intensity. Our procedure is to enter organizational intensity as an independent variable into the regression equation along with mass support and metropolitanism. The last two variables were selected because of their powerful performance in predicting organizational intensity. If intensity makes an independent contribution to issue arousal, it should be under conditions that put it to a severe test. As we observe in the upper portion of Table 6-8, both mass support and organizational intensity make an appreciable impact upon issue arousal. As mass support declines and organizational intensity increases, the issue climate of the school district becomes heated. Surprisingly, the complexity of the environment makes virtually no impact upon issue arousal once the contribution of the other two factors is taken into account.

TABLE 6-8
Conditions Associated With Issue Arousal

Issue Arousal Index

	Simple r	Beta	
Mass Support	-.66	-.39	
Organizational Intensity	.66	.38	
Metropolitanism	.41	-.03	$R^2 = .50$
Racial Problems			
Organizational Intensity	.62	.33	
Mass Support	-.58	-.24	
Metropolitanism	.51	.17	$R^2 = .44$
Criticize Teachers			
Mass Support	-.51	-.36	
Organizational Intensity	.47	.21	
Metropolitanism	.31	-.01	$R^2 = .28$
Financial Problems			
Organizational Intensity	.50	.38	
Metropolitanism	.37	.10	
Mass Support	-.41	-.08	$R^2 = .26$
Fire Teachers			
Mass Support	-.38	-.32	
Metropolitanism	.11	-.18	
Organizational Intensity	.33	.20	$R^2 = .17$
Superintendent Turnover			
Mass Support	-.28	-.45	
Metropolitanism	-.02	-.22	
Organizational Intensity	.15	-.07	$R^2 = .12$
Financial Defeats[a]			
Organizational Intensity	.26	.34	
Mass Support	-.15	.10	
Metropolitanism	.14	-.02	$R^2 = .07$

[a]Based only on districts where financial referenda had been held in past 3 years.

We have mentioned the affinity between mass support and organizational intensity; we now add that, as a consequence of their interaction, a school district can find itself immersed in a climate of hostility *whether or not the environment is socially complex.* The latter point is especially significant in view of the earlier discussion of the link between complexity and organizational intensity. In terms of the *consequences* of these patterns, we are far better off knowing the level of organizational intensity than knowing the degree of social complexity.

We should be careful to disclaim any clearly established causal chain in these events. Since we cannot be sure whether issue arousal or organizational intensity comes first chronologically, we might argue logically, if not empirically, that the stimulation of the debate over issues leads to organizational intensity rather than the reverse. However, when we construct the same regression equation with organizational intensity instead of issue arousal as the dependent variable and issue arousal as one of the independent variables, the beta coefficient for issue arousal is .22. Issue arousal predicts organizational intensity less well than intensity predicts arousal (.22 vs. .38). We still do not wish to make too much of the argument simply on the basis of regression coefficients despite this support.

If one examines the "real world" of educational politics in local districts it would probably be very difficult, indeed impossible, to construct a causal chain. Perhaps it is more fruitful to think in terms of interaction between issue arousal, decline of mass support, and organizational intensity, with each contributing to the other. The more action on the part of the interest groups, the more trouble there is for the school board — regardless of causal flow. It is little wonder that school board members shudder when group action proliferates.

Organizational intensity stands as a strong predictor of the overall level of issue arousal, as represented by the index based on six specific issues. Since the issues represent a wide range of concerns, however, it is quite possible that organizational intensity is less consequential in some areas than in others. That possibility is borne out by the remaining figures in Table 6–8. One notable feature of these figures is that the amount of variance explained for each separate issue by all three predictor variables is lower than it is for the multi-item indicator of issue arousal. The latter gives a much better overall indication of the issue-arousal climate within the district and, in turn, is better predicted by the three variables of mass support, metropolitanism, and organizational intensity.

Within the framework of weaker associations for the specific issues, it is nevertheless reassuring to see that organizational intensity continues to fare well on five of them. Organizational intensity is the best predictor of financial defeats, racial problems, and financial problems. For the issues dealing with teachers and superintendents there is a greater link with mass support, but organizational intensity still makes an appreciable contribution except for superintendent turnover. The pattern is for issue arousal to increase with proportional increases in organizational intensity. One is hard pressed again to assert a causal chain in which organizational intensity exists prior to issue arousal. It might work the other way; racial problems, for instance, might motivate interest groups to become involved.

Yet the regression coefficients with organizational intensity treated as dependent upon the issue-arousal items are uniformly lower than those presented in Table 6–8. To take one example, the beta involving racial problems as the independent variable and organizational intensity as the dependent variable is .21, compared to .33 when the order of the variables is reversed, as is the case in the table. Thus, there is clearly a reciprocal effect operative; organizational intensity increases board members' awareness of, say, racial problems, but as the problems become more apparent organizational intensity increases. Nevertheless, there is more "cause" if we adhere to the model suggested in the table.

The Contributions of Specific Organizations

It is true that some groups are more active and effective than others. Given the nature of the dependent variable of issue arousal, we might expect that the more ideologically oriented groups would have more of an impact. Since the goals of left- or right-wing groups differ fundamentally from the goals of groups such as service organizations, does it necessarily follow that their effect will differ? To answer this question, we perform a regression using mass support, metropolitanism, and each organizational type individually. When this is done, the only groups whose betas are not diminished to the point of triviality are left-wing (.32), teachers (.18), and right-wing (.13). These diminished coefficients demonstrate the importance of multiple versus simple types of organizations in generating issue arousal. What an intense single group might not do, a combination of them will.

The most significant type of group, insofar as issue arousal is concerned, is the left, far more so than the right. As expected, the dominant groups are ideological; but this does not tell us why the left is associated so much more with issue arousal than the right is. It is useful here to recall that left-wing groups are more *active* (according to the perceptions of board members) than right-wing groups; perhaps sheer activity at least partially explains their greater impact. Although left-wing groups are *not* more active than teachers organizations, for instance, they have greater impact. Indeed, if we perform a regression using *only* organizational types as independent variables (with the index of issue arousal as the dependent variable), left-wing groups rank first, and right-wing groups rank last! The beta for left-wing groups is roughly five times that of right-wing groups (.46 versus .09).

One explanation is that the left-wing groups cast a wider net than the right-wing groups, and hence are more effective on more issues. It is quite possible that groups will concentrate their energies in a few areas of controversy. Taxpayer associations, for example, are likely to be more involved with financial issues than with the dismissal of teachers. It is unnecessary to require that all groups compete in an equation with mass support and metropolitanism if we want to make a point about the distribution of influence. For instance, even though in a given issue area a group has less impact than mass support or social complexity, it still might be the most efficient group *in competition with other groups*.

If we enter all groups into the stepwise regression equation for each issue area, it will give us a better notion of differential organizational impact. In Table 6-9, the entry of the group into the equation is listed next to the beta coefficient. If we concentrate our attention on the first three groups for each issue area, we can observe that there is very little overlap between issue areas. Only four types of organizations appear in the top three more than once. They are: religious groups (2), citizens advisory committees (2), left-wing groups (3), and teachers (3). Further, if we examine those groups that rank first, only left-wing groups repeat. Compared with right-wing groups the average beta for left-wing groups is demonstrably higher — 28.3 versus 11.0. These results help explain why left-wing groups have a greater overall influence than right-wing groups: they have impact upon more issue areas.

We should not necessarily argue that emergence as a strong predictor is equated with influence in a planned direction. Organizational intensity may often be a consequence of an inflamed issue area. It is apparent, for example, that not all of these groups take the same position on financial issues. Presumably, the League of Women Voters and teachers organizations are most likely to favor the passage of the issue while taxpayers associations are not. Yet the direction of their influence is the same irrespective of the ideology of the group. What seems to happen is that such groups excite the election environment and, possibly, stimulate a higher turnout. Generally, higher turnouts spell doom for school financial elections since they draw a disproportionate turnout from negatively inclined lower status people.

Ironically the result of activity by proschool forces and antischool forces is the same. The effect, if one can call it that, seems to be independent of the goals of the organization. A similar effect can be observed with regard to racial problems, where left-wing and civil rights groups have the greatest impact. What probably happens in this case is that the racial problem has been there all along, and group activity simply brings it to the surface. Hence the school board defines it as a problem because interest groups have made the problem salient. Therefore, it is probably more accurate to say, for example, that left-wing groups while seeking integration, hiring of black teachers, and the teaching of black history crystallize an issue which may lead to its partial resolution.

There are instances where the relationships are less ambiguous, with the goals of the organization and the result of its activity being compatible. The positive association between right-wing group and teacher firing is a case in point. In this case, right-wing groups have harassed school boards to get rid of various kinds of allegedly subversive teachers; and the table indicates that they have done a good job. Similarly consider these negative associations between activity and issue areas: PTA efforts with superintendent turnover; labor organization intensity with teacher firings; and League of Women Voters activity with teacher criticism. These are reasonably clear examples of the intended consequences of group efforts and the actual consequences of their efforts being congruent.

One can interpret the evidence in Table 6-9 from another perspective. On the one hand, the fact that most organizations have impact upon a single issue

TABLE 6-9
Contributions of Specific Organizations in Specific Issues[a]

Type of Organization	Race Problems	Financial Defeats	Financial Problems	Teacher Criticism	Fire Teachers	Superintendent Turnover
Left-wing, Civil Rights	.55 (1)	.11 (11)	.41 (1)	.40 (1)	.12 (7)	.03 (12)
Teachers	.18 (2)	.19 (8)	.12 (6)	.23 (4)	.05 (9)	.11 (6)
Neighborhood	.13 (3)	.47 (1)	– _b	.11 (9)	-.09 (8)	.12 (5)
Religious	.12 (4)	.21 (6)	-.06 (8)	-.04 (11)	.17 (4)	.22 (2)
PTA	-.11 (5)	-.18 (9)	-.19 (3)	-.06 (10)	.04 (11)	-.21 (3)
Service Clubs	.11 (6)	.35 (3)	.19 (4)	.24 (3)	-.05 (10)	.03 (11)
Labor	-.10 (7)	-.29 (5)	-.03 (9)	.02 (12)	-.14 (6)	.09 (7)
Citizens Advisory Committee	.08 (8)	.41 (2)	.14 (5)	.12 (8)	.18 (3)	-.18 (4)
Taxpayers	.07 (9)	.30 (4)	.20 (2)	-.13 (7)	.20 (1)	– _b
Business and Professional	.07 (10)	.05 (12)	.02 (10)	– _b	-.15 (5)	-.03 (10)
League of Women Voters	.06 (11)	.21 (7)	-.11 (7)	-.34 (2)	-.03 (12)	.03 (9)
Right-wing	.05 (12)	-.15 (10)	.02 (11)	.20 (5)	.19 (2)	.09 (8)
Political Party	.02 (13)	– _b	-.02 (12)	.15 (6)	– _b	.32 (1)
R^2	.46	.46	.34	.32	.32	.23

NOTE: Entries are beta weights.
[a] Controlling for the effects of the other organizations. Number in parentheses indicates the rank order of the beta weights.
[b] See note b, Table 6–6.

area argues for a pluralistic interpretation. On the other hand, the fact that two types of organizations (left-wing and teachers) dominate half the issue areas, leaving the remaining groups to contest for influence in the other issue areas, suggests a concentration of influence. Further, it is possible that in a given district at a particular time, a single issue (and hence a single group) is most salient. For example, if there is a struggle to oust the superintendent, then political organizations will appear most influential. If there is an effort to remove allegedly subversive teachers, then right-wing and taxpayer groups will dominate. In short, neither a concentrated power structure nor a pluralistic one receives unequivocal support.

Yet while it is true that issues and salient groups vary, two issues appear to attract a disproportionately high level of organizational interest. Judging from the multiple correlations, group effort abounds in the areas of financial defeats and racial problems. Such a finding fits well with a "commonsense" view of what is likely to arouse extraschool involvement in educational politics. Many school districts have been caught up in the "taxpayer revolt" and have, simultaneously, had to cope with federal and local pressures toward integration. These issues not only require the mobilization of the resources of the school district, they also are likely to excite the passions of the various publics which normally may not be especially attentive to school affairs.

As identified in the introductory section, we have been dealing with two unresolved problems in the study of interest groups and school district governance. On the one hand, there is the empirical question of the origins and consequences of group activity. On the other hand, there are serious problems of measurement if we are to move toward providing at least tentative answers to the empirical questions.

One purpose of this chapter was to contribute to the resolution of these kinds of problems by identifying the subsystem under investigation as the unit of analysis, rather than the individuals who comprise the subsystem. This methodological decision places the study in a somewhat different light than previous studies of interest groups. By using school boards rather than school board members as units of analysis, we were able to develop a measure of organizational intensity which could then be linked with other systemic variables. The cost of such an operation should not be ignored. We were unable to take into account the potentially significant behavior of the leaders of particular groups, and the unique behavior of individual board members. Thus we can provide no direct answer to the Salisbury-Olson theories of interest group origination. Nevertheless, we were able to account for the intensity of group activity by using indicators which made no reference to individual behavior. Perhaps the unexplained variance in our equations can be accounted for by the activities of individual entrepreneurs, as is suggested by Salisbury and Olson.

With regard to the antecedents of group activity, the "traditional" theories which Salisbury and Olson seek to modify hold up rather well. Both social complexity and the lack of mass support are quite helpful in predicting organizational intensity. It is with the consequences of group activity that traditional group theory leaves much to be desired. Here we have tried to go beyond the linking of a specific group with a single policy outcome; we have sought to explain the general role of interest groups in defining the climate of issue arousal in school districts. In so doing, we can isolate two general categories of organizations. First, there are non-issue-specific groups, such as PTAs, League of Women Voters, and service organizations. These organizations provide support for the ongoing system, but inject little conflict into the system. They constitute a resource from which decision makers may draw in times of crisis. Then there are ideological and issue-specific groups whose role is to inject conflict into the system and to make conflict salient for decision makers. Intense activity by such organizations usually has an effect, but not necessarily the effect that such groups desire. The unanticipated consequences of such groups may be a result of the fact that they have the influence to make an issue salient by expanding the scope of conflict but apparently have less ability to control the outcome of a conflict once it has developed.

A somewhat surprising finding lies in the comparison of left-wing and right-wing groups. For one thing, the intensity of the left is much more predictable than that of the right, thereby suggesting more of a flash or idiosyncratic pattern for the latter. Of course some would argue that the views of the right — presumably residing in at least part of the so-called "silent majority" — may not need the explicit articulation of the left in order to be incorporated into school district policies. But our findings also provide a useful corrective to the popular views of social and educational critics that the right-wing is the better organized, more spirited participant in school district politics. Issue arousal and disposal were actually much more reflective of left-wing energies than of the right-wing. The prominence of one or the other of these wings probably varies over time. During the late 1960s the left was the more prominent, if our data are a guide.

Finally, there is the notion of the feedback or interaction between issues and organizations. Once an issue is raised, partially as a consequence of group activity, other organizations enter the arena. In using survey research to describe this phenomenon, we are using what amounts to a stop-action camera. We get a picture of the situation at a single point in time; therefore, we can do no more than speculate upon the question of issues engendering groups or groups generating issues. We have suggested a pattern of development in which interest groups play the leading role in raising issues, but what is clearly needed is the development of dynamic methods of observation in order to resolve this impasse.

NOTES

1. Arthur Bentley, *The Process of Government* (San Antonio, Texas: Principia Press of Trinity University, 1949); David Truman, *The Governmental Process* (New York: Alfred A. Knopf, 1951).

2. See Lester Milbrath, *The Washington Lobbyists* (Chicago: Rand McNally, 1963); Raymond A. Bauer, Ithiel de Sola Pool, and Lewis A. Dexter, *American Business and Public Policy* (New York: Atherton, 1963); Harmon Zeigler and Michael A. Baer, *Lobbying* (Belmont, Calif.: Wadsworth, 1969).

3. See, for example, Thomas R. Dye, *Politics, Economics, and the Public: Policy Outcomes in the American States* (Chicago: Rand McNally, 1966).

4. Harmon Zeigler, "Interest Groups in the States," *Politics in the American States*, eds. Herbert Jacob and Kenneth L. Vines (Boston: Little, Brown, 1965), pp. 101–147; Lewis A. Froman, Jr., "Some Effects of Interest Group Strength in State Politics," *American Politicial Science Review*, 60 (December, 1966), pp. 952–962.

5. Wayne Francis, *Legislative Issues in the Fifty States: A Comparative Analysis* (Chicago: Rand McNally, 1967).

6. Robert H. Salisbury, "An Exchange Theory of Interest Groups," *Midwest Journal of Political Science*, 13 (February, 1969), pp. 1–32.

7. Salisbury, *loc cit.*; Mancur L. Olson, Jr., *The Logic of Collective Action* (Cambridge: Harvard University Press, 1965).

8. Neal Gross, *Who Runs Our Schools?* (New York: Wiley, 1958).

9. Eugene R. Smoley, *Community Participation in Urban School Government* (Washington, D.C.: USOE Cooperative Research Project S–029, 1965), p. 180.

10. David Rogers, *110 Livingston Street: Politics and Bureaucracy in the New York City School System* (New York: Random House, 1968); and Marilyn Gittell, *Participants and Participation: A Study of School Policy in New York City* (New York: Praeger, 1968).

11. These figures are based upon *all* mentions, including those which could not be placed within a specific category.

12. Robert A. Dahl, *Who Governs?* (New Haven: Yale University Press, 1961); see also James D. Koerner, *Who Controls American Education? A Guide for Laymen* (Boston: Beacon, 1968).

13. Louis Wirth, "Urbanism as a Way of Life," *American Journal of Sociology*, 64 (July, 1938), p. 20.

14. Betty H. Zisk achieves similar results, using similar measures, in her analysis of the Bay Area City Council study. See her "Local Interest Politics and Municipal Outputs," in Hahn, *op. cit.*, pp. 231–54, especially pp. 241–43.

15. It should be stressed that neither in this chapter nor elsewhere in this book have we actually employed causal modeling in our analysis. The beta weights and partial correlations used do not take into statistical account indirect effects.

16. Zisk was able to make inferences about interest group impact on specific public policy outputs of a financial variety. Impact was discernible especially in the area of local amenities. See Zisk, *op. cit.*, pp. 252–53.

17. The composite index was constructed in the following manner. For each board, the percentages of members answering in the affirmative on the questions about teacher criticism, firing of teachers, financial problems, and racial problems were summed. To this total was added 100 percent if one or more financial referenda had been defeated, and 100 percent if the superintendent's departure had been voluntary. The addition of 100 was necessary because the other indicators were all scored from 0–100. The total sums were divided by four if no budget referenda had been held and no superintendent turnover had occurred, by five if all but one of the conditions held, and by six otherwise.

Chapter 7

Shared Orientations

between Boards and their Constituents

Representation takes many forms in school districts.[1] We have considered some
of those forms in the previous two chapters. What we have not done yet is to
treat one of the most basic ways in which the concept of representation is visualized
in democratic societies, namely, the degree to which leaders and led share the same
public policy preferences. We are fortunate in having separate soundings from
school district constituents to complement those obtained from school board
members and superintendents. These soundings will enable us to make modest in
roads on the question of shared preferences, a question which — for many people —
is the primary one of representation.

We will consider four main topics. First, in what measure do the rank
and file and elite hold that the basis of policy making should rest on the assumption of congruent preferences? Second, to what degree do the citizenry and the
elite hold the same priority schedules with respect to problems in the school
district? Third, what is the level of concordance with respect to opinions on
specific issues? Finally, how does the concordance of mass publics and boards of
education compare with that between mass publics and the other major policy
maker, the superintendent?

Despite the obvious utility of pairing political leaders with their constituents, this has rarely been done in the study of American politics, or the
politics of other countries for that matter. Only the Miller-Stokes study of Congressmen and their constituents[2] and the Verba-Nie study of community leaders and
citizens[3] have employed such an approach on the national level. Certainly a major
obstacle to these designs has been the sheer cost of mounting the research. In our

own case the ability to employ such a design derives from the fact that the school districts included in the sample were drawn almost entirely from primary sampling units which the Survey Research Center uses in its national cross-section studies. To the extent that the sample segments for a particular survey fell within the boundaries of the school district we had the opportunity to match up school district residents with their respective board of education officeholders.

The national survey used by us was the 1968 postelection study, conducted less than six months after our school board survey. Included in the interview schedule were a number of questions which paralleled those in the board and superintendent forms, as well as other questions more appropriate for the mass public. By utilizing the place information for each respondent we were able to allocate 513 into the districts included in our board sample. A comparison of these respondents with those not included in our districts shows a surprisingly high resemblance both in sociological and political characteristics.

Of greater importance is the fact that 70 percent (raw $N = 60$, weighted $N = 130$) of the augmented board sample can be paired with district constituents. This high coverage stems primarily from the presence of districts which either encompass large numbers of people (such as those in the large cities) or which encompass a large area (such as whole counties). A certain price is paid for this circumstance. Compared with the full sample, the districts with matches are found slightly less often in the Northeast (18 percent versus 27 percent for the entire sample), more often in the South (35 petcent versus 28 percent), and more often in cities of 150,000 or larger (35 percent versus 25 percent). Significantly, however, there are scarcely any differences on the political features of included districts versus excluded districts. Therefore, remembering these modest demographic differences, we conclude that the subset of districts in which we matched board members and their constituents is quite representative of the entire augmented sample of districts.

In most of the following we use data grouped at the district level. That is, board member responses from a given district were grouped into a single score for that district. The responses of the cross-section national survey respondents were grouped similarly.[4] More details on the mass public sample are found in Appendix A.

HOW SHOULD THE GOVERNORS MAKE DECISIONS?

Having said that we are seeking indicators of shared orientations does not let us elude the most time-honored puzzle of all: should the representatives represent the *interest* or the *will* of the represented? Where interest and will converge the dilemma disappears in an operational sense. Many have argued that the entire dichotomy is false, and that we are still suffering from the straitjacket imposed by Burke in his famous address to the electors of Bristol.[5] As indicated in the two preceding chapters, our own interpretation of the representation process does not hinge on the two polar positions. And recent work in the field has tried to work around the classic formulation.[6]

Yet the contrast stands. Academics and theorists may wish it away or write it away, but the public and public officials live with the choice (or blending of choices) constantly. Even the theorist who has done the most to clarify contemporary thinking about the issue warns that if the preferences of those being represented and those doing the representing diverge appreciably, then the representatives should be able to show good and legitimate cause for the divergence.[7] Moreover, school government is a sector in which the two philosophies have exceptionally fertile grounds for clashing. Standing against a growing professionalism and aura of expertise is the long tradition in this country stating that education should be controlled by representatives from the lay public and that those representatives are directly responsible to the people whom they serve — especially the parents of children in school and those who use the schools' basic product (e.g., local employers).

One might, therefore, expect the general public to favor the instructed-delegate model rather than the trustee model. Board members, recognizing the complexity of governing and being situated between their constituents on the one hand and a professional bureaucracy on the other, will almost assuredly be less in favor of the instructed delegate model than their constituents are. At the aggregate level these predictions are borne out with a vengeance. We employ a three-point indicator, where 1 represents the position that the board members should do what the public wants despite the members' own opinions, 3 represents the position that the board members should rely on their own judgment, and 2 represents being undecided and pro/con responses. The mean score for constituents across districts is 2.10, or barely leaning toward the trustee model. In sharp contrast the mean score for board members is 2.56, that is, skewed markedly toward the trustee version of representation. In percentage terms 48 percent of the mass public, versus 68 percent of the board members chose the trustee orientation. We have a wide gap here, and we shall proceed later to see if that gap is reflected in low correspondence between board members and their own constituents.

First, however, it is worth examining the superintendents' preferences on this question. Their mean score of 2.76 demonstrates a trustee orientation of even greater magnitude than that of the board. This score remains remarkably stable regardless of district characteristics. If we may assume that superintendents prefer to see lay "meddling" in educational affairs kept at a minimum, this finding is not surprising. Since a school board composed of delegates will tend to base its decisions on the wishes of its lay constituents more than on the professional standards of the superintendent, it is a difficult board for the superintendent to control. A trustee-oriented school board, on the other hand, is more susceptible to superintendent leadership because it does not feel obliged to adhere to every demand expressed by the public. It sees itself as serving the public best by acting in accordance with its own judgment. All the superintendent has to do in such circumstances to control educational policy is to convince the board that his position is in the best interest of public education. The job of convincing the board, as we shall see in subsequent chapters, is not a difficult task for many district superintendents.

The reasoning behind these contrasting views of representation is hardly surprising, but it goes to the heart of much of the debate about popular rule in the nation's school districts. Table 7-1 contains the distributions for the major response categories offered by members of the mass public and board members. Entries are percentaged against the total number of responses made as justifying the respondent's choice on the basic question of whether trustee, delegate, or combined role orientation was preferred.

Overall, the mass public and board members do not differ much in terms of why they believe the trustee role is the appropriate one. Board members emphasize more the inherent difficulty of trying to be a bona-fide instructed delegate whereas the mass public stresses more the role requirements and the superior advantage of the board members compared with the public. However, the bulk of the board responses are also in the latter categories. What really supports the belief in the trustee orientation is 1) that board members have a far better perspective and more information; and 2) even more importantly, that by selecting board members to represent them the public is giving up its option to make those decisions directly. They have placed a trust in the hands of the board, and the board should prosecute that trust.

Arguments in support of the delegate role (third heading in Table 7-1) cluster much more. The basic rationale is that a 1:1 relationship should exist between public preferences and leader preferences because attainment of office, rather than giving the office holders carte blanche, simply gives them opportunity to sum up the preferences of those who elected them. Most people did not go beyond this rather simple line of reasoning. Interestingly, it was members of the public who occasionally amplified their remarks, as in citing the economic sanction. Others claimed that over the long pull what the public prefers will produce the best policy, so that should be the appropriate decisional rule. Still others noted that education is for the benefit of children, so the guardians of those children should have the prime say in major decisions that are made about the children's educational world.

If pressed, many of our respondents – in both the elite and mass samples – would undoubtedly have gone on to qualify their position in favor on one extreme or another. Some did this without prodding: 13 percent of the mass public and 19 percent of the board members. These people explicitly recognized the ambiguities, paradoxes, and perhaps even fatal consequences which might flow from complete subscription to one or the other viewpoint. They most often suggested what high public officials often say in public: that public opinion should certainly be considered (and sought) and then used as one element in the decision-making calculus. Board members more frequently worked the other way around from consulting and then acting. These members say, "Make up your mind but have the anticipated reactions of the public in mind. If necessary alter your position a bit to make it palatable to the public." Others, especially the public, believe that the basis of action should be situationally dependent, a convenient if not very explicit guideline.

TABLE 7-1
Arguments Favoring Trustee versus Delegate Role
for Members of Education Board

	Mass Public	Board Members
Reasons for Trustee Role		
Philosophical — representing means acting for the people	08%[a]	11%
Board role is to make judgments, provide leadership, exercise responsibility — that is why they are chosen	42	28
Members are better informed and qualified than public; latter shortsighted and uninformed	34	28
Members can't know exactly what public thinks, can't satisfy everyone, can't get consensus — ergo must use own judgment.	10	14
Members should do what's best for students and the schools	04	10
Members have to decide ultimately on basis of principle and conscience	01	06
Other	01	03
	100%	100%
Reasons for Combination of Trustee-Delegate Role		
Members should seek out opinion, and consider what people want, then use own judgment	46	57
Situational; sometimes members should rely on public preferences, other times should use own judgment	32	10
Public is not determinative but should count — members should temper judgment with what is politically acceptable	12	26
Respondent is ambivalent; can't make up mind	05	05
Other	06	03
	101%	101%
Reasons for Delegate Role		
Members are elected to represent public so should follow preferences of majority	70	91
What majority wants is usually best	08	04
Public pays the piper, so public should call the tune	12	—
It's the public's children, so public should prevail	07	—
Other	02	06
	99%	101%

[a]Percentage base is all responses under each major heading in this table.

The striking differences at the aggregate level between board members and the public are echoed at the district level, where the correlation between the two is but .12. Thus there is virtually no relationship between how the constituents and their (usually) elected leaders interpret the classic representation roles. Typically the understanding of the basic contract between the two is not at all well understood or agreed upon. The norms, guidelines, or decisional rules are at issue. Little wonder that violent clashes sometimes emerge between the public and the board not only over substantive issues, but also over the decisional rules to be used. In the real world of school governance, boards will most often act somewhere in between the two poles of pure-trustee versus pure-delegate orientations. Even the most callous board will not completely ignore public preferences and even the most public opinion-conscious board will not completely eschew a commitment to a conception of the larger public good. But it is not uncommon for board members to rationalize their actions with one of the two arguments. And indeed sometimes intraboard conflicts develop in which the two approaches form the lines of cleavage.

Are there some kinds of districts where agreement on representational roles is higher and some where agreement is weaker? For the most part the answer is no. There are occasional aberrations, most of which are beyond explanation. For example, congruence is much lower in the Midwest than in the other regions; similarly it is lower in the very largest districts than in others. One key finding is that there is no difference between appointive versus elective boards. Whatever may be the virtues of elective boards, one of them is not to bring members and their constituents closer together on this age-old dilemma. Nor are partisan boards more like their constituents than nonpartisan ones; in fact the tendency is in the opposite direction. On two other selection characteristics, though, the "unreformed" districts have higher levels of agreement. In ward districts the correlation is .48, compared with –.04 for at-large districts. And when state and/or federal elections are held with school elections the correlation is .27 versus .02 when the elections are not coterminous. Overall, there is some indication that districts with manifest political forms do achieve greater elite-mass concordance.

But the strongest demarcator is an indicator of competition in the district. Where there was no opposition in the immediately past election the correspondence between board and constituency was .53; where there was a contest it was .01. The less competitive the district, the greater the agreement about representational roles. Traditional electoral theory argues that greater competition increases the concordance, because competitors are trying to bring themselves into close accord with the electors in order to gain office. Such theory is predicated on a view of politics as issue-oriented, parties as dominant actors, and officeseekers as being motivated by a strong desire for political careerism. As we have seen, such conditions do not describe school district politics very well, nor most other levels of local politics.[8] One cannot be led to say that competition drives down mass-elite congruity. Rather it seems to be just the reverse: where concordance is reasonably high, there is little reason to be excited about the electoral process, to make sure that competition exists, or to turn the rascals out since they are not perceived as rascals at all.

Does the basic correlation of .12 between constituents and board members reflect complete board ignorance of public preferences about representational roles, or are board members interposing their own judgments between what they know the public prefers versus what they, the leaders, prefer? To answer this question the board members were asked what they thought their constituents preferred, members who used their own judgment or those who followed the wishes of their constituents. Replies to this question show that board members concede that there is a discrepancy between their own interpretation versus their constituents' interpretations. Although in the aggregate they still lean heavily toward the trustee role, the correspondence at the district level moves to .27. Even this increase means that board members are reading their constituents rather poorly, but there is at least some visible evidence of convergence.

AGREEMENT ON THE DISTRICT AGENDA

Our effort here is to determine if the governors and the governed have the same sort of agenda. One indicator of substantive representation is whether the governors and the governed assign the same weight to problem areas. To the extent that they do we would say that substantive representation is occurring, that the problems and needs as defined by the constituency are reflected in those of the board members. Since the definition of the agenda is a key function in any governing process because it reflects priorities and the potential commitment of resources, it becomes important to know the degree of congruency between elites and masses on that score.

Whether concordance comes about because of direct information flow from the mass public to the board members is a crucial but not decisive point in this context. Especially in school matters one might expect the flow to be the other way: the school governors would take the lead in defining problems for the public. Or both mass publics and elites could be responding to the same stimuli. Nevertheless, since influence is distributed asymmetrically, the essential point in terms of substantive representation is the degree to which elites share the agenda of their constituents.

An identically worded question was put to both board members and the mass public: "In your opinion, what is the most important problem facing education in this school district?" In order to obtain a full range of answers, the board members were asked a specific question about the second most important problem. Well over half of the board members gave more than two important problems, whereas the mass public sample averaged barely over one. Responses to this question produced a wide array of answers; in all we coded over seventy distinct mentions. The diverse replies tended to fall under broad rubrics and we have taken advantage of that tendency by collapsing the responses into five major families, realizing that much of the rich texture is thereby sacrificed. In many respects these families resemble the categories of campaign issues used in Chapter 2.

Before considering the nature of these responses, it is important to observe that three of every ten persons in the mass public sample could not specify any problem at all, and another one in twelve said that there were no problems at the current time. Although the incidence of such responses across social and political strata is worthy of study, the key point for us is that such a large proportion of the populace has no items to put on the school district's problem agenda. From a strict standpoint, board members best representing the will of these people also have no agenda. This is a bizarre example of why the concept of representation has to include more than the representation of will and preference. We realize that by looking only at shared orientations that we are viewing only one aspect of the representational process. Another important consequence of this sizable block of people who see no problems is that the base for comparing board members and the mass public is reduced substantially. All comparisons to follow, then, are based on the attentive public on the one hand and the school board on the other.

Let us first consider the gross distributions of board members and the mass public. These are presented in two forms in Table 7-2. First, school boards were scored according to what percentage of the members mentioned a problem in each of the five broad areas. Thus on the average 60 percent of the board members in the various districts said that there were financial problems in the district. Similarly, the mass public respondents in each district were scored according to what proportion mentioned a problem in each area. As the second column of Table 7-2 shows, an average of 38 percent of the respondents across the districts said that there was a money problem in their district. Partly because the board members were more voluble (and were actually asked a specific "second problem" question) it is appropriate to adjust the replies of each sample so that a common base number of responses rather than respondents is used. Columns 3 and 4 show these adjusted figures and give a better indication of the relative attention each sample attaches to the various items on the district agenda. These figures will be the basis of the following discussion.

Taking boards and mass publics as a whole, there is a remarkable amount of congruence in the overall shape of the priority schedule. Thus both are unequivocal in saying that financially related problems are the most severe. Given the salience of taxes and bond issues to the public, plus the inflationary costs of education and the growing difficulty during the late 1960s of gaining public support for financial proposals, it is not surprising that both groups place dollar-related difficulties at the top of the agenda. There are subtle variations in the specifics of these differences across the two groups but generally these are differences incumbent in the amount of detailed knowledge and sophistication possessed by the leaders versus the led.

Nor is there much division in the relative importance attached to difficulties in the area of teachers and teaching. Teachers, as the most visible part of the schools aside from the students, are a natural focus of attention and to some extent serve as lightning rods. On the parental side, dissatisfaction with the schools often takes the form of complaints about the quality of teaching, the deportment of teachers, the demands of teachers, and the treatment of children by the teachers. Parents are also concerned about the loss of good teachers and the inability to hire those with high potential. These latter themes and the competitive disadvantage of their districts are especially prominent in the responses of the board members.

Staffing and financial problems stand out in contrast to the lesser emphasis on the remaining three areas. And the consensus breaks down somewhat when the other three major problem areas are considered, although general similarity is still prevalent. Problems in the educational program are specified with nearly equal relative frequency. Compared with board members, however, the public attaches much greater significance to such matters as discipline, deportment, and morality than to the more formal parts of the curriculum.

The major differences between mass publics and the board elites appear in the differential emphasis attached to racial problems rather than those of district governance. Whereas the public more often wants to see racial problems put on the agenda, the board is more concerned about the difficulties of governing the district. Given the emotional salience of the race issue, it is not surprising to see this small edge for the mass public. Significantly, racial problems is the only area in which the mass public virtually matches the board members in the absolute, unadjusted frequency of mentions (cols. 1 and 2). Therefore, even though the adjusted difference is not large, the unique place of race-related concerns is apparent.

District governance, on the other hand, is a domain of peculiar significance to board members, in that much of the substance involves somewhat arcane and inner-circle matters. For example, the difficulties of board organization, inter-governmental relations, district autonomy, community relations, and maintenance of the proper balance between professional administrators and a lay board are topics about which none but the most sensitive citizens are aware. On balance, it seems in the nature of mass public behavior that a racial incident or the threat of busing acquires a salience well beyond its "objective" importance, whereas crucial questions of district governance might go begging in the public's attention frame.

When one canvasses boards and their constituents in the aggregate there are differences, but in general board members and their constituents see the agenda in about the same way nationwide. One might be tempted to conclude that the priorities of the public are well replicated among their leaders. To make such a statement would be equivalent to saying that a congressman's constituents are achieving substantive representation if the agendas of a national sample of Americans coincided with that of the House of Representatives as a whole. Clearly such a statement would be out of order. Congress at least convenes as a collective body,

TABLE 7–2
Identification of School District Problems
by Mass Public and School Boards

Problem Area	*Unadjusted Mean Responses*		*Adjusted Mean Responses*		*Correlation between Boards and their Constituents*
	Mass Public	*School Board*	*Mass Public*	*School Board*	*r*
Financial – need more money, revenue base inadequate, plant expansion, lack of public support	38%	60%	35%	31%	.25
Teaching and teachers – quality of staff declining, hiring difficulties, teacher demands, loss of teachers, inadequate salaries	29	44	26	23	.06
Racial – integration, busing, white-black conflict	18	21	16	11	.79
Educational program – quantity and quality of curriculum offerings, special groups neglected or indulged, disciplinary and moral decline	16	33	15	17	.03
District governance – board-public relations, lack of public interest, composition of board, board procedures, board-supt. relations	09	33	08	17	.38

and in a sense represents the 435 congressional districts collectively. Obviously such a condition does not apply to local boards of education.

To locate shared orientations, as in the congressional case, we must match up board members and their constituents within districts. A number of procedures could be used to define the degree of concordance between board member and constituent. One of the qualities we wished to maintain, however, was the degree of congruence within specific educational arenas. It seemed possible that greater mass-elite congruence might be achieved with respect to some items on the agenda than for others. It is one thing to know the overall or average articulation between the two parties, but quite another to know how they stand with respect to a specific area.

A simple device can be used to look at congruity across issue-areas — the product moment correlation.[9] We can correlate the (grouped) mean percentages of the constituents with the (grouped) mean percentages of their respective board members. Positive relationships simply mean that the more emphasis constituents attach to a problem area the more emphasis the board also attaches. The fact that board members were more verbose than their constituents is no problem in this regard.

Viewed in the light of the strong aggregate patterns, the range of correlations is striking. Standing on the side of essentially no relationship are the two arenas comprising the essence of the system — teaching and the educational program. This negligible association is perhaps the most remarkable finding we encountered when looking at a variety of mass-elite comparisons. Whereas financial and governance matters are presumably means to other ends, and race matters represent a unique blend of concerns, teaching and the educational program lie at the heart of education — they are the ends of education.

We are not talking about specific preferences with respect to instructional and curriculum problems. Rather, we are talking about whether there *are* major problems in those areas. As the figures demonstrate, there is no agreement between constituents and their representatives that problems exist in these areas, let alone that the two would agree on the appropriate solutions. Substantive representation is, if one takes these figures literally, nonexistent. Of course, one should not take the figures literally. If pressed, most board members who did not see teaching and curriculum as major problems in their districts would probably have agreed that there were at least minor problems in those domains. Still, the degree of importance assigned by constituents and leaders works, on the whole, at cross purposes.

Why should this be, especially since concordance in the other domains ranges from moderate to very healthy? The answer would seem to lie in the experiential base utilized by the two sets of actors in defining whether there are difficulties in these areas. We suggested that the specific details offered by board members contrasted rather sharply with those presented by the mass public. Constituents drew much more from their own personal encounters with the school system or from the encounters of friends, neighbors, and relatives. Several of these comments were in the form of direct or vicarious grievances growing out of the way particular children or groups of children have been treated, the kind of training they received, the amount of counseling, etc. In sum the mass public takes a micro view. It is also heavily influenced by widely publicized events of a dramatic nature.

By contrast, board members take a more macro approach. They are not as touched by single incidents and the individual case. Rather, they are concerned about the overall flow of teachers in and out of the system, the quality level of the staff, the negotiations with teacher organizations, the grand structure of the curriculum, and specialized aspects of the program. While a widely publicized event can galvanize a board into action in a specific instance, usually problems of more district-wide and longer standing interest preoccupy them. These two different experiential bases mean that districts wherein the constituents feel that curricular and staffing problems are paramount need not be the ones wherein the board feels that way.

Agenda setting in two other areas exhibits more consistency between constituents and their representatives. Financially related issues and those of district governance are brought up with at least moderate coincidence by both parties within districts. In the case of money matters this is perhaps not too surprising. Although the ordinary citizens see the money problem from a different angle than the political elites do, the presence of a severe problem will probably be recognized by both. Most commonly the lay citizen verbalizes the problem as a simple need for more money to run the system and build a school plant, or with the lament that education is a very expensive proposition. Board members go into more of the details of the problems, including alternative sources of revenue, problems of budgeting, and so on.

The concordance on matters of district governance, while considerably higher, is more difficult to comprehend. We saw that board members emphasize this problem twice as much as the lay public. The kinds of specific issues mentioned by the public which fall under this general rubric are generally not the kind which would grow out of idiosyncratic experiences with the school system — the kind which characterized a good share of those in the instructional areas. Rather, they are of a more systemic nature. Concern about decentralization, consolidation, educating the public to the needs of the schools, and board-superintendent relationships are topics that have a macro rather than a micro cast. Some of these are also matters that only the more informed and alert citizens may understand. If a concern about these kinds of problems has penetrated to the public stratum, it is probable that there is also some elite concern with them.

The potential agenda topic generating highest congruity between masses and elites is that of race-related problems. Racial difficulties are not new to this time in the country's history, but beginning at least with the 1954 Brown versus Board of Education decision, the implications of racial strains on the education system have been enormous. A sizable literature has also developed about education, race, and the politics and economics thereof. In both a literal and figurative sense race problems in American's school districts are very visible. As the correlation of .79 indicates, whether race problems should be placed on a district's agenda tends to be a jointly perceived function in most districts. More correctly, one would say that the proportion of a board which sees race as a problem rises and falls along with the proportion of the constituency which sees it that way.

To some extent this congruence is a direct consequence of whether there are any minorities in the school district or in surrounding districts. Most districts, however, have at least a visible component of nonwhites. Neither the degree of correspondence in these districts nor the absolute rate of specification of race as a problem is a direct function of the proportion nonwhite. Rather, the tight fit between leaders and led seems to be a reflection of what both see or fear in the real world. It is a striking commentary that the issue-area fostering the highest level of priority scheduling is the one which best illustrates a pathologic condition of the society in general and its school system in particular.

Although the degree of shared orientations about what should be on the school district's agenda is one indicator of representation, the question of how the items on the agenda should be handled is equally compelling. It would be quite possible for board members and their constituents to be in substantial agreement about what sort of problems faced the school district and at the same time have sharp disagreement about the proper solutions to these problems. Indeed, the gravest conflicts in a school district seem to break out over solutions of problems rather than their specifications. The controversy over busing as a way to achieve racial integration is a classic case in point.

In an effort to catch this side of the representation process we asked both the board members and their constituents how they would solve the problems that they cited. There were plentiful remedies, with respect to the elites, although some of them were not particularly thoughtful or even practical. Answers from the mass public were disappointing but not surprising. The 30 percent which saw no problems in the district obviously were not asked to submit solutions. The number of cases for analysis and potential pairing with their respective board members is, therefore, reduced immediately. Also, a fair number of citizens who saw problems were not able to offer any sort of solution (15 percent). The base is again reduced. Among those offering a solution, most ventured only one. Finally, the quality of these solutions was often so poor that the problem was simply restated. For example, if lack of financial resources was singled out as a problem, a leading solution was to "find more money." Or if crowded schools was seen as the district's prominent problem, a common remedy was to build more schools. Clearly, the majority of the mass public has only the slimmest grasp of cause-effect relationships with respect to school district problems and their solutions. More properly one might say that in the space and context of an interview, most people cannot articulate in clear fashion how district problems should be handled. More extended inquiry would undoubtedly improve the quantity and quality of the solutions.

The meagerness of the mass public's descriptions of remedies had a direct bearing on our attempt to assess congruency between the leaders and the led. We felt that the quality and quantity of the data were insufficient to permit carrying out the kind of analysis used for defining the agenda. In one sense, however, it is still possible to draw an inference about the representation process. If we consider the number of people who see no problem, the number not advancing solutions, and the number having only the most rudimentary and circular solutions, it is obvious — given the evidence of much better solutions proposed by the board members — that in an absolute sense congruence on solutions cannot be much more than minimal.

Structural Determinants of Agenda Congruency

A number of factors might affect the likelihood of concordance between citizens and board members. Many of these lie at the micro level. We might expect to find, for example, that the more participative citizens were more likely to have their concerns echoed by board members than their less active fellow citizens. By the same token certain qualities among board members might enhance mass-board linkage. While not gainsaying the utility of such explanatory approaches, we will confine our analysis to socio-political features inhering in the district. This approach is in keeping with our general tendency to look toward structural determinants of school governance whenever feasible. And we shall use some of the same measures employed in previous places to denote the socio-political environment in which the school district is embedded.

It will be recalled that in two of the issue areas — educational program and staffing — there was virtually no correspondence between the laity and the elite. This lack of correspondence for the total sample could be disguising systematic fluctuation within particular strata. That was not the case, however, so for most purposes we will exclude these two areas from our discussion.

In previous chapters we have found that social complexity, as measured by metropolitan status, had a profound effect on the political life of the district. Both the style and substance of district governance vary according to whether the district lies within or outside a Standard Metropolitan Statistical Area (SMSA). When we turn to the question of the district agenda, we find again that metropolitanism is a sharp demarcator, as the figures in Table 7–3 show.

TABLE 7–3
Relationship of Metropolitanism and Congruence on District Agenda

	Financial	Racial	Governance
Non-SMSA	.38	.91	.40
SMSA	.14	.64	.41

There is no difference on the governance issue, but on the other two problems the correspondence between constituents and their representatives is much stronger in districts inside SMSAs rather than outside. It is not too difficult to imagine why articulation is higher in the less complex areas. Communication flows more freely, issues are more visible, and the schools are more often the center of community attention. The friends and neighbors atmosphere more often found in the nonmetropolitan areas seems conducive to a greater sharing of perspectives between the leaders and the led.

Size alone is not the crucial element here. We divided the districts into four size categories, looking especially at the two extreme cases: those where the district population < 10,000 and those ≥ 150,000. Although congruency was considerably stronger on financial matters in the small communities than in the larger ones (r = .53 and .25, respectively) the pattern was actually reversed with respect to race (r = –.02 and .48, respectively).

Again it should be stressed that higher agreement about what should be on the school board agenda does not necessarily indicate higher agreement about how the problems should be solved. Indeed, we shall present evidence below which goes to this very point. Simply because citizens in a non-SMSA are more likely to have their priority schedules shared by their board of education does not mean that the board would necessarily share in the citizens' preferences about problem resolution. For the moment, however, those who have traditionally argued that linkage between leaders and the public is closer in the less complex environments are vindicated.

In passing we should note that another place characteristic, region, was also introduced into the analysis. There were no plausible or systematic patterns in the results, except that concordance on the whole was somewhat lower in Northeastern districts than in districts located elsewhere.

The other set of structural determinants is manifestly political. We have argued that certain structural properties built into the selection (and election) process can have visible and meaningful outcomes for school district governance. More specifically, we have suggested that the more explicitly political the selection process is the more open, responsive, and competitive is the process of governance. And this relationship may exist in a direct sense or in an intervening, mediating fashion. In the current analysis we employ four such indicators: whether the board is appointive or elective; whether the system is de facto nonpartisan or partisan; whether elections are strictly at-large or ward-based; and whether state and federal elections are held coterminously with school board elections.

Our hypothesis is that the more explicitly political, unreformed districts will exhibit greater mass-elite linkage than the reformed, less explicitly political districts. This hypothesis follows from our contention that in the former there is a more vigorous, open form of politics, that less transpires behind the hidden doors of good government and keeping politics out of education. By forcing district governance into a more open and competitive environment, these rules, regulations, and structures bring the constituents and their leaders closer together in terms of defining issue priorities.

So runs the gist of our argument. In the financial issue area it is completely vindicated. Concordance regarding financial problems increases dramatically in elective districts, those with partisan elections, those having ward-based elections, and those holding elections coterminously with state or federal balloting. Mass-elite agreement about whether there are financial problems which the district should solve would, therefore, appear to be very much affected by the conditions of board selection and by the political climate which these selection rules help create.

If one stopped with the financial arena, our hypothesis would be fully supported. The other two dimensions lend only moderate support, however. In the racial sector greater concordance is definitely found among elective districts, but there is essentially no difference according to the other three characteristics. On district governance the pattern holds very nicely for nonpartisan versus partisan districts (r = .10 versus .56), but the relationship is actually reversed for elective versus appointive districts (r = .35 versus .74). Altogether, of the twelve possible relationships (three issues times four selection characteristics) concordance is higher in the more political districts in eight instances — but a couple of these are statistically insignificant. Of the remaining four, one is a dead heat, one is clearly statistically significant, and the other two are marginally so.

One obvious conclusion to draw from this is that the consequences of political structural variables depend in part on what kind of problem area is being considered. In the present instance the fact that financial proposals so often are carried to the public is a probable reason for greater articulation in the more politicized environments. Obviously, financial proposals are carried to the public in the "nonpolitical" districts also. So why should there be a difference?

The answer would seem to rest in the fact that the explicitly political features sharpen the salience, visibility, and group-relatedness of financial issues. Candidates running for office can scarcely avoid the financial issue. Partisan candidates, as we have seen, emphasize issues more and campaigns for bond and millage proposals often witness (bi-) partisan support. Board members representing wards are also more issue-oriented and also presumably stay in somewhat closer contact with their specific constituents on an issue such as finances, which is dear to constituents. Finally the presence of state and/or federal elections with their partisan and more heated nature, probably develops a more sensitized and sensitizing issue environment for the handling of financial referenda.

Some of this is conjecture, of course. Specific case studies would be necessary to verify the reasoning. Yet it is the combination of substantial salience for both public and elite actors plus the frequent resort to the public vote which sets off the financial arena from the other two arenas of race and governance. Since we lack alternative solutions, the presence of the two factors of salience and mass decision making seems to account for the importance of the political determinants.

One additional selection variable can be employed, although it is not a formal rule as are the other four. We have commented before that competition for office is not always lively in America's school districts. Illustratively, of the subset of districts included in the present analysis one-fifth had absolutely no competition for office in the last election held before our study entered the field in 1968. Does the absence of competition mean that elections are being manipulated, that there is a great deal of apathy, or that the citizens are satisfied with having incumbents and novices attain office without challenge? Traditional democratic theory — and much of our previous argument — would hold that the more opposition there is the more the winning candidates and officeholders would strive to converge with their constituents. From this perspective we should expect to find that mass-elite congruency would be higher in those districts where the recent electoral climate was warm enough so that there was at least some opposition to candidates on the ballot. That is not the case at all, however, as the figures in Table 7-4 demonstrate.

Clearly board members and constituents more often share the same agenda ordering when the recent election was a foregone conclusion. Contrary to the theories of representation based on electoral accountability, linkage is highest when there is no contest!

TABLE 7-4
Relationship of Opposition and Congruence on District Agenda

	Financial	*Racial*	*Governance*
No opposition	.60	.92	.83
Some opposition	.32	.82	.36

How do we account for such a state of affairs? The simplest explanation is the best, if we think about the probable sequencing of events. Assuming that there is a high degree of congruence at the time of the last election as well as at the time of our soundings, then there is probably also less dissatisfaction. To use the clichés of politics there is less desire to throw the rascals out, to clean house, to change the guard, or perhaps even to rock the boat. At least one set of motivating factors, disagreement over the agenda, is noticeable by its absence. Just as Miller found that congressmen from the safest districts were in highest agreement with their constituents,[10] so too we find that districts with the least competitive elections have the highest levels of board-public concordance.

We must ask whether this flies in the face of our contention that the more "political" districts yield, on the average, higher congruence. Not necessarily. In the first place, although nonpartisanship and at-large elections are related to the lack of opposition in the previous election, the correlations are modest (about .30 at the bivariate level) and there is no relationship with the presence or absence of coterminous state/federal elections. Thus lack of opposition is only weakly dependent on the two structural forms. In the second place, the argument about the effects of nonreformed structures by no means rests completely on whether they foster more absolute competition for office. As we saw in Chapter 4 they are related to the quality of competition also. More importantly, the general, ongoing climate of educational politics differs, regardless of whether a particular election happens to have a contest for office. Finally, we are talking about less than a fifth of the districts, and one may assume there is something distinctive about districts *sans* competition. Still, the interaction effects created by the presence or absence of office competition should not be downplayed, for they run against the grain of conventional theory, and also suggest the conditions under which challenge will not occur.

The meaning of no opposition takes on an added dimension if we consider the two other issue arenas, educational program and instructional staffing. We considered some possible reasons why the articulation between mass and elite was so slender on these two issues and concluded that a major reason lay in the experiential base prompting constituency concern versus the quite different base prompting board concern. The salience of these problem areas, as seen by the public, may have a difficult time being translated into the electoral arena.

Graphic evidence is supplied if we consider those districts where no contesting occurred in the last election. As compared with the overall correlation of .06 for teaching-related problems, the correlation in no-contest districts was −.26. Similarly, the overall figure for educational program problems was .03, but in the no-contest districts it drops to −.26. Clearly, the penetration of issue salience in these two areas is poor; indeed the lack of election contesting prospers (in a manner of speaking) when the masses and elites disagree on whether these are problem areas.

Congruence on Specific Issues

Perhaps the most common way that people say they are well-represented is that their representatives feel as they do on specific, substantive issues. Given the range of decisions most legislative bodies take, including a good deal of esoterica and trivia, even the staunchest exponents of "representing the will of the people" would not expect representatives to be perfect microcosms of their constituents' preferences. There is still no denying, however, that one of the major criteria used in evaluating representatives is whether they reflect the majority sentiment of their constituents on specific issues — however that sentiment might be measured, and whatever nuances might actually be involved in the definition of the issue.

Several issue questions were put to both the elite and mass samples in our study. Unfortunately, these were few in number with respect to the mass sample. They are also mainly single indicators of attitudinal dispositions. Obviously, it would have been more preferable to have had multiitem indicators of attitudes in a wide number of substantive areas. Given this limitation, we will confine ourselves to an overview of the results and offer the findings as suggestive of the nature of mass-elite symmetry on education-related issues.

Let us first consider responses in the aggregate. These are of more than usual interest, because board members are influenced by the opinions of board members in other districts, partly through the National School Board Association. Nor are members of the public completely ignorant of how people in other parts of their state and in the rest of the country may feel about particular issues. Table 7-5 contains the response patterns for six issues. The first two deal with very controversial issues tapping strong emotions. On both counts the mass public is more conservative than school board members, and particularly so with respect to the issue of prayers in school. Despite the court rulings and despite growing disuse, there is still exceedingly strong sentiment in the public at large in favor of allowing prayers in the classroom. Of course, even the board members have a mean score well over the midpoint in the direction of allowing prayers. The gap is not as wide on the federal role in integration, but even here board members on the average are more "liberal" (1968 version) than the public. Those who speak of greater tolerance and subscription to basic civil liberties on the part of elites will find support in these data.

The next two issues deal with teachers and their roles. In decided contrast to the two issues just discussed, board members emerge as more conservative than the public in general. Board members are less favorably disposed than the public toward the right of teachers to strike and toward teachers having a greater voice in making major decisions affecting school policies; moreover the differences are sizable. Hence any inclinations one might have to ascribe a generally more liberal image to board members must be tempered by these results. One might argue that when board members are in a potentially adversarial relationship, this more liberal orientation dwindles.

The final pair of items deals with an evaluation of the amount of control which the federal and state governments exercise over local education. Not surprisingly, board members more often see the higher levels as exercising too much control. Historically, local boards have been preoccupied with the goal of maintaining local autonomy (although not always averse to higher level subventions) even in the face of an increasingly nationalized educational network. Federal intervention in particular is resented, especially since it has often come in sensitive areas where the desire for local option runs high. Both integration and religious instruction would fall into that category.

Ordinary citizens are less convinced about the deleterious effects of higher level control, but even they are loath to say that state and federal governments exercise too little control. To the extent that federal intervention has been on the side of liberalism in the past decade or two — and most observers would agree that on the average the federal position has been more liberal than the sum of

TABLE 7-5
Opinions of Board Members and the
Mass Public on Political Issues

	Mass Public $\bar{X}$	Board Members $\bar{X}$	Correlation between Boards and Constituents[a] r
Use of prayers in schools (1 = against, 5 = for)	4.34	3.70	.52
Federal role in school integration (1 = for, 5 = against)	3.09	2.80	.09
Right of teachers to strike (1 = for, 5 = against)	3.74	4.26	.02
Stronger voice for teachers (1 = for, 5 = against)	2.71	3.25	.38
Federal control over local education (1 = too much, 5 = too little)	2.42	2.24	.49
State control over local education (1 = too much, 5 = too little)	3.23	2.83	.20

[a]Correlations are based on mean scores developed from responses to each question.

local positions — the board members emerge as again more conservative than the public. Faced with the variable nature of state governments and their departments of education, we find it hazardous to speculate about the relative ideology of board members and the citizenry in that domain.

So much for the overall picture. When one approaches the district level it is obvious that, as with the problem agenda, there is great variance in the range of board-constituency agreement. Concordance runs from a very healthy .52 on the question of prayers in the classroom down to the miniscule .02 on the issue of the right of teachers to strike. Nor is there a consistent pattern in these results. Illustratively, even though the prayer and integration issues are both salient and controversial, the concordance values are widely disparate. Similarly, even though both of the teacher items would seem to hit the same vein among both elites and masses, there is a moderately high correspondence on the "greater voice" question and none on the right to strike question. Only on the two questions about higher level control is there a significant correlation in each instance, albeit the amount of agreement on state control is quite modest.

What can one make of these results, which seem to show little systematic variation? Part of the difficulty may be on the measurement side. As we indicated at the outset, we were severely restricted in the number of questions which could be put to the mass public. Multiple-item indicators in a variety of issue areas would undoubtedly increase the quality of the measures, and perhaps attenuate what appears to be an element of idiosyncrasy in the data.

On the other hand, it is also true that each of the six items utilized in Table 7–5 deals with a quite different set of attitude objects, even the two concerning higher level control over local education. One dimension of the response to each question certainly would rest on the axis of higher control qua higher control. But another would assuredly rest on one's feelings about the federal government as such and one's feelings about a particular state government. That is, people would employ different frames of reference in answering each question; and mass and elite samples could vary between themselves on the importance accorded the respective dimensions.

Consequently, to the extent that our individual indicators are tapping true attitudinal dimensions, the great range of mass-elite congruence accurately reflects the "real" state of affairs. Of course, we still have not explained why the range exists. Nor do we intend to dwell upon that important topic here. It is sufficient at this stage of inquiry to note that the degree of shared issue orientations is not invariant and that much must be done to uncover the processes whereby some come to be more shared than others.

One additional point is that we have clear evidence that agreement on the shape of the agenda does not necessarily lead to agreement on how particular issues should be settled. We noted earlier that board-public agreement on whether the district had a racial problem was quite high ($r = .79$). Yet on one of the signal issues involved in race and the schools — the federal government's role in integration — the board-public agreement is nil (.09). Defining a problem and solving that problem may tap quite different perspectives and motivations among elites and masses, producing in one instance congruence and in another noncongruence. In this sense representation through shared orientations is complicated still further.

LINKAGES WITH THE SUPERINTENDENT

It has become a commonplace of modern democratic theory to recognize that representation occurs through the appointed and career professionals of the bureaucracies as well as through the holders of elective offices. Often these professionals — department and agency heads, staff officials, budget makers, and the like — represent particular interests and special constituencies. Others serve more general clientele. At the local level of government the city manager's office is a good example of the latter. The alert city manager and his aides engage in a tremendous amount of interaction with the public and as one of their functions they represent the public (or parts thereof) to the city council and other relevant parties.

The school superintendent's office is analogous to that of the city manager's. If anything, the superintendent and his staff have built into their roles a much more prominent function of representation. They are directly or indirectly beseiged by students, parents, teachers, principals, interest groups, and others to do this or that with respect to the school system. As a focal figure in most school districts, the superintendent inevitably comes to serve representational roles in addition to the strictly technical and administrative. Indeed, some have argued that superintendents are often better representatives of the public's interest and its will. To test this proposition we need to compare the superintendent and board as representatives of constituency will.

Since the superintendents were asked the same set of questions which were put to board members and the general public, we were able to match superintendent responses with those of district residents in the same fashion as we did in the board-public pairing. In order to expand the range of comparisons we have added a few measures not previously introduced.

First we may take a quick look at how superintendents compare with board members and the rank and file. On the whole superintendents order the school district problems in about the same fashion as do the rank and file and the board. The major difference, surprisingly enough, is the superintendents' lesser concern with teaching-related problems. This neglect is counterbalanced by a slightly greater concern with educational problems.

On the civil rights issues of federally-promoted integration and the ban of prayers in schools the superintendents more often take the liberal position. In each instance the gap between them and the citizenry is greater than that between them and board members. One interpretation of this is that superintendents are more likely to take refuge in their professional role as policy administrators, because on each issue they more often sided with what was the federal government's position (via court rulings and other actions). Board members and ordinary citizens would not feel this constraint. This rather uncharitable view may be misplaced. Superintendents may indeed have a stronger liberal streak, although their mean scores are not terribly convincing in an absolute sense.

Further discrediting of their liberal image comes in observing their views on the two questions about teachers' rights. Superintendents are more supportive than boards and mass publics of a greater voice for teachers. But in the crucial, emotional issue of the right to strike they even outdistance board members in their opposition. When it comes to activities that are most likely to win an expanded role for teachers in decision-making processes — a goal to which superintendents give heaviest support — superintendents are more inclined to draw the line.

Superintendents feel about the same as others do on the issue of federal control, claiming there is too much or about the right amount. But they are less worried about excessive state control. Finally, they put relatively less of their trust in the national government than in their state and the local governments.

Table 7-6 demonstrates that shared orientations are much more prevalent between board members and their constituents than between superintendents and these same constituents.[11] On defining the agenda of district problems, for example, there are no differences in two of the areas; but of the other three, board-public concordance is appreciably higher on two of them. The pattern is more exaggerated on views of intergovernmental relations, with all four issues showing a hefty advantage for the board. Finally, on the four specific issue questions, board-public congruity is substantially higher on two of the four with the other two showing essentially no difference. Altogether, on only one measure — the specification of instructional staffing as a district problem — is there a significant and positive advantage for the superintendent.

Certainly the measures we were able to use do not begin to exhaust the range of issues and broader orientations on which it would be desirable to make comparisons. Yet it seems unlikely, for a number of reasons, that a more extended listing would produce grossly different results. One reason involves role definition. Despite their nominal trustee orientation, the board members made it clear throughout the interviews that they felt a heavy obligation at least to try to take their constituents' preferences into account. In contrast to the superintendent, board members exist in a fiduciary relationship to the public whereas the superintendent has a contractual one with the board of education.

A second reason is demographic. Although a vast gulf exists between board and public in terms of social status, they are both drawn from the same general pool, with at least a moderate amount of shared history and perspectives uniting them. Superintendents, on the other hand, are professional vagabonds. They tend to be as much or more oriented to their profession as they are to their particular contemporary districts. It seems likely that this duality of focus would hinder the superintendent's converging toward the preferences of the mass public.

To the extent that the representational function is best fulfilled by shared orientations between leaders and led, board members rather than superintendents are likely to fill the role. Not that even board members can be said to do

TABLE 7-6
Comparison of Concordance for Board-Constituency and
Superintendent-Constituency Preferences

Measures	Board-Constituency r	Superintendent-Constituency r
District Problems		
Racial	.79	.55
Governance	.38	.39
Financial	.25	.00
Staffing	.07	.25
Education Program	.03	.01
Intergovernmental Relationships		
Federal Influence on Schools	.41	.11
State Influence on Schools	.20	.02
Level Trusted Most	.30	.12
Level Trusted Least	.52	.01
Specific Issues		
Prayers in School	.52	.32
Federal Role in Integration	.09	.00
Right of Teachers to Strike	.02	.06
Stronger Voice for Teaching	.38	.14

this very faithfully across a variety of measures. But on balance they do a much better job than do the superintendents.

One final piece of evidence along these lines may be offered. Both board members and superintendents were asked how often they thought the district residents disagreed with actions of the board. Their answers were matched with what the residents reported. Agreement between board and constituency was positive but modest, $r = .27$. In sharp contrast the superintendent-constituency figure is slightly negative, $r = -.09$. While neither judged the temper of the district with much acumen, board members fared much the better. Here is another indication of greater closeness between board and public, and it occurs on a subject of relevance for the representational process.

In assessing the significance of our findings with respect to issue preferences, issue identification, and the need to act on the basis of shared orientations it is important to bear in mind the fact that we were analyzing the opinions held by public officials and *not* their actual decision-making behavior. The implications for the quality of public representation in educational government differ if there is a discrepancy between the two. It is possible that the sentiments of the public are represented with greater or lesser accuracy in educational policies than our findings would indicate.

Although we admit this possibility, we nevertheless hold to the belief that dramatic differences between the policy-related opinions of decision makers and their policy-making behavior are unlikely. Research conducted by Miller and Stokes as well as subsequent work done by Cnudde and McCrone[12] indicates that whatever the correspondence between constituency attitudes and the final decision-making behavior by representatives may be, the path of causality passes through the attitudinal structure of the representative. In other words, it has been ascertained (at least with respect to Congress) that the attitudes and opinions of representative decision makers have a direct bearing on the translation of constituency preferences into policy. Although the extent to which such translation occurs depends in part on the type of issue in question, the representative's own attitude has at least a marginal impact on the quality of representation. It follows that where representatives' own attitudes correspond closely to constituency attitudes the potential for public representation is greatest.

With respect to representation within the local educational governments in our study we may conclude that representation is best achieved through the school board rather than through the superintendent. Although this may be the general case, we are able to identify certain variations that exist within specific contexts. Board attitudes appear to be more closely associated with public attitudes when episodic public issues are involved both with respect to recognition of problems and to preferences for the alternative policies. Advocates of public control will no doubt be disappointed by the moderate level of correspondence even in this area.

Less socially complex districts tended to have greater concordance on priority schedules, but the results were inconsistent on specific issue preferences. Some support was also noted for the contention that unreformed, "political" school boards perform their representative function better than reformed boards, but the evidence here too is far from compelling. Such differences are most pronounced when issue identification is involved. A seemingly anomalous finding is that the districts having had no contest for office in the previous election tended to have the greatest mass-elite congruity. On reflection we concluded that if indeed the electorate perceived harmony between itself and the board, a harmony which in fact frequently existed, then there was less cause for electoral challenge. Mechanisms other than electoral challenges were bringing the representatives and the represented into line.

Overall, the potential for the representation of public will in local educational policy-making systems is very uneven and very much issue specific. As such, the school district representational process resembles that for congressional districts and most probably for other units of representation as well.

NOTES

1. One of the few attempts to draw together the diverse empirical work in representation and organize it theoretically is Norman Luttbeg, *Public Opinion and Public Policy: Models of Political Linkage* (Homewood, Ill.: Dorsey, 1969).

2. Warren E. Miller and Donald E. Stokes, "Constituency Influence in Congress," *American Political Science Review*, 57 (March, 1963), pp. 45–56.

3. Sidney Verba and Norman H. Nie, *Participation in America: Political Democracy and Social Equality* (New York: Harper, 1972), especially chapters 17–19.

4. While the sampling error for the mass public sample in any one district might be sizable in some cases (due to the small N's in some of those districts), the gains to be achieved by including such districts outweigh this danger. We are guided here very much by the arguments and procedures of Miller and Stokes (see note 2).

5. Edmund Burke, "Speech to the Electors of Bristol" (1774), *Works*, Vol. 2.

6. See Paul E. Peterson, "Forms of Representation: Participation of the Poor in the Community Action Program," *American Political Science Review*, 64 (June, 1974), pp. 491–507. We have been particularly influenced by his conceptualizations and have borrowed freely from them.

7. Hannah Pitkin, *The Concept of Representation* (Berkeley: University of California Press, 1967), pp. 209–10.

8. The leading work here is Heinz Eulau and Kenneth Prewitt, *Labyrinths of Democracy: Adaptations, Linkages, Representation, and Policies in Urban Politics* (New York: Bobbs-Merrill, 1973).

9. For a different approach, see Verba and Nie, *op. cit.*, Chapter 17 and Appendix I.

10. "Majority Rule and the Representative System of Government," in *Cleavages, Ideologies and Party Systems: Contributions to Comparative Sociology*, eds. Erik Allardt and Yrjo Littunen, (Helsinki: Transactions of the Westermarck Society, 1964), pp. 343–76.

11. Because the board scores are grouped measures, and thus have smoothed out deviations, the likelihood is that board-constituency pair correlations will automatically be somewhat higher than those for superintendent-constituency pairs. We have run the analysis at the individual board member level as well. Although the magnitude of the correlations decreases somewhat, the essential edge of board over superintendent is still present.

12. Miller and Stokes, *loc. cit.*; Charles K. Cnudde and Donald J. McCrone, "The Linkage Between Constituency Attitudes and Congressional Voting Behavior," *American Political Science Review*, 60 (March, 1966), pp. 66–72.

PART III

Conflict and Cooperation between

Boards and Superintendents

Chapter 8

Toward Understanding

Resources and Governance

It is an axiom of science that the empirical applicability of any set of generalizations based on specific observations is dependent upon the theoretical framework employed in interpreting those observations. That which links the unique even to a much larger class of events is the abstract theory which is used to order and to categorize the various observations. Since it is our objective in this part of the book to form generalizations about power relations between boards and superintendents, we must adopt a theoretical framework appropriate to the task. Fortunately, the work done by social and political theorists such as Blau, Cartwright, Gamson, and Zald is uniquely suited to our needs.[1]

INFLUENCE

Briefly, our theory views decision-making power as a function of the resources actively employed by each of the parties which desires to control a particular decision. Control will be exercised by that party which is willing and able to commit resources having the highest aggregate value. Some resources are expendable; like money in economic exchange, once they have been used to purchase an object they are no longer available for use by their original owner. Other resources are nonexpendable. Again referring to an economic illustration, as long as actors maintain a reputation for reliability and integrity, that reputation is a resource upon which they can draw repeatedly in financial transactions. A strong reputation exemplifies a third quality that is characteristic of certain resources —

146

appreciation. The more one employs an intangible resource such as a reputation for dependability, that reputation will appreciate in value, provided that one's objective behavior is consistent with the reputed quality.

Resources possessed are not necessarily resources used. In Gamson's phrase, resources can be "in repose."[2] In the case of our own study, school boards have the *potential* power to exert leadership over local educational policy by virtue of their formal authoritative positions within educational systems. If superintendents emerge as the dominant actors in school governance, it is because the boards have given way. Dykes makes this point succinctly:

> *Because of the nature of the legal structure which gives to the board, in most instances, complete executive and legislative power over the schools at the local level, the participation of the superintendent in board decision making is determined by the board. The degree to which the superintendent shall participate and the role he will play as a participant are, in the final analysis, dependent upon board wishes and desires.*[3]

It would seem that the determination of decision-making power is a straightforward counting operation, that the resources commanded by the interested parties need only be totalled and the party with the highest value be declared the winner. If this were the case, our task would be simplified immeasurably. It would also be less challenging. However, parties involved in these relationships exercise discretion over the resources which they control. Rarely do they mobilize all the resources available to them in any single influence situation. When a resource remains dormant, it falls within the category of potential political resources. The willingness and the ability of an actor to convert potential resources into active ones will vary depending upon the nature of the decision and the circumstances surrounding it. In some cases a decision maker may deem it inadvisable to spend or to risk a given resource on a particular issue. Other situations may exist in which decision makers do not possess sufficient skills to activate their potential resources. Therefore, the maximum amount of insight that the influence model provides can be gained if we direct attention to the factors which affect the resource conversion process and if we analyze the pool of potential resources available to decision makers. We shall return to this point after considering the types of resources that are generally available to the principal elite participants in educational policy making — school boards and superintendents.

School Board Resources

The main potential resource of the school board is, of course, its formal authority. The school board is legally the policy-making body for the school district. Not only does it have the authority to set policy, but also it is the superintendent's employer, with the formal power to fire and to hire. With such formidable resources at its disposal the board might be expected to emerge as the dominant decision maker in virtually all school districts. Historically, however, this has not always been the case. For a variety of reasons, school boards do not uniformly transform their de jure authority into de facto decision-making power. One of the explanations frequently cited for this uneven pattern of assertion was identified by Minar as the distinction between the *rank authority* of the school board and the *technical authority* of the superintendent.[4] We will explore this distinction more fully later. It is now sufficient to observe that social scientists have postulated several distinct types of authority, each of which, when skillfully employed, may produce dominance for its possessor within a decision-making system. Available evidence suggests that school boards vary in the utilization of their formal, or rank, authority.

A second reason given for the boards' difficulty in exerting their authority is that they are multimember bodies. There are usually from five to seven individual members sitting on the board, although the number ranges from three to 15 depending on the locality. As anyone who has ever served on a committee will appreciate, the task of coordinating the decisions of even relatively small numbers of individuals is no mean feat. Yet if the school board is to exert its authority effectively, it must avoid developing severe internal dissension. Moreover, the men and women who constitute the board may not be fully cognizant of the authority invested in the board. As one educational authority has put it:

> *The role of school board member is perhaps the most ill-defined in local government. The individual board member has no legal power, though the board itself is considered a corporation. The board's rights and responsibilities are rarely spelled out by the state except in the most general terms, and the board rarely undertakes to define them itself. The board's entire role and that of its individual members is simply an accretion of customs, attitudes, and legal precedents without much specificity. Many school board members . . . move in a sea of confusion about their powers.[5]*

Another potentially powerful resource which is available to the school board is popular support stemming from its representative nature. We have seen that the public attaches great importance to the concept of local control over its schools. The demand for local control calls for policy decisions to be made at the community level by members of the community or by persons who act on behalf of everyone. It is a demand for grass roots representative democracy. Localism implies that there is a certain degree of mistrust directed toward outsiders and toward experts, and that it is the people who are served by the school system who are the rightful directors of that system. To the extent that localism prevails, it provides appreciable support to the school board that maintains the trust of the community. As was the case with formal authority, however, school boards vary considerably in their ability to exploit the potential resource of popular support. Among the conditions which affect a board's ability to draw upon this resource are the manner in which board members are recruited, the visibility of the board to the public, and the overall salience of educational issues to the community.

As Zald, in particular, has asserted, the linkages between a board and the representative public is a resource in any interaction with an appointed official. In the mythology of lay control, this resource should be powerful indeed. However, the manner in which a board views its constituency — its response style — is clearly variable. Consequently, representation as a resource may be underutilized.

Of course it is trite to say that elected bodies should engage in policy practices while administrators should be the obedient executors of policy. Generations of students of public administration have scoffed at the separations of policy and administration. However, the educationalists' corollary to the separation of policy and administration — the separation of education and politics — has contributed to an ideological rationalization for board impotence which may undermine strong representation resources. The resources of the board, then, are sometimes "slack,"[6] i.e., not utilized to their full potential.

Underutilization of resources is certainly not a problem unique to school boards. Rarely do policy actors ever learn to display their available resources to the fullest. Representative bodies such as state legislatures and city councils frequently find themselves giving ground, grudgingly or willingly, to an executive or bureaucratic unit. Merely being a legally authoritative decision-making body is no guarantee that the "voice of the people" will be efficiently transformed into policy.

For example, state legislatures vary enormously in both legal and actual authority. Gubernatorial power also varies. We frequently hear of weak or strong executives, terms referring not only to legal authority but also to the ability of a governor to convert potential resources into actual power.

Similarly, the effective power of boards is subject to substantial variation; and in this part of our book we will seek out explanations of this variation. We should not, however, carry the analogy with other representative bodies too far. The strong emphasis upon the nonpolitical nature of educational decision making, an emphasis not found in most representative assemblies, is an important consideration in assessing the ability of boards to live up to their potential.

Kerr, among others, has identified the traditional separation of education and politics as a strong factor in undermining popular support as an effective resource. His argument is that depoliticization obscures the representation character of the school board and tends to suppress all conflict concerning education.[7]

Board resources can be further impaired by the inadequacies of the electoral process. As we saw in Part I, the formal and informal processes by which the few are chosen from among the many does not contribute very much to a viable linkage between board and constituents. A strong base of sustained political organization is lacking in most districts. As is the case with most organizations, boards attract those who will fit in.[8] Both the informal recruitment process and the formal electoral process contribute substantially to the insulation of some boards and the active engagement of others. Our position is that the political structures and practices should provide us with clues as we seek to unravel the variations in board-superintendent relations.

Although formal authority and public support are potential resources which are available to every school board, there are other resources that may be available in varying degrees in specific districts. One resource is support from key members of the community, alternatively referred to as ruling elites or community influentials. Vidich and Bensman, for instance, found a close alliance between the powerful few of Springdale and the school board.[9] Similarly, Kimbrough reviews a number of case studies in which the members of community power elites lent their weight to educational decision makers. Interestingly, such support did not always flow to the school board but went on occasion to adept superintendents.[10]

 The subject of elite support is one that must be approached with caution for, as students of community power have frequently pointed out, power elites (like beauty) are often in the eye of the beholder. The expectations of a researcher, the form the research hypothesis takes, and the methodology used in testing it can determine the nature of one's findings regardless of the objective quality of the observations.

 Other resources that may be available to individual school board members include knowledge of the educational system, personal prestige, and social status. Such personal attributes may be of value in certain influence situations, but we will concentrate more of our attention on properties of the district and board as a whole.

Superintendent Resources

The superintendent's potential resources, although more limited in scope than those of the board, are no less effective when judiciously employed. His primary resource is his reputation for professional expertise in matters pertaining to education. It is a curious anomaly in American popular attitudes that while the concept of local, lay control of public schools is valued so highly, the alien educational expert is accorded greater deference than perhaps any other professional in public life.[11] The value placed upon education in this country undoubtedly helps to account for this seeming paradox. Schools of high quality are universally desired, and the quality of the educational program is thought to be best assured by placing it under the control of an acknowledged expert. Moreover, the tendencies to divorce politics and education and to suppress conflict over educational issues produce a drive for consensus. The focal figure around whom such consensus tends to be formed is the ranking expert within the district, for he is presumptively the best equipped to determine what is in the best interest of education. Frequently, the lay public seems to have only the role of assuring that the physical and financial needs of the expert are met.[12]

 Educational administrators have worked diligently to capitalize on the tendency of lay persons to regard the administrators' professional qualifications with deference. In fact, according to a number of observers, administrators have been instrumental in perpetuating this public tendency. For instance, Eliot reported a bit of advice to school board members offered by the American Association of School Administrators several years ago:

 Curriculum planning and development is a highly technical task which

> *requires special training . . . Board members do not have and cannot be*
> *expected to have the technical competence to pass on the work of expert*
> *teachers in this field. . . . Nor can the board pass on specific textbooks.* [13]

One former superintendent asserts the same thing in a recent book "intended as a
ready reference for busy board members":

> *The superintendent should expect the board to look to him for leadership*
> *in the educational affairs of the district, and corollary to this leadership*
> *in the supporting business and service areas. He alone is in a position to see*
> *the total picture, and, furthermore, he must carry the responsibility*
> *implicit in the role of chief school officer.* [14]

Although many scholars have identified the superintendent's expertise as being
perhaps his foremost resource, it is difficult to establish precisely its impact on the
allocation of decision-making power with school districts. The subtle manner in
which the adroit superintendent utilizes his professionalism makes such an assessment highly conjectural. Nevertheless, under certain conditions we would expect
professionalism to be used with greater frequency and to greater effect than under
others. One condition, the depoliticized, consensus-oriented school district, has
previously been mentioned. Another case is the district in which issues are seen to
involve techniques of implementation rather than political questions of value
allocation. As Minar has so aptly stated:

> *The technical expert, the district superintendent, is likely to flourish in*
> *those community settings where* expertise *and division of labor are*
> *assigned intrinsic value. . . . Where his "employers" on the board and in*
> *the community trust and value* expertise, *he [the superintendent] is likely*
> *to have much more discretion and initiative, right up to the highest policy*
> *level.* [15]

Political support as a potential resource is not the exclusive property of
school boards. Superintendents, regardless of the extent to which they pay lip-
service to the shibboleth of a depoliticized educational system, often court public
opinion. They do so in speeches before Rotary Clubs and Parent-Teacher Associations, in statements issued to the press, and in a variety of ways that may be
summarized under the heading of community relations. Typically, these activities
are not the overt appeals for support normally associated with political figures,
because that would violate the unwritten rule of separating schools and politics and
would elevate conflict to a visible level. Instead, the public utterances of educational officials tend to be presented as attempts on the part of the enlightened
professionals to inform the laymen of the district. Controversy is avoided, and if
the educator has done his job well, his reputation as a knowledgeable expert will
be enhanced. The net effect of such tactics over time will be a gradual accretion of
trust and support from the public.

The fact that superintendents participate in this form of political behavior should not be viewed with alarm or indignation. After all, they *are* public officials who perform political functions. The inconsistent element in the pattern is not the political activity of the educational administration; it is the misplaced belief that educational government is not a political process. This belief, however, creates an environment within which the skillful superintendent can develop and utilize public support with greater ease and to greater effect than if it were recognized for what it is, a *political* resource.

Let us compare the school superintendent with an analogous figure in local government, the city manager. Each is a professional administrator, and each is formally responsible to a representative body selected from the community. Furthermore, each is charged with the responsibility of overseeing the day to day operations of complex public service facilities. Each is interested in the policies established by his governing board, for he will have developed a set of preferences about the direction of the policies. At the very least the board will make his job easier or more difficult; but he has probably formulated larger goals, and to reach these he is dependent on board or council policy.

Like the city manager, the school superintendent is a politically neutral figure in the minds of most Americans. He maintains a certain degree of public visibility, but he is careful to project an image of a person who possesses the knowledge and the desire to follow that course which is in the best interest of public education. He makes no obvious appeals for partisan or special interest support, because the educational system is to be kept above these influences. He definitely attempts to attract popular support; however, like the city manager, his tactics are untarnished by the taint of politics. He appeals to the public on a subtle level by projecting himself as the foremost authority in the community over a policy area where knowledge rather than political influence should prevail. And in so doing he "has emerged . . . not only as an influential policy maker but also as an active politician in the popular understanding of the term."[16]

The sources of political support that a superintendent may command are not limited to the undifferentiated public. Although he must avoid the appearance of courting the favor of special interest groups, he may assure that his visibility is greater among certain influential groups than among others whose support he deems less valuable. If he is particularly adroit in his public relations, he may so thoroughly capture the allegiance of a civic organization that it can be used to increase further the scope of his support. Parent-Teacher Associations are frequently used in this manner. "The PTA," as Koerner has observed, "is usually a creature of the local administration."[17] Many others have noted the closeness of the relationship between educational administrators and PTAs, but perhaps none have described it quite so well as Dahl:

> The functions of the PTA are rather like those of party sub-leaders. The PTA supplies a group of people whose loyalty and enthusiasm can occasionally be mobilized for educational purposes important to the leaders.[18]

Another source of potential support for the superintendent consists of local influentials. There is nothing inherent in the existence of community elites which assures that their influence will result in a strong school board actively asserting its dominance over educational policy. Several studies have found instances where superintendents had been successful in gaining access to key members of the community's leadership, thereby effectively enhancing their own power vis-à-vis the school board.[19]

Even in communities where once powerful elites no longer hold the reins of power, the superintendent can find it expedient to align himself with either the old establishment or with an emerging set of influentials.[20] If the traditional pattern of power in the district consists of generalized leadership executed by the few, political change is likely to take the form of one elite supplanting another. Although the monopolistic character of leadership may not change, those who exercise that leadership do. During the transition from one set of elites to another it is often difficult for a public figure such as the superintendent to avoid being drawn into the conflict.

A final resource that is available to the superintendent is what Minar has described as his "access to the tools by which decisions are made and organizations controlled."[21] A list of these resources includes such diverse items as the district's administrative staff, data processing equipment, communications facilities, funds available in the administrative budget, and time. One could spend an inordinate amount of energy in compiling detailed inventories of the organizational and decision-making tools available to the superintendent. Fortunately, that tedious undertaking is not necessary for purposes of the present discussion. For all of the items that would be included relate to the fundamental resource of information.

Information is the raw material from which policy decisions are formed. In the absence of adequate knowledge no individual can either satisfactorily evaluate a problem or adequately assess the merits of alternative solutions. Moreover, most people are reluctant to assert themselves actively in areas about which they do not feel competent. Thus a practical precondition for policy leadership within any decision-making system is a sufficiency of information. It is a characteristic of the field of education that the informational requirements which are required to make a person feel comfortably informed are sometimes quite demanding. Unquestionably, the growth of school districts and the technical developments in educational facilities and procedures have magnified the complexity of educational government manyfold during the twentieth century.

Compounding this national trend is the tendency for the educational establishment to inject what many consider to be elements of false complexity, a jargon designed to confuse the uninitiated, and a voluminous amount of "technical" literature and data bordering on trivia. Well-intentioned citizens who obtain a seat on a local board of education may understandably feel incompetent to assert a position on a question concerning which so many experts have had so much to say. They will probably defer to the leadership of trained professionals. They will probably not develop their own informational resources to the point where they are no longer dependent upon the superintendent, for they have neither the time nor the access to raw data that the superintendent enjoys. Pois described this facet of the school board-superintendent relationship when he wrote:

> *[A] crucial factor in the ascendancy of the general superintendent vis-à-vis the board is the latter's almost complete dependence upon the general superintendent as the source of information . . .*
>
> *The lack of adequate information is bound to confirm a board member's tendency to take refuge in the more humdrum matters while dealing gingerly with difficult or elusive problems, or amiably concurring in the desires of the superintendent. The layman who "takes on" the professional frequently assumes a calculated risk of being rebuffed decisively — if not put to rout — by the expert who has ready access to the pertinent data or background material.* [22]

What are the "humdrum matters" in which board members take refuge when they feel that their information is inadequate? Those who have studied the issues upon which school boards devote most of their time have found that they tend to concentrate on tangibles such as physical facilities and finances, leaving control over the actual educational program largely in the hands of the administration. [23] Superintendents possibly seek to encourage this division of labor.

Apart from using his superior informational resources to increase the apparent disparity in competence between himself and the board, the superintendent can exert control over the *kind* of information to which the board is privy. Control of this sort is not necessarily confined to information concerning issues that are before the board, and it may determine whether or not an issue is brought up at all. The most visible means of controlling the definition of issues is through the formal preparation of the board's agenda. In his study of the Chicago educational system, Pois recognized the significance of this technique when he reported that "the general superintendent's ability to channel the board's deliberations has been enhanced immeasurably by the practice of having the agenda for board meetings consist almost exclusively of reports transmitted by the general superintendent for board consideration." [24]

Social scientists have long recognized that the ability to determine the agenda of a decision-making body and to define the alternatives to be considered is a powerful resource. [25] On the topic of the extent to which this resource has been transformed from a potential to an active one by educational administrators, Pellegrin has observed that the superintendent and his top aides

> *are the ones who initiate action, who make proposals for change, who recommend that this or that be done. The school board and the community at large may accede wholly or in part to these proposals, or they may turn any of them down. But in the main the school board and the public pass upon the alternatives proposed by the administration. They rarely initiate proposals themselves. On a long-run basis, those who initiate*

the proposals will be the top figures in the educational power structure (emphasis added).[26]

The competition between the board and the superintendent has, therefore, all the earmarks of the classic jostling between representatives and bureaucrats. One speaks as the authoritative representative of "the people"; the other speaks with the authority of the expert. Who wins? The answer is by no means clear cut. In spite of the justifiable tendency to bemoan the decline of board power, we should acknowledge the vigor of some boards. A superintendent of San Francisco or St. Louis would probably be amused by an assertion that boards have no power. To use another case, the superintendent in "Springdale," were he to try to bully his board, would find himself placing an ad in the classified section of a newspaper seeking employment. Why do such situations exist? Are there systematic explanations for variance in board influence?

THE EDUCATIONAL-POLITICAL ARENA

The mere existence of a potential resource is insufficient to warrant the conclusion that it will necessarily be converted into political influence. "Power requires resources," write Hawley and Wirt, "but [it] also depends on the will and ability of the individual who holds the resources, and *the relevance of the resources to the desired object*" (emphasis added).[27] The relevance of a given resource to a particular object cannot always be judged solely in terms of the resource and the object in question. Frequently, contextual considerations determine how effective a resource is. A hypothetical superintendent may count the active support of his community's mayor among his resources. The effectiveness of mayoral support, however, varies depending on the power of the mayor with respect to the school board. If the mayor appoints members to the board, for instance, his support is more valuable than if board members are elected by the public. Likewise, whether the school district is coterminous with the city affects the value of this resource. Thus the context within which resources are evaluated directly affects their worth. We shall refer to evaluative contexts as educational-political markets.

A market is more than a physical or conceptual space within which these transactions take place; it is also a set of norms which affects those transactions. As we have seen, one type of market norm provides criteria by which resources are evaluated. Since there are no conventional standards of evaluation within educational-political markets comparable to that of money in economic markets, conversion rates for comparing the relative value of resources may vary widely from market to market.

It is the school board that in most instances is in a position to dictate the norms under which resources are to be evaluated. The board is also the prime (though not exclusive) determinant of public and interest group influence. As we demonstrated previously, boards differ markedly in how they respond to demands emanating from the community. Some are more receptive to the demands of formal groups, whereas others respond more to communications from individuals. The representational style of the board has a direct effect on the worth of interest group resources. If a board is not responsive to groups in the first place, then it is of little importance whether there are increases or decreases in the absolute levels of group resources, which are assigned negligible value in any case.

The style of response, although it is an important market variable, is not the only source of differential resource evaluation for nonelite actors. The role orientation of the board is equally important. Boards vary not only in representational style, but also in the degree to which they assume a representational role. While the precise wording of their definitions may differ, role theorists usually agree that a role is a set of behavioral norms which constitutes a standard of action for the occupant of a social position.[28] A board which sees itself principally as a mechanism through which various segments of the community can participate in the formation of educational policy will behave much differently than one which views its role as being a protective buffer between the professionals who actually run the schools and the public which finances the schools. The former type of board is likely to place a higher value on public resources than is the latter type of board. The variations in interest group and individual resource evaluations that are due to differences in representational style, therefore, are more properly viewed as marginal variations on the more fundamental pattern of public rather than professional resource evaluation. Again, however, the determination of what weights are to be assigned to what resources is left up to the board. Although external constraints exist, the board's own image of its responsibility needs to be accounted for.[29]

The importance of examining different educational-political arenas stems from the fact that various norms for resource evaluation result in identifiable biases. These biases, in turn, influence the amount of effective power at the disposal of the respective actors. Consequently, each arena situation affects the ability of the superintendent to exert leadership over the making of public educational policy by imposing certain standards of resource evaluation on the school board. Since the superintendent's "fundamental power resource . . . [is] his perceived expertise,"[30] it follows that he is most likely to dominate his school board when the educational-political arena places a high value on expertise. We can expect such a market to exist whenever the school board perceives the issue under deliberation to involve routine, administrative policies and procedures which lend themselves to rationalized decision making. Conversely, when an issue is deemed pertinent to the distribution of community values or the establishment of community goals, the principal board resources of public support and legitimacy are likely to have the highest conversion rate. Board leadership should result. Various sets of descriptive labels have been applied to these types of issues (routine-extraordinary, administrative-political, esoteric-exoteric, etc.); however, each set maintains the distinction outlined above.[31] For example, Agger, Goldrich, and Swanson write:

> *An* administrative *demand or decision-making process is regarded by its maker or participants as involving relatively routine implementations of a prior, more generally applicable decision; it implicates relatively minor values of a relatively few people at any one time and has "technical" criteria available to guide the technically trained expert in selecting one or another outcome as* the *decision. A* political *demand or decision-making process is thought to involve either an unusual review of an existing decision or an entirely new decision; it implicates relatively major values of a relatively large number of people and has value judgments or prefer- ences as the major factors in determining selection by "policy-makers" of one or another outcome as* the *decision.* [32]

For the sake of consistency, we shall hereafter refer to the former type of issue as "internal" and the latter as "public," as Martin has suggested.[33] Regardless of the label attached, it should be noted that the crucial factor in defining an issue is how the school board perceives it and not the intrinsic content of the issue itself. Therefore, an objective of actors who desire maximum influence over educational decision making should be to arrange for the board to define issues in such a way that their resources will command a high value. Evidence attesting to the efforts of superintendents to influence board perceptions is legion. Most issues are defined by superintendents as internal, and many boards appear to have difficulty in staking out a legitimate territory. As Koerner so aptly wrote, "The local board's customary failure to distinguish between fundamental policy and housekeeping details is one of the abiding anomalies of local control of education."[34]

Although in the final analysis it is the board which makes the authorita- tive decisions affecting the quality of the educational political arena, the fact that perceptions of issues play such an important role in the process indicates that the school board enjoys decidedly less than absolute free will in this vital area. A variety of forces, many of which are independent of board control, influence the nature of the board-defined arena. Collectively, these forces indirectly determine the arena structure by circumscribing the range of collective behavior in which the board may engage or by constraining its perceptual freedom. In general it may be argued that the forces which depoliticize educational government and remove it from the public sphere produce a bias in the arena which devalues the resources of the board and of the groups and individual citizens who seek a voice in educa- tional policy through school board representation. Frequently the void that is thus left in educational policy leadership is filled by the district's professional edu- cational administrators. Nearly all issues come to be viewed as technical problems internal to the educational system, and the market becomes biased in favor of the professional resources such as expertise. When this sort of situation exists, the result is likely to be that which Gittell found in New York City:

> *In the last two decades, education in New York City has become amazingly insulated from political and public controls. One could accurately des-*

cribe the situation as an abandonment of public education by key forces of the political power within the City. . . . Weber's theory of the emergence of a specialized bureaucracy monopolizing power through its control of expertise characterizes the role of the educational bureaucracy in New York City. The claim that only professionals can make competent judgments has been accepted. Civic and interest groups have responded ambivalently. On the one hand they accept the notion of the professional competence of the bureaucracy, but at the same time express a hopelessness regarding their ability to change the system.[35]

We can infer that when educational government is *not* depoliticized, the arena will be structured to devalue the resources of the superintendent and inflate the resources of the board and community-interest groups. It is frequently argued that educational decision making is becoming more involved with the political process. If we find districts in which this is true, we should expect to see a radically different picture than the one drawn of New York.

NOTES

1. Peter M. Blau, *Exchange and Power in Social Life* (New York: Wiley, 1964); Dorwin Cartwright, "Influence, Leadership, Control," *Handbook of Organizations*, ed. James G. March (Chicago: Rand McNally, 1965), pp. 1047; William A. Gamson, *Power and Discontent* (Homewood, Ill.: Dorsey Press, 1968); and Mayer N. Zald, "The Power and Functions of Boards of Directors: A Theoretical Synthesis," *American Journal of Sociology*, 75 (July, 1969), pp. 97–111.

2. Gamson, *op. cit.*, pp. 93–109.

3. Archie R. Dykes, *School Board and Superintendent: Their Effective Working Relationships* (Danville, Ill.: Interstate Printers and Publishers, 1965), p. 152.

4. David W. Minar, "Community Characteristics, Conflict, and Power Structures," *The Politics of Education in the Local Community*, ed. Robert S. Cahill and Stephen P. Hencley (Danville, Ill.: Interstate Printers and Publishers, 1964), pp. 132–133.

5. James D. Koerner, *Who Controls American Education? A Guide to Laymen* (Boston: Beacon Press, 1968), p. 122.

6. Gamson, *op. cit.*, pp. 97–98.

7. Norman D. Kerr, "The School Board as an Agency of Legitimation," *Sociology of Education*, 38 (Fall, 1954), pp. 34–59.

8. Gamson, *op. cit.*, pp. 117–120.

9. Arthur J. Vidich and Joseph Bensman, *Small Town in Mass Society: Class, Power, and Religion in a Rural Community* (Garden City, N.Y.: Doubleday, 1960).

10. Ralph B. Kimbrough, *Political Power and Educational Decision-Making* (Chicago: Rand McNally, 1964); see also Laurence Iannaccone and

Frank W. Lutz, *Politics, Power and Policy: The Governing of Local School Districts* (Columbus, Ohio: Charles E. Merrill, 1970).

11. Roscoe C. Martin, *Government and the Suburban School* (Syracuse, N.Y.: Syracuse University Press, 1962), p. 50.

12. Calvin Grieder, Truman M. Pierce, and William E. Rosenstengel, *Public School Administration* (2nd ed.; New York: Ronald Press, 1961), p. 198.

13. Thomas H. Eliot, "Toward an Understanding of Public School Politics," *American Political Science Review*, 52 (December, 1959), p. 1037.

14. Lloyd W. Ashby, *The Effective School Board Member* (Danville, Ill.: Interstate Printers & Publishers, 1968), p. 48.

15. Minar, *op. cit.*, p. 141.

16. Martin, *op. cit.*, p. 61.

17. Koerner, *op. cit.*, p. 147.

18. Robert A. Dahl, *Who Governs? Democracy and Power in an American City* (New Haven: Yale University Press, 1961), pp. 155–156.

19. Kimbrough, *op. cit.*, pp. 221–236.

20. Iannaccone and Lutz, *op. cit.*, pp. 41–44.

21. David W. Minar, *Educational Decision-Making in Suburban Communities* Cooperative Research Project No. 2440, research supported by the U.S. Office of Education (Evanston, Ill.: Northwestern University, 1966), p. 93.

22. Joseph Pois, *The School Board Crisis: A Chicago Case Study* (Chicago: Educational Methods, 1964), p. 430.

23. Grieder, *et al., op. cit.*, p. 198.

24. Pois, *op. cit.*, p. 429.

25. E. E. Schattschneider, *The Semisovereign People: A Realist's View of Democracy in America* (New York: Holt, Rinehart, and Winston, 1950); and Peter Bachrach and Morton Baratz, "The Two Faces of Power," *American Political Science Review*, 57 (December, 1962).

26. Roland J. Pellegrin, "Community Power Structure and Educational Decision-Making in the Local Community," a paper read before the American Association of School Administrators, Atlantic City, N.J., February 15, 1965, quoted in Koerner, *op. cit.*, p. 138.

27. Willis D. Hawley and Frederick M. Wirt (eds.), *The Search for Community Power* (Englewood Cliffs, N.J.: Prentice-Hall, 1968), p. 214.

28. Neal Gross, Ward S. Mason, and Alexander W. McEachern, *Explorations in Role Analysis: Studies of the School Superintendency Role* (New York: Wiley, 1958), pp. 3–13.

29. Dykes, *op. cit.*, p. 11.

30. Iannaccone and Lutz, *op. cit.*, p. 40.

31. See Alan Rosenthal, "Community Leadership and Public School Politics: Two Case Studies" (Ph.D. dissertation, Princeton University, 1960) and William D. Knill, "Community Decision Processes: Research Strategies," in Cahill and Hencley, *op. cit.*, pp. 83–85.

32. Robert E. Agger, Daniel Goldrich, and Bert E. Swanson, *The Rulers*

and the Ruled: Political Power and Impotence in American Communities (New York: Wiley, 1964), p. 48.

33. Martin, *op. cit.*, p. 61.

34. Koerner, *op. cit.*, p. 124.

35. Marilyn Gittell, *Participants and Participation: A Study of Local Policy in New York City* (New York: Center for Urban Education, 1947), p. 46.

Chapter 9

The External Context of

Opposition to the Superintendent

Our analysis of the linkage between school boards and their constituencies indicates a pattern of semi insulation and sporadic community influence. We turn now to an analysis of the exchange between the school board and the superintendent, for it is here that we find a key to understanding local educational policy making. Our major goal is to explain variations in the degree to which boards are dominated by their superintendents. Stated conversely, we seek to account for opposition to the professional expertise represented by the superintendency. Superintendents have developed over the years several techniques for coopting the school boards in such a manner that the superintendent's resources gain primacy in the educational-political market, but superintendents, like other executives, are sometimes challenged. We want to know the kinds of boards which challenge. We will describe the board-superintendent contest in terms of the role-orientation of the board, the socio-political environment in which the competition takes place, and the levels of tension and demand articulation in the district. Each of these categories of variables should influence the results of the board-superintendent contest.

    As noted previously, superintendents are products of the demand for managerial efficiency in educational policy making. As schools grew in complexity during the nineteenth century, it became apparent that lay boards had neither the time nor the inclination to continue their original managerial role. School boards began to hire professional administrators who slowly and inexorably began to assume not only administrative but also policy-making authority.[1] At the turn of the century, boards fought off an attempt by superintendents to take over full

161

responsibility for educational policy and to become independent of school board supervision,[2] but the growing complexity of school district management increased the value of superintendent resources. Since 1932, over four-fifths of the school districts in the United States have disappeared, while pupil populations have risen by 15 million. The ratio of board members to student population increased from one to 46 in 1932 to one to 300 in 1967.[3]

Hines's fifty-year history of an Oregon school board illustrates how superintendents have gradually expanded their powers. His study shows the gradual assumption by superintendents of the responsibility for the instructional program, and then for the selection and supervision of the professional staff. From these beachheads the superintendent expanded his domain to budget preparation, fiscal control, purchasing, school site selection, plant management, and public relations. The first erosion of board power occurs when the superintendent and his staff assume control over the instructional, or educational program. Curiously, the educational program is the one area where boards have theoretical legitimacy; yet it is the first to undergo erosion.[4]

MEASURING THE COMPONENTS OF EDUCATIONAL PROGRAM OPPOSITION

Our assessment of the board-superintendent interaction will be made in terms of two dependent variables: the extent of opposition to the superintendent and the probability of a superintendent succumbing to the opposition. With regard to opposition, Minar's research suggests that school board opposition to superintendents develops when boards function in situations characterized by high levels of community conflict.[5] In partial corroboration of Minar's thesis, Crain discovered that school boards could seize the initiative and operate the schools in ways which displeased the superintendents with regard to decisions about integration, primarily because the issue escalated community conflict.[6] One line of congruence between the findings of these two scholars is the notion of episodic control. When faced with the superintendent's expertise, his greater technical resources, and his commitment to his career, the board member will try to avoid a challenge to professional authority. But there is no administrative maxim which enables superintendents to posit the correct way to deal with the demands of civil rights organizations. Such crises arouse fierce antagonisms, propel interest groups into the policy-making process, and provide little opportunity for the exchange of professional resources.

Episodic crises, by definition, constitute the exception rather than the rule in most districts. More customarily, boards of education make decisions about the educational program, the components of which usually do not have the salience and symbolic significance of more controversial issues. Professional educators are understandably inclined to make most issues fit within the framework of the educational program, that is, within a framework of what kinds of policies and practices will produce the "best education" for the students. To the extent that they are successful in doing that, their roles as experts become highly valued and evoke deference.

In this chapter and the next we deal with opposition to the superintendent with respect to the educational program. Although various definitions of educational program exist in the minds of board members, responses to an open-ended question revealed that the great majority of board members defined the educational program in terms of the curriculum structure, student problems, and teacher quality. These are topics which presumably lie at the heart of school system performance. Our task is to assess the variability of opposition between the lay board and the professional educator on these central topics.

We work from general rather than specific indicators of opposition. The interview schedule contained a number of specific questions dealing with the educational program, and it would have been possible to estimate the level of opposition between boards and superintendents on these. That procedure would have run the severe risks of overlooking certain topics which occur in some districts rather than others and of creating "artificial" opposition about issues which had not arisen in the district. Similarly, we could have asked whether the board overruled the superintendent on specific issues. Again, that would have excluded, across the broad and diverse range of districts in our sample, a number of issues which we did not have the foresight (or interview time) to include. Therefore, we have utilized responses from more general questions about opposition in the expectation that the board members have a variety of specific issues and instances in mind.

A board's propensity to oppose the superintendent on the educational program was tapped by asking this question: "Does the board ever disagree with the superintendent about the content or nature of the educational program?" Board members as a whole were divided on this question: 38 percent gave an unequivocal "yes," 12 percent a qualified "yes," and 50 percent an outright "no." Aggregating to the board level resulted in a mean disagreement or opposition score of 39 percent. Not surprisingly, members of particular boards tended to agree with each other about the presence of opposition, as Table 9-1 indicates. About one-third of the boards were in moderate disagreement, since from one-quarter to one-half said conflict existed whereas their colleagues denied its presence. Some of the disagreement undoubtedly stems from some board members thinking of others as opponents when those others in fact exclude themselves and perhaps all of their colleagues. Despite these inconsistencies the percentage of members reporting opposition to the superintendent can be taken as a gauge of the intensity, if not the absolute frequency, of board-superintendent conflict.

Degree of opposition does not convey sufficient information to measure policy leadership fully. Schattschneider and Bachrach and Baratz, for instance, have pointed out that policy may be controlled by preventing conflict over a threatening issue from ever being joined.[7] It is conceivable that an adept superintendent could avoid overt board disagreement over a potentially controversial issue which he opposes by practicing the tactics of nondecision making and controlling the entry of such issues to the board's deliberative proceedings. Likewise, a superintendent

TABLE 9–1
Distribution of Boards According to Percentage of
Members Citing Disagreement with
Superintendent about Educational Program

Percent of Opponents	*Percent of Boards*	*N*
None	17	17
0–24%	16	17
25–49%	32	35
50% or more	35	38
Totals	100	107

who is passive or dominated by his school board may anticipate board opinion and never take a stand that he believes will attract opposition. In neither of these hypothetical cases will the simple measure of board disagreement tap the element of policy leadership that we are after. Therefore, we have also utilized data concerning the subjective probability which board members attribute to the likelihood of their winning an overt contest between themselves and the superintendent over proposed changes in the content of the educational program.

Board members were asked: "If the superintendent wanted to change the educational program and the board disagreed with the change, how likely is it that the board would eventually approve the change anyway?" At the individual level the responses to this question are distributed in a compressed bell-shaped pattern across the four response categories: 23 percent said very likely, 31 percent fairly likely, 34 percent not too likely, and 13 percent not at all likely. As with the board opposition measure, we need to convert the probability of board victory into a board level variable. In this case it means taking the obverse of superintendent victory estimates. Thus boards predicting superintendent defeat are, of course, predicting board victory. In order to achieve an equitable distribution of boards according to estimates of their overcoming the superintendent we calculated the mean percentages believing it was anything except very likely that the superintendent would prevail. This is a very generous measure of estimating board victory. More conservative approaches would have yielded far fewer boards judging themselves capable of overcoming the superintendent. The overall board mean is 46; the grouped distributions are shown in Table 9–2.

Before delving into the corollaries of opposition it would be well to set in place the relationship between our two indicators of opposition. It might be hypothesized that boards which regularly oppose the superintendent regarding the educational program would also be those which have a sense of confidence that they can overcome the superintendent's preferences. After all, why oppose if the outcome is foreordained? There is, however, only slight support for the hypothesis. The correlation (r) between frequency of opposition and the likelihood of winning is .17. Although the relationship is in the direction posited, the magnitude suggests

TABLE 9–2
Distribution of Boards According to Percentage of
Members Estimating Board Victory
over Superintendent[a]

Percent of Estimating Victory	Percent of Boards	N
0–24	18	19
25–49	34	37
50–74	26	27
75+	22	23
Totals	100	106

[a]Strictly speaking this is the percentage which did not say it was "very likely" that the superintendent would prevail.

that the factors associated with opposition are probably different than those associated with winning. As we discuss the results of our analysis it will be evident what these factors are and why they operate as they do.

Role Orientation and Board Vitality

Strictly speaking, our first example of external context is an attitudinal state rather than an environmental property. But this particular role orientation is so reflective of how board members define and weight the environment that we will introduce it at this point. Role theorists tend to agree that a role is a set of behavioral norms which constitutes a standard of action for the occupant of a social position.[8] Our interest in working with this concept is to assess the manner in which school boards define their responsibilities with respect to the public and to the superintendent, for our hypothesis is that variations in responsibility will result in different educational markets.

Dykes asserts that "what the school board does depends in large measure on the board's view of itself in relation to its responsibilities."[9] A board which sees itself principally as a mechanism through which various segments of the community can participate in the formation of educational policy will behave much differently from one that views its role as being a protective buffer between the professionals who run the schools and the public whose children are educated in them. In the former instance, public support is expected to be the most salient consideration in decisions pertaining to public issues. Boards of this type are characterized by what we will call a *fiduciary* role orientation. *Professionally-* oriented boards, on the other hand, will be less inclined to perceive the extent to which popular values and community goals are involved in any given issue and, therefore, will rely more on technical expertise to resolve what they define as internal issues.

The fiduciary-professional distinction should not be confused with the classical concepts of "delegate" and "trustee." Both of the latter terms are used to describe styles vis-à-vis the public. Neither the delegate nor the trustee would challenge the assertion that the first consideration of the representative should be the welfare of his constituents. They differ only on how best to achieve this goal. Consequently, both fall within our concept of a fiduciary role orientation. With respect to school board roles, however, we believe that a more fundamental distinction is warranted. The board that confuses its responsibility to the public with its perceived responsibility to the professional educators is likely to permit professional values to obscure its regard for the public interest in many instances.

The critical element which we must tap in measuring the school board's role orientation is its ability to discriminate between its public responsibility and its allegiance to school administrators.

Therefore, each school board member in our sample was asked the question: "Do you ever feel any conflict between your responsibility to the public and to the school administration?" Each board was then given a score to reflect the percent of its members which responded negatively. High scores indicate relatively high degrees of professionalism in board role orientations, whereas low scores indicate fiduciary boards.

The distribution of scores (mean = 60) shows that American local school boards tend to perceive no conflict between the two sets of allegiances. Initially, one would infer that these boards define their roles in a manner consistent with the values of professional educators, thus defining the educational market to the advantage of the superintendent.

Such an inference, of course, goes well beyond the data and is, at best, suspect. Alternative explanations come readily to the mind. The "professional" boards may simply be saying that the administrators and the public see eye to eye. Hence the problem of determining allegiance simply does not exist. The level at which such harmony is perceived could be quite vague; for example, both the public and the administration want "good education." Still, perceived agreement might mask an actual conflict in the absence of systematic input from the community.

Support for the notion that the professionalism of boards is evidence of deference to the superintendent can be mustered by an examination of an earlier study by Gross, Mason, and McEachern of 105 school districts in Massachusetts. These scholars found a majority of boards to be professional in that they performed such tasks as helping to sell good education to the community, avoided direct communication to the superintendents' subordinates, and avoided intraboard cleavages.[10]

Such behavior and attitudes add up to a board with primary identification with the superintendent, a negation of the role normally associated with representatives of the community. If so, we would expect to find professionally-oriented boards less likely to resist the superintendent. Our data support this argument. There is a negative correlation (−.38) between professional role orientations and the intensity of board opposition regarding the educational program. Our other measure — the estimated likelihood of prevailing over the superintendent when there is conflict about the content of the educational program — provides corroboration. As professionalization *increases*, the likelihood of victory *decreases* (−.41). Thus there is evidence to support the idea that deference to the superintendent is linked to a resolution of role conflict against the community; the job of board member becomes one of representing the administration's program.

Urbanism and Opposition

We found the role played by district social complexity to be quite important in affecting the electoral and linkage processes. Given that importance, it seems probable that it will also have an impact on superintendent leadership and school board behavior. Most commonly we operationally defined social complexity in terms of whether the school system was inside or outside an SMSA. That categorization proved quite workable for our earlier concerns. As we shall proceed to document, however, important subtleties in board-superintendent interaction are masked by the dichotomy. Consequently, for some purposes our gross indicator of social complexity will be different in this and the following chapter.

    A distribution of districts based upon the two-fold categorization of SMSA versus non-SMSA was modified primarily by reassigning districts in the SMSA category, those in counties which have a central city of 50,000 population or greater. If the district was located in the major urban center of its SMSA, it was put into the city category; if it was not in the largest center but was located within the same county (or collection of counties defining the SMSA), it was placed in the suburban category. All other districts are in non-SMSAs, and we will refer to them as small town districts even though they range from essentially small, semirural districts to medium-sized town districts located in counties without a city of at least 50,000. This scheme produced a distribution in which slightly less than half of the districts (48 percent) are in "small towns," while city and suburban districts each constitute approximately one-fourth of the sample (25 percent and 27 percent, respectively). For convenience we will refer to the three categories as different levels of urbanism.

    Social scientists have generally held the assumption that larger communities are more conflict-prone because of their complexity. Typical is the Prewitt and Eulau study of city councils which noted that:

> *Unlike in larger and heterogeneous cities, where various social groups are present and likely to make their demands known to the city council, in the smaller, more homogeneous settings, the group life is likely to be less developed and the public pressures brought on the council are probably less frequent or urgent.*[11]

Our own findings, it will be recalled, are comparable to the city council study: group life is associated with the complexity of the urban setting.

Of course, the more aroused citizenry which is associated with group conflict may not penetrate the board-superintendent exchange. Under conditions of community tension the board and superintendent might be drawn closer to ward off an assault. However, if boards succeed in their representative capacity, community conflict could evolve into intraboard or board-superintendent conflict.

In a manner typical of urban political systems, the more urban school districts have a heterogeneous public, a plurality of interests within the community, large and growing populations which produce extremely high levels of strain on the capacity of the school system, and proportionally fewer "free" resources to alleviate strain from mounting problems in other sectors of city life. Since the cities have ample pools of well-educated, high status personnel from which to draw, their school boards are often composed of members who are of uniformly high status, who are well-versed in the practices of rational management, and who are able to deal with the complexity and the diversity of the problems in urban communities. Indeed, we found that the social status of board members was highest in city districts, next in suburban districts, and lowest in small town districts. Thus we might expect opposition frequency to vary accordingly.

At the same time, the territorial boundaries of the metropolitan center and its school district tend to be coterminus.[12] This overlap may blur the traditional distinction between the city's political system and that of the school district. Although there may be a sufficient supply of elites within the district, partisan political considerations may result in boards which are heterogeneous in the interests they represent. Furthermore, such "politicized" boards might be less impressed by the superintendent's reputation as an educational expert.[13]

The peculiarities of the small town district have been less fully explored than have the urban and suburban situations. No doubt such slighting of these districts can be accounted for in part by the fact that the most dramatic changes and the most pressing problems are experienced in the latter two types of school systems.

Fortunately for our purposes the work that has been done on small town school districts has shed sufficient light on them to permit us to develop some expectations concerning the quality of the educational environment the districts provide. Perhaps the most illuminating of these studies, although it is only one part of a larger study of a single community, is Vidich and Bensman's description of Springdale in rural New York.[14] The picture that emerges from their writing is one of a community that has a relatively homogeneous populace and is dominated by a single monolithic elite group that exerts generalized leadership over virtually all aspects of civic life. The school district includes both the town of Springdale and the surrounding rural area. Although there is not a perfect coincidence of interest between the town's businessmen and farmers, their values are sufficiently similar to conclude that this small community is highly consensual.

Curiously, at least in comparison to more metropolitan environments, the school is a focus of interest for the community. Therefore, the school and the policies concerning it are highly visible objects of concern — more so in fact than other areas of public institutions. "In contrast to the village and town boards," Vidich and Bensman reported, "the school board is faced with making important decisions on issues which have far-reaching consequences in the community at large."[15] It is in the governance of the school system "that all aspects and pressures of all phases of community life are expressed in politics."[16]

This portrayal of the small town district is not unique to Springdale. Alford's study of the intense opposition generated against a proposal to unify two small California districts also illustrates the special home town chauvinism that can prevail in the smaller districts, where the school and the community are integrated, as Bidwell observes, "both socially and culturally."[17] The hallmarks of the small town district are: (1) homogeneity of public interests and values, (2) generalized political leadership exercised by a single elite group, and (3) the general salience of educational government.[18]

In this type of atmosphere the superintendent is usually an alien expert. As such he may develop powerful leadership resources, but he must be careful to employ them in backing policies that conform to the dominant values of the community.[19] At best he can become only a highly regarded outsider whose technical knowledge is recognized; he typically remains unintegrated, both politically and socially, with the community he serves. Power over all aspects of community life rests with the monolithic elite group which jealously preserves its power and defends the values of the community. The extent to which the small town superintendent can win the confidence of the ruling elite group in his district will determine the extent of his effectiveness as an educational leader. In order to establish such confidence he must not pose a threat to the sacred values of the community. Even though there may be potential conflict seething beneath the surface of the small town's sea of tranquility, it is not channeled into conflict laden activities. A "mobilization of bias" prevents conflict from erupting;[20] hence, small towns should have fewer board-superintendent head-on clashes.

Our expectations regarding opposition in suburban school districts are mixed. In general, however, we would expect them to lie midway between the urban and small town configurations. Part of the difficulty in speculating about suburban districts is that suburban areas assume such a wide diversity. Contrary to popular beliefs, all suburban areas are not middle to upper middle class nor are they all satellite communities. Taken as a whole, the suburban districts have some properties of the larger cities, within whose orbits they lie, as well as some properties of the small towns, which they resemble in terms of size and greater homogeneity.

With the foregoing discussion in mind, we turn now to the relationship between urbanism and opposition. In large part our expectations are fulfilled. Looking first at the question of the extent to which the board disagrees with the superintendent about the educational program, we observe little difference between city and suburban districts (Table 9-3). In small towns, however, there is much less opposition. If the small town board is as jealous of its prerogatives as it has been portrayed to be, it is unlikely that the superintendent will back a position contrary to the board's position. Although low levels of opposition result, superintendent dominance is not automatically assured. When we examine the second of the two leadership-related variables, this interpretation of the small town situation emerges more clearly. The likelihood that the board will persevere to victory is significantly higher in small town districts than in either of the other two categories. Likewise, the suburban board is more likely to prevail over a superintendent than is the city board.

TABLE 9–3
Urbanism and Board Opposition

Type of District	Opposition to Superintendent $\overline{X}$	Probability of Board Victory $\overline{X}$
City	45	36
Suburban	48	46
Small Town	28	52

From the point of view of the superintendent there is less middle ground, less opportunity to play one faction against another in the small town system. The costs of generating opposition are high. Once opposition is begun, it is likely to sweep aside the protestors. Thus the drive toward consensus in small towns may not indicate an absence of competition in the board-superintendent exchange; but it does suggest that there will be less opportunity for superintendents to develop countervailing power once a conflict appears. The sensible superintendent will anticipate those issues which are likely to generate conflict and avoid raising them.

One of the additional reasons small town superintendents are less likely to raise conflict issues in the first place is that they share more compatible backgrounds with their boards. This compatibility is certainly influenced by the clear, homogeneous pattern of superintendent recruitment. Like most board members everywhere, superintendents are Waspish, Republican, and devout. Here, however, the similarity ends. Superintendents are far more likely to have been reared in a small town and to have a lower middle class background. Few of them are urban or professional in origin. While such origins place them out of context on the typical urban board, with its high status, they are very much compatible with the substantially lower status small town board.

ELECTORAL CONTEXT AND OPPOSITION

Our findings so far would lead us to believe that the more "political" the school system, the more probable it is that the superintendent will face meaningful board opposition when it comes to the educational program. If our assumptions are correct, the presence of structured and intense competition should lead to boards which are less intimidated by professional expertise, more influenced by public demands and discontent, and (consequently) more willing to challenge the super-intendent. We consider the same range of categories of electoral variables that we utilized in previous chapters, and group them under the general rubrics of legal constraints and competition structure.

In terms of sheer opposition virtually all of the electoral variables have an impact. The less reformed and the more competitive the district the more likely will opposition arise. One legal constraint violates this pattern. There is virtually no difference ($r = .04$) according to whether the board is appointive or elective. Whatever the conventional wisdom may be about appointive boards being more likely to fall under the sway of the professional bureaucracy, it is disputed by these data.

Ward versus at-large elections and, to a lesser degree, coterminous school district referenda heighten opposition levels (Table 9-4). We see that the same devices which contribute to the politicization of a district — enmeshing it in the aspirations of heterogeneous groups — also make life more difficult for the super-intendent. Any device which links the educational with the broader political system tends to increase conflict within the educational system. One can interpret these findings in accordance with Schattschneider's theories of expanding the arena of conflict to include more competing values. When the educational process remains isolated from a more general conflict of values, the superintendent can look forward to a more compliant board. When board membership is politicized, the superintendent is vulnerable. An expert can be challenged when expertise is not the sole resource.

Additional support for these arguments is provided by the negative correlation between length of term of office and opposition. Anticipating the next chapter, we interpret this finding as suggestive of the cooptation process whereby board members become identified with the school system. They learn something about the day to day problems of the system, become sympathetic with

TABLE 9-4
Correlations between Electoral Structure
and Board Opposition

	Opposition to Superintendent	*Probability of Board Victory*
At-Large/Ward	.31	.15
Coterminous Referenda (no/yes)	.18	-.03
Length of Term (short to long)	-.22	-.11
Partisanship (no/yes)	.39	.11
Electoral Opposition (no/yes)	.37	-.04
Forced Turnover (low to high)	.26	.12
Office Sponsorship (low to high)	-.21	.16

the admittedly difficult problems of administration, and gradually shift their
reliance to the experts. Identification with the administration by those legally
charged with regulation of administration is a classic problem of bureaucracy. As
Gamson states: "They acquire a stake in the organization, having gained some
control over resources. . . . they may come to identify with the collectivity to such a
degree that it will mute and subdue their original loyalty. . . ."[21]

The competition structure (partisanship, office sponsorship, electoral
opposition, and forced turnovers) should have a similar relationship with opposition. The electoral structure should illuminate the dimensions of insulation as they
contribute to the superintendent's relations with his board. From the superintendent's standpoint spirited, open competition probably means potential danger.
To the extent that he embodies the school system's organizational image and
manager, selective entry helps minimize control problems. Organizations which
have little control over whom they admit frequently find it difficult, if not impossible, to maintain a stable decision-making situation.[22]

Our measures of district competition structure indicate how well these
notions of permeability and impermeability are borne out. Without exception the
more competitive activity a district displays, the more likely the board is to
develop opposition to the superintendent. Closure from electoral competition
provides a safe haven for the superintendent.

A distinction should be made between the quasi-legal parameter of
partisanship and the other indicators of competition, which are more in the nature
of informal constraints. It turns out that metropolitanism is also associated with
opposition (.43), as our earlier analysis by urbanism would suggest. Even though
metropolitanism is but weakly associated with partisanship (.12), it is still possible
that the effects of partisanship may be vanquished when metropolitanism is held
constant. With Blau, however, we believe that political institutions have "an
independent influence upon political life in a society."[23] Our evidence lends
support to Blau in that the correlation between partisanship and opposition is
dented but not destroyed by controlling for metropolitanism (.20). The other
competition measures are also maintained under this control. We may conclude
that the competition variables function independently. However, as we have done
previously, we will also explore the question of the mediating role of electoral
factors (below).

These results remind us of the findings in Chapter 4, where it was shown
that involuntary superintendent departures covaried with electoral heat.[24] More
importantly, the fact that competitive districts nurture opposition-prone boards
suggests that board and superintendent do not necessarily huddle together to create
a protective shell against a common foe. Competitive structures help create
conduits between the anxieties of various publics and educational governors.

Office sponsorship, the extent to which boards consciously seek control
over recruitment, is especially intriguing since it bears directly upon Gamson's
ideas of selective entry and control in organizations. Significantly, office sponsorship is more prevalent in the relatively closed political system of small towns and
in suburbs than in central cities, where the relative intensity of conflict apparently

widens the arena enough to make entry control difficult. The inability to control entry results in an incomplete socialization of members, since a major criteria of selection is compatibility with the existing value structure.

Other studies indicate that the main purpose of board self-perpetuation, especially in less urban areas, is the avoidance of abrupt shifts in policy. For instance, Minar concludes:

> *The main task performed by the caucus – indeed, the formal reason for its existence – is the selection of qualified, "acceptable" candidates for school board openings. . . . Most significantly, caucuses ordinarily nominate only one candidate for each vacant board position, and in most caucus communities caucus nominees are not opposed by candidates from the "outside."*[25]

Similarly, McCarty and Ramsey describe the remarkably closed selection process of a small town board:

> *The school board itself urged people to run . . . and they usually did so unopposed . . . Candidates were always suggested by the superintendent . . . in terms of their name, the person's prestige with community, his talent for being down to earth on crucial issues, and his compatibility with the other board members.*[26]

Finally, Vidich and Bensman, in referring to the fact that only members of the dominant elite of Springdale had an effective voice in board selection, write that "the most invisible act of local politics is the process of selecting nominees for school board membership."[27]

In short, it is clear that the reason for entry control and the results of entry control are to avoid conflict, and that the superintendent benefits. However, *he benefits only as long as he is able to anticipate the expectations of the board.* If he encounters opposition, he runs a small risk of losing, as indicated by a .16 correlation between sponsorship and the likelihood of board victory.

As is the case with sponsorship, all of the other electoral variables show an attenuated relationship with the probability of board victory as compared with the occurrence of opposition. Most of these relationships are too weak to be of any significance. It is worth noting, however, that ward-based elections, partisan structures, and degree of forced turnover do have a slight salutary effect on increasing the confidence of the board that it could win in a contest with the superintendent.

THE EFFECT OF COMMUNITY TENSION AND DEMANDS UPON OPPOSITION

So far we have seen that both personal orientations to governance and socio-political parameters play an important role in determining the level and success of board opposition. Now we want to look at the impact of mass public behavior. Boards receive input from the community and can be expected, when the input process becomes intense, to respond. To what extent does this response manifest itself as opposition to the superintendent? The answer is by no means apparent, for it is alternatively possible that community tensions and demands fracture the board into factions, thus encapsulating it and contributing to superintendent domination. We consider first a multiple indicator of overall tension and then a specific indicator of demand for changes in the educational program.

A large number of specific questions asked of our respondents had an intuitive relationship with what we had in mind. Therefore, it was possible to factor analyze these items and determine the extent to which they actually measured aspects of the same phenomenon. One principal dimension emerged which accounted for approximately 36 percent of the common variance. We have called this dimension the tension factor. Of the 13 variables included in the factor analysis, eight were loaded significantly on this factor. These eight and their respective loadings are listed in Appendix B. Factor scores were computed for each board. The range of the tension index (standardized) is from a low of $-.82$ to a high of 2.17.

One extremely noteworthy corollary of tension levels should be mentioned immediately. As described in the next chapter, boards were characterized according to their levels of intraboard cohesion. Not surprisingly, tension levels have a dramatic impact upon board cohesion. Consensual boards are associated with low levels of community tension ($\bar{X}$ tension of $-.49$), pluralistic boards with less tension ($-.01$), and factional boards with high tension ($.48$). Of greater immediate interest is the strong correlation ($.42$) between community tension and opposition. Thus both intraboard behavior and the board-superintendent relationship reflect what is going on at the district's grassroots.

Further, the linkage between community tension and opposition varies with the complexity of the community, although the direction is the same. The linkage appears more immediate in metropolitan districts ($.47$) than in nonmetropolitan districts ($.25$). Perhaps the simple, more unified influence structure of the latter provides their boards and superintendents more insulation from community tension.

Nevertheless the central message of the findings is that discontent and conflict within the constituency do find expression in board opposition regarding the educational program. Under assumptions of responsive governance that is the expected relationship. Two forces might nullify the correctness of the assumption. First, perhaps the educational program as such is not part of the tension configuration. We purposely did not include measures of (perceived) public satisfaction with the educational program in this overall measure. Yet it seems most likely, given the results, that some component of tension does embrace dissatisfaction with the educational program.

A second way in which the relationship might have been nullified is if the board members refuse to pay any heed to signs of tension. For those observers characterizing lay boards as having deaf ears and idle hands, that refusal is a real possibility. But the translation of tension into greater opposition points decidedly toward boards as conduits and translators of public discontent and political activity. In this sense, a classic representative function of democratic governors is being fulfilled.

Tension level has only a weak relationship to the probability of board victory; moreover it is a negative association (−.16). Raising issues does not necessarily lead to board domination of the educational program. On the other hand, there are environments in which the probabilities are enhanced. In metropolitan areas tension lessens the probability of board victory (−.33), but in non-metropolitan areas tension strengthens the hand of the board (.17). Such findings appear compatible with our general assessment of big town and small town educational market places. Anticipating the consensual nature of small town boards, it is not surprising that they serve as an effective counter to the superintendent. The tension in small town districts is less diffuse, more focused, and more immediately translatable into explicit demands. In contrast, metro boards under conditions of tension are more inclined to fragment and produce board factions that reflect the demands of conflicting interest groups.

Public Demands

Kerr has suggested that one reason school boards develop a tendency to evaluate the superintendent's resources higher than they do public support or constituency wishes evolves from the fact that the public is generally uninterested in educational government and ill-informed about the operations of the school system.[28] In such circumstances, there is little incentive for the board to adopt a fiduciary role orientation. This theme is echoed by others. Koerner notes the particular lack of public concern manifested over the educational program:

> *One must regretfully recognize that dissent in suburbia, or elsewhere for that matter, is very rarely over matters relating directly to the quality of education. Apart from recent outbreaks of parental disaffection in racially segregated schools, the layman rarely raises a question in public over standards or the curriculum, over whether social studies should be allowed to swallow up history and geography, over the quality of reading instruction, over whether girls should be compelled to take home economics or boys industrial arts, or over whether to establish a means of regular assessment of the district's schools.[29]*

Such observations led us to hypothesize that the lower the level of public demands in a district, the greater is the tendency for the school board to eschew a fiduciary role orientation in favor of a more professional one. A corollary to this is that low levels of public demands will result in relatively high levels of superintendent dominance. In short, we are construing public demands as a major aspect of the educational climate that characterizes a school district.

We placed board members in the role of observers and asked them to

assess the extent of public demands in their districts: "Have any persons or community groups ever tried to have parts of the educational program changed?"
At the individual level 37 percent of the board members responded affirmatively.
The percent of positive responses for each board was taken as the measure of
public demand articulation. In approximately one-half of the districts, fewer than
one-third of the members could recall any efforts of this sort.

As was the case with community tension, the articulation of demands for
changes in the educational program is directly related to the occurrence of board
opposition to the superintendent ($r = .35$). Here is another strong indication
that public dissatisfaction can be transmitted to and translated by the public's
authorized representatives. Charges that the boards are insensitive to the public
would seem to be refuted. Of course this positive association does not prove that
boards are acting simply in response to public expression. Boards and the public
may both be responding to the same stimulus. Yet the congruency of dispositions
at the very least does not deny the linkage between constituents and their representatives.

Whatever may be the salutary effects of public articulation on board
opposition they clearly do not carry over to successful confrontation with the
superintendent, for there the relationship is on the negative side ($-.27$). As we shall
see momentarily, a likely reason for the counterrelationship lies in the types of
districts in which demands for educational change are voiced.

Recalling that estimates of board victory occur more often in less urban
districts, we examined the extent to which demands vary according to urbanism.
The results are dramatic. Demand articulation is much greater in the cities ($\bar{X}$ of
71) than it is in the suburbs (41) where, in turn, it is greater than in small towns
(21).

In view of this finding, correlations were calculated between the opposition variables and the public demand level within each of the urbanism categories
(Table 9–5). Public demands produce no significant results in small town districts.
This stands to reason in view of the uniformly low levels of board opposition
and public demands in small town districts along with the low probability of the
superintendent overcoming board opposition when it does occur. Moving up
to the suburbs, we find increased levels of opposition that result from more highly
articulated demands. However, there is a correspondingly higher probability that
the board will lose when demands increase. The same pattern is observed in city
districts but in a more exaggerated form.

Thus it appears that our earlier findings about the simple associations
between the type of urban environment and the leadership variables is a function
of the manner in which public demands vary among the types of communities.
In absolute terms, demands are highest in city districts, next highest in the suburbs,
and lowest in small towns. Moreover, the effects of any given level of demand
articulation also differ. Demands are most likely to produce opposition to the
superintendent in city districts, less likely to do so in suburban districts, and have
no apparent effect in the small towns. At the same time, however, a given level

TABLE 9-5
Correlations between Board Opposition and
Public Demands, Controlling for Urbanism

	Opposition to Superintendent	Probability of Board Victory
City	.53	−.57
Suburban	.39	−.23
Small Town	−.04	.13

of demand is most likely to result in the board losing to the superintendent in metropolitan centers, less likely to do so in suburban communities, and unlikely to have that effect in the smaller districts.

The only logical explanation for these anomalous results relates to the complexity of the districts involved. The large city board, which is more politicized than others, reacts to expressions of public dissatisfaction over the educational program by advocating policy changes in order to maintain public political support. It is most likely to oppose the superintendent, who is the person most visibly associated with the existing program. The complexity of the educational system in larger cities, however, makes it virtually impossible for the lay board to master its intricacies. Therefore, despite the board's attempt to change the system, its complexity renders it almost impervious to challenge. The technical resources of the superintendent are required to bring about change. Board opposition notwithstanding, the superintendent's chance of prevailing is great in the complex environment of the city school district.

Suburban boards are less politicized than urban boards. All other things being equal, we would expect them to display less concern for the maintenance of public support. Consequently, the suburban board should be less likely than the urban board to translate public demands directly into opposition to the superintendent, as our data confirm. The suburban school system also differs from its central city counterpart in that it typically serves a smaller, more homogeneous public and is, therefore, less complex. Consequently, the problems and the intricacies of the suburban school system are less difficult to fathom than those of urban systems. In suburban systems knowledge is easier for the board to obtain, and the board is less dependent on the expertise of the superintendent. When the suburban board does advocate change in the educational program contrary to the wishes of the superintendent, it should be more likely to prevail than the city board. The data support this view. Even though the suburban board is still more likely to predict defeat than victory, the suburban educational-political market is not as strongly biased in favor of the superintendent as the city district is.

Finally, the small town board's observed lack of opposition even when segments of the public may demand change, may be a result of the fact that the elites are so secure in their positions and so confident in the merits of the traditional educational program that they feel no pressure to advocate policy change. Given the value consensus that is characteristic of the small town, one suspects that members of the public who express dissatisfaction with the educational program are a small minority who are perceived by the board and the community as cranks or troublemakers. Hence, their demands tend to be disregarded by the school board. The firmly established feeling of power of the small town school board is, however, again demonstrated by the positive association between public demands and the probability of board victory in the event that the board should oppose him. When the board responds to public requests for educational change, the technical resources of the superintendent are of much less value in small towns than in complex districts. Additionally, the relatively uncomplicated nature of the small district makes the board less dependent on expert advice than either suburban or city school boards.

THE MEDIATING EFFECTS OF ELECTORAL STRUCTURES

In Chapters 5 and 6 we emphasized that electoral constraints mediate between environmental complexity and board-community linkages. We observed that certain structures amplified the linkages while others depressed them. Now we are interested in whether the same electoral factors cause variations in the previously established relation between tension and opposition. The first problem is that tension is associated with various electoral constraints, as well as with opposition. Nevertheless, the correlations between electoral factors and opposition are weakened but hardly vanquished when they are entered into a regression analysis including public tension.

By holding electoral factors physically constant and allowing the tension-opposition relationship to vary, we can see to what extent electoral constraints have a mediating role. Table 9–6 leads one to suspect that the educational reformers were employed by superintendents to devise ways to maximize their power! The consequences of reform strengthen the hand of the superintendent, while muting the voices of those in the community protesting the directions of educational policy. Judged by these results if schools are to respond to the demands of constituents promptly, then much of what was done in the name of reform needs to be undone.

Among the legal constraints the presence of ward-based elections, coterminous referenda, and shorter terms all exaggerate the correlations between tension and the occurrence of opposition. At the same time they reduce the basic negative relationship between tension and probable board victory. Clearly, the legal parameters within which educational governance transpires are important conditioners of political translation. This interpretation takes on added weight in view of the fact that the legal parameters vary scarcely at all according to urbanism or metropolitanism, our other major structural variables.

In part the pattern according to the competition structure resembles that

TABLE 9-6
Relationship between Public Tension and
Board Opposition, by Electoral Factors

	Opposition to Superintendent	*Probability of Board Victory*
All Boards	.42	−.16
Election Area		
Wards	.49	−.12
At-Large	.40	−.19
Coterminous Referenda		
Yes	.51	−.11
No	.26	−.18
Length of Term		
2–3	.61	−.09
4	.42	−.12
5–6	.28	−.21
Electoral Opposition		
Yes	.50	−.07
No	.34	−.26
Forced Turnover		
Hi	.46	−.02
Low	.17	−.12
Sponsorship		
Low	.27	−.19
Hi	.35	.09
Partisanship		
No	.46	.07
Yes	.39	−.33

for the legal structure. The more heated and recurrent the competition for school board seats, the greater is the association between tension and expressed opposition to the superintendent over the educational program. Similarly, even though boards are still unlikely to prevail in a conflict with him, the probability of loss is at least reduced somewhat. Especially impressive are the consequences of the two "hardest" indicators of quantitative competition, namely, the presence of electoral opposition in the preceding election and the rate of forced turnover over the past several elections. New blood and electoral challenge stir up the governing process, and two of the most immediate signs of this emerge in the board taking a closer look at the educational program as designed by the superintendent's office and in modestly elevating the board's sense of confidence about confronting him.

Office sponsorship and the presence of partisan (and slate) elections have a different bearing on the tension-opposition nexus. With respect to opposition, per se, the level of sponsorship and the presence of partisanship make for little difference, although what difference there is runs contrary to our expectations and the flow of the other findings. The results are more confounding in the domain of expected board victory. High sponsorship increases, if ever so modestly, the likelihood of board victory. This result suggests that sponsorship may occasionally heighten the board's sense of unity and responsiveness to community pressures. The fact that the tension-victory probability relationship is actually lower in nonpartisan than partisan districts is anomalous given the other results and the known corollaries of partisanship school districts.

A central dimension guiding our analysis in this chapter has been the balance between authorized representatives of the public and the expertise of the professional administrators. Our concern is not that boards should obstruct simply for the sake of being obstreperous or creating diversions; rather, our concern is that the balance between the decision rules of commonweal organizations and the decision rules of service organizations will be weighted inappropriately toward the superintendency. The properly functioning board is one with respect for professional expertise. We do not suggest that the expert knowledge possessed by superintendents be discounted. We are not suggesting a revolution against expertise, but rather a return of educational governance to the principles of responsive government.

Our quest for responsive government — defined in this context as opposition to the superintendent — leads us once again down the path of the traditional political process. As we have mentioned so often, the injection of a healthy dose of politics proves benevolent. Not surprisingly, intensity of opposition to the superintendent is greatest in the politically heated environment of large urban centers. Here, community tension and the subsequent articulation of demands virtually propels a school board to reflect some of the antagonism of the political community. Similarly, those districts which have remained unreformed, for example, those with ward rather than at-large elections, are able to produce boards that are not totally committed to the goals of the superintendent. In general, the more union between the political and educational arenas, the more viable the opposition to the superintendent. Political institutions also enhance the process of linkage between community tension and board behavior — a crucial link between the rulers and the ruled.

The most ironic link in the chain of responsiveness between the community and the ultimate policy of the governance is found in the widely varied behavior of small towns and large city boards. Small towns, without the high level of tension normally associated with metropolitan areas, nevertheless produce boards with a taste for combat if necessary. The very factors leading to board opposition in large cities — the factors associated with the normal political process — are generally absent in small towns. Yet when tension does appear, the hand of the board is strengthened. Tension in large cities strengthens the hand of the superintendent. As a city system fights, and as the warring factions find their representation on the board, the superintendent is able to assert his authority to govern with more vigor.

In small towns, community tension has a more unidirectional mode and hence produces a more united board. It is a rarer, but more lethal, phenomenon.

NOTES

1. H. Thomas James, "School Board Conflict Is Inevitable," *The American School Board Journal*, 154 (March, 1967), pp. 5–9.

2. Raymond E. Callahan, "The History of the Fight to Control Policy in Public Education," *Struggle for Power in Education*, ed. Frank W. Lutz and Joseph J. Assarelli (New York: The Center for Applied Research in Education, 1966), pp. 16–34.

3. James, *loc. cit.*

4. Colen Hines, "The Development of the Superintendency in the Eugene, Oregon Public Schools, 1891–1941" (Ph.D. dissertation, University of Oregon, 1950).

5. David Minar, *Educational Decision-Making in Suburban Communities*, U.S. Office of Education Cooperative Research Project No. 2440 (Evanston, Ill.: Northwestern University, 1966).

6. Robert L. Crain, *The Politics of School Desegregation* (Chicago: Aldine, 1968).

7. E. E. Schattschneider, *The Semisovereign People: A Realist's View of Democracy in America* (New York: Holt, Rinehart and Winston, 1960); and Peter Bachrach and Morton Baratz, "The Two Faces of Power," *American Political Science Review*, 57 (December, 1962), pp. 947–52.

8. Neal Gross, Ward S. Mason, and Alexander W. McEachern, *Explorations in Role Analysis: Studies of the School Superintendency Role* (New York: Wiley, 1958), p. 233.

9. Archie R. Dykes, *School Board and Superintendent: Their Effective Working Relationships* (Danville, Ill.: Interstate Printers and Publishers, 1968), p. 11.

10. Gross, *et al.*, pp. 228–230.

11. Kenneth Prewitt and Heinz Eulau, "Political Representation: Prolegomenon to a New Departure from an Old Problem," *American Political Science Review*, 43 (June, 1969), p. 431.

12. An exception to this rule is found in the south, where school districts tend to be countywide.

13. Laurence Iannaccone and Frank W. Lutz, *Politics, Power and Policy: The Governing of Local School Districts* (Columbus, Ohio: Charles E. Merrill, 1970), p. 67.

14. Arthur J. Vidich and Joseph Bensman, *Small Town in Mass Society: Class, Power, and Religion in a Rural Community* (Princeton, N.J.: Princeton University Press, 1958); see also Robert R. Alford, "School District Reorganization and Community Integration," *Harvard Educational Review*, 30 (Fall, 1960), pp. 350–71.

15. Vidich and Bensman, *op. cit.*, p. 174.

16. *Ibid.*, pp. 175, 220.

17. Charles E. Bidwell, "The School as a Formal Organization," *Handbook of Organizations*, ed. James G. March (Chicago: Rand McNally, 1965), p. 1010.

18. It has been pointed out that these characteristics are not necessarily unique to small towns. They may be found in other demographic environments as well; however, in the interest of simplifying the present discussion we shall contend only that they summarize the modal rural or small town educational environment. See Ralph B. Kimbrough, *Political Power and Educational Decision Making* (Chicago: Rand McNally, 1964); and Iannaccone and Lutz, *op. cit.*

19. In this regard, Iannaccone and Lutz's discussion of the "sacred community" is most informative. Iannaccone and Lutz, *op. cit.*, pp. 29–68.

20. Schattschneider, *loc. cit.*

21. William Gamson, *Power and Discontent* (Homewood, Ill.: Dorsey Press, 1968), pp. 135–6.

22. *Ibid.*, pp. 112–120.

23. Peter Blau, *Exchange and Power in Social Life* (New York: Wiley, 1964), p. 243.

24. See also Iannaccone and Lutz, *op. cit.*, pp. 86–88.

25. David Minar, "The Community Basis of Conflict in School System Politics," *American Sociological Review*, 21 (December, 1966), p. 825.

26. Donald J. McCarty and Charles E. Ramsey, *The School Managers* (Westport, Conn.: Greenwood, 1971), pp. 173–4.

27. Vidich and Bensman, *op. cit.*, p. 180.

28. Norman D. Kerr, "The School Board as an Agency of Legitimation," *Sociology of Education*, 38 (Fall, 1964), pp. 53–55.

29. James D. Koerner, *Who Controls American Education? A Guide for Laymen* (Boston: Beacon Press, 1968), p. 151.

Chapter 10

The Internal

Context of Opposition

Our discussion shifts now to a fundamentally different class of explanatory variables, while our attention remains riveted upon the same dependent variables of board-superintendent exchange. In this chapter we take up three classes of variables. First, we consider the behavior of boards of varying status, remembering the over representation of upper SES groups. Does variation in status produce accompanying variation in board-superintendent competition?

The second class of variables deals with efforts by the superintendent to influence, if not control, the board. He can lobby the board bluntly or gently; he can present information persuasively or neutrally; he can become a community politician and try to build coalitions. Should he be an active mobilizer, or should he rely solely upon his status as expert?

Finally, we link the internal decision style of boards (whether they are consensual, have "floating" coalitions, or stable factions) with their strength vis-à-vis the superintendent. What unites these three classes of variables is that they pertain to properties inherent to board members and superintendents, rather than to the community.

SOCIOECONOMIC STATUS

There is disagreement among authorities about the relationship between school board status and decision-making behavior. Gross, for instance, noted that it did not matter whether a board was "made up of bus drivers and electricians or of lawyers and business executives. Both kinds of boards are just as likely to adhere to professional standards for school board behavior."[1] Of the three status indicators — occupation, income, and education — only the latter, he found, was related to the professionalism of the board. Bowman's study of Illinois school boards, on the other hand, found that both educational and occupational status were related to the degree of decision-making latitude that boards are willing to grant their superintendent. Better educated and higher status boards displayed a tendency toward permissiveness, whereas the opposite was true of lower status and more poorly educated boards.[2]

It is possible that the educational environments in Illinois and Massachusetts are so dissimilar that status has a decidedly different impact on board behavior in each of the two states. Perhaps the different measurement techniques used by Bowman and Gross created indicators which themselves were not comparable.

Social status deserves more thorough analysis. We documented in Chapter 2 the middle and upper class bias in board recruitment, making no inference that board behavior is inextricably linked with status. However, we have argued that a major consequence of the reform movement was to place board position beyond the grasp of the lower classes and into the hands of the classes with the greatest sympathy for the professional role of the superintendent. Upper and middle class people should understand, due to their own occupational experience, the necessity for "sound management."

We developed board-level indicators for occupational status, educational attainment, and income for our school boards and examined their interrelatedness. Then we analyzed the effects of each on school board behavior in establishing local educational markets. For occupational status the head of household's occupation was used. Each occupation was transformed into a decile rank score according to the Duncan Socioeconomic Index.[3] Board means were computed by averaging these individual scores. Board education level was computed by calculating the mean score of the individual board members. Each respondent was coded 1 for a high school education or less, 2 for undergraduate college education, and 3 for postbaccalaureate work. Slightly over 60 percent of the boards sampled attained values greater than 2.0. Income refers to the mean family income of the board members in each district.[4] With a mean average income in excess of $19,000 it is obvious that American school boards do not include many financially impoverished members. Even our poorer boards are among the economic elites of relatively poor districts.

These variables are too weakly associated to permit us to conclude that they are equivalent indicators of status; yet intuition tells us that the concept we call status must be related to all three. Therefore, we subjected them to a factor analytic procedure which yielded a principal factor solution. Eighty percent of the common variance was accounted for in the initial factor, which we call general status.[5] In the remainder of this analysis, when we speak of socioeconomic status without qualification, it will be the general status score to which we are referring for our empirical indicator. However, we shall also inspect each of the three specific components of status more closely.

Turning now to questions relating to status and board behavior, we examine the associations between each of the status variables and variables that pertain to the board-superintendent relationship. Table 10-1 presents the relevant correlations with which we are concerned.

Contrary to our expectations after reviewing the findings of both Gross and Bowman, none of the status indicators is related to a professional role orientation. Our initial reaction was to suspect that partial correlation coefficients for each of the three original variables, controlling simultaneously for the influence of the other two, would produce more discrimination. Again, however, no significant results emerged. In short, we are forced to conclude that general board status, occupational status, education, and income are all unrelated to the professionalism of the board's role orientation. Whatever relationship status may have to superintendent leadership, then, must be independent of role orientation.

TABLE 10-1
Association between Status Variables and
Board-Superintendent Relationships

	Profes-sional Role Orienta-tion	*Opposition to Super-intendent*	*Probability of Board Victory*	*Importance of Super-vising Super-intendent*	*Board Devotes Time to Educational Program*
Occupational Status	−.08	.18	−.38	−.28	.20
Income	−.01	.13	−.12	−.20	.26
Education	−.08	.21	−.28	−.44	.24
General Status	−.06	.20	−.30	−.33	.26

The first component of board assertion, opposition to the superintendent over the educational program, yielded consistently significant though modest positive correlations. Thus higher status breeds more opposition. However, all status-related variables, with the exception of income, also produced moderate but negative results when laid against the probability that the board would win in the event that it came into conflict with the superintendent over the educational program. Regardless of the particular indicator of status used, the higher the mean status of the board the greater is the likelihood that the superintendent will dominate in the face of board opposition. Direct relationship between board status and board influence is indicated. Higher status boards, although they do not always expect victory, exert more opposition to the superintendent over the educational program than do their lower status counterparts, even though the latter are less likely to see the superintendent as the eventual victor.

It has been suggested that one characteristic of low status boards is their

failure to distinguish between public policy and administrative detail. After
observing that less well-educated and lower status boards "are expected to be
'harder' for the superintendent to 'work with,' [and] more inclined to participate
in the handling of administrative detail," Minar contends that:

> *The differences in decision-making we would suppose to derive from
> differences in conditioning to, understanding of, and outlook on expertise
> and the division of labor [are] differences rooted in the experience of
> status groups. Thus the better-educated and those in professional and
> managerial occupations are those who respect and understand specializa-
> tion and delegation, those who see it in their own life routines.*[6]

According to this view, lower status boards tend to define their relationship with the superintendent as an employer to an employee. They should, therefore, attach greater importance to the function of supervising the superintendent
than should higher status boards. In order to test this proposition board members
were asked how important they felt it was for the board to supervise the superintendent and his staff. Board level scores were then assigned by calculating the
percent of the members on each board who believed this to be an important
function. The resulting correlations between this variable and our status indicators
were all significant and in the predicted direction. Of the three raw status indicators,
education emerged as the most strongly associated with the supervisory function.

Similarly, we were led to expect lower status boards to devote relatively
more time to routine, internal issues at the expense of the educational program.
This expectation follows directly from Minar's contention that low status boards
are less likely to be versed in the managerial practices of delegating responsibility
over routine matters. One of the questions administered to school board respondents
asked them to estimate the time they spend on the educational program as a percent of the total time they devoted to school-related matters. Each board was
assigned a score equivalent to the mean estimate of all individual members. Again
our expectations were confirmed. As indicated in Table 10-1, each status variable
is positively related to the proportion of time devoted to the educational program.
This finding, in conjunction with the preceding one, results in a picture of lower
status school boards being overly concerned with administrative detail, failing
to delegate authority over routine matters to the superintendents, and defaulting
on their responsibility to oversee the general educational program.

In a final probe of the relationship between status and superintendent
leadership we computed partial correlation coefficients between the status indicators and the two components of board opposition while controlling for the relative
amount of time devoted to the educational program. Our reasoning was that the
failure of low status boards to come into conflict with the superintendent over the
educational program might be an artifact of their devoting less time to that issue
area in the first place. By controlling, our aim was to remove any confounding
influence which would mask the basic relationship between status and leadership.
The controlling procedure caused all correlations to increase infinitesimally.

Consequently, we conclude that the amount of attention school boards give to the educational program does not mask the relationship between board status and opposition proclivities.

Our analysis has shown that occupational status, education, and income are neither equivalent indicators of a single attribute nor equivalent predictors of school board behavior. Of the three, income is consistently the poorest predictor. Occupational status and education are roughly comparable in their effects. When they diverged by more than a few hundredths of a point, however, one is as likely as the other to produce the higher correlation. The general status factor score which is, in a sense, a weighted average of the three individual indicators, produced associations not consistently stronger than the strongest of the single indicators.

No clear association was found between any of the status indicators and the fiduciary versus professional board role orientation, although the data indicate that lower status boards tend to view their district superintendent as an *employee* rather than as a *professional*. Lower status boards place relatively high importance on supervising the routine administrative work in the school district while paying concomitantly less attention to the educational program. In terms of the economic analogy previously introduced, the lower status boards' emphasis on administration and supervision is indicative of a market in which the superintendent's resource of professional expertise carries relatively little weight. We were led to conclude that superintendent leadership over educational policy is directly related to the status of the school board.

This proposition was only partially borne out empirically, however. Superintendents confronted with low status school boards encounter less overt board opposition than their counterparts who must deal with higher status boards. But due to the fact that their boards do not respect their professional resources, superintendents are less likely to win any contest that does develop. Hence, the analyst as well as the superintendent is left with a paradoxical situation. The higher the board status, the greater is the weight attached to the superintendent's resources, and the more cognizant is the board of its responsibilities in the area of public educational policy. Under such conditions the superintendent is expected to prevail over the board when the two conflict over the educational program. Lower status boards, which spell trouble for the superintendent, are relatively scarce. Higher status boards lack the tenacity of lower status boards, and they are less successful as antagonists. While higher status boards, themselves possessors of expertise, are more likely to assert the decision-making authority of the board, they are also more easily overcome.

EFFORTS BY THE SUPERINTENDENT TO INFLUENCE THE BOARD: COOPTATION AND PERSUASION

Superintendents, of course, are not necessarily passive, blandly and meekly following the lead of the board. They can, and often do, intervene directly into board affairs, hoping to coopt the board into their own sphere of influence.

Cooptation, as Selznick observed, may take one of two forms, or it may combine aspects of both.[7] *Formal cooptation* involves the inclusion of representatives of previously unrepresented sectors of a constituency among the office holders of a government or an organization. Frequently, a ruling elite will resort to this tactic in order to mollify a disaffected portion of its clientele and to reestablish elite legitimacy. This sharing of power is usually more symbolic than substantive.

Informal cooptation, on the other hand, involves the de facto sharing of power. Selznick writes:

> *Cooptation may be, however, a response to the pressure of specific centers of power within the community . . . Legitimacy and confidence [in formal authorities] may be well established with relation to the general public, yet organized forces which are able to threaten the formal authority may effectively shape its structure and policy.*[8]

He goes on to observe how informal cooptation, because it involves the sharing of decision-making power with "unauthorized" actors, frequently occurs below the level of public visibility.

> *If adjustment to specific nucleuses of power become public, then the legitimacy of the formal authority, as representative of a theoretically undifferentiated community (the people as a whole), may be undermined. It therefore becomes useful and often essential for such cooptation to remain in the shadowland of informal interaction.*[9]

As reflection will indicate, these two types of cooptation are decidedly dissimilar. In addition to the fact that they vary with respect to the visibility of actual decision makers and with regard to the distribution of de facto decision-making power among officials, the flow of influence which produces informal cooptation is the reverse of that which results in formal cooptation. In formal cooptation the formal authoritative actor manipulates the unofficial actor in order to neutralize dissent or challenges to its legitimacy. The flow of influence is from the authoritative actor to the nonauthority. Informal cooptation, however, involves the manipulation of formal authorities by nonauthoritative actors. Hence, the direction of influence is from the unofficial sphere to the authoritative sphere.

We deal with informal cooptation in the present chapter, for we are interested in examining the prevalence and the effects of attempts by the superintendent to informally coopt the school board. If such attempts are made and if they are successful, they should result in the board's sharing its formal policy-making power with the superintendent.

Kerr contends that even independent, reform-oriented individuals are often subjected to cooptation tactics during the course of their early socialization to the board with the result that their potential threats to the educational status quo never achieve realization. He emphasizes the fact that "the school board's attitudes often originate in the socialization process, rather than in a uniform predisposition on the part of candidates regarding the professional prerogatives of the superintendent."[10] There are two kinds of informal cooptation that we assume are prevalent in the superintendent-school board exchange, persuasive cooptation and political cooptation.

Cooptation by Persuasion

The superintendent who desires a stronger voice in public policy decisions need not merely wait for the board to recognize its need for his expertise. There are tactics of persuasion that he may use to foster such recognition, for persuasion, in Gamson's words, "involves some change in the minds of the authorities without adding anything new to their situation. It involves making them prefer the same outcomes that the influencer prefers."[11] In the present context, of course, the influencer is the superintendent and his preferred outcome is an educational-political market in which his technical resources are highly valued. The school board must perceive its need for technical knowledge and expertise if informal cooptation is to be possible. Furthermore, the board must believe that it is incapable of developing such resources internally or it must be unwilling to do so. We may conclude that the school board that recognizes a need for the voice of the expert in its policy-making activities, that feels incapable to provide such expertise, and that acknowledges its superintendent's technical competence provides a fertile setting for informal cooptation that may lead to superintendent leadership. The superintendent can engage in two tactics of persuasion that will encourage such recognition by the school board: gatekeeping and propaganda.

Gatekeeping is the exercise of control over the information received by the board. A superintendent who occupies a gatekeeping position with respect to the flow of information to the board is ideally situated to select only what he wants the board to hear.[12] Most observers acknowledge that many, if not all, superintendents occupy a strategic gatekeeping position, particularly where technical information is concerned.[13]

But information control is not the only feature of the superintendent's strategic position that permits him to influence the conduct of educational policy making. To the extent that he can control the selection of issues and the definition of alternatives he may cause the board to perceive that issues are more internal to the educational system and require more technical expertise than it otherwise would. Consequently, the superintendent who controls issue definition indirectly controls the type of educational-political market within which policies are decided. As Schattschneider once observed, "The definition of the alternatives is the supreme instrument of power."[14] In general, the more securely the superintendent is established as a gatekeeper for the board — either through information control, agenda control, or both — the more likely it is that he will be able to persuade the board to value his technical resources highly in the determination of public educational policy.[15]

A second technique which may lead to informal cooptation is somewhat less subtle but no less effective than gatekeeping: the direct propagandizing of the school board. This technique may occur as a low key "indoctrination" of new board members to the educational system by the superintendent or by professionally socialized incumbent board members. To avoid conflict, administrators are urged by their colleagues to assume responsibility for proper orientation:

> *The superintendent and carryover board members all have a responsibility to educate new board members on their duties. The board chairman in particular should aid in orienting new members. State Departments of Education and state school board associations should also sponsor orientation programs.* [16]

While the specific contents of such socialization efforts vary, there are some uniform themes. The superintendent is portrayed as the expert whose judgment should be regarded as valid. He is the *one* person with a clear understanding of the total school program. School board members are also given the unappealing choice of supporting the superintendent or firing him. The more moderate course, one of supervision, is discouraged on the grounds that such a course allows boards to "fall into the trap of becoming involved in administration. . . ."[17]

We shall accept as a working hypothesis that superintendents who indoctrinate newly selected members and who interact frequently with their boards have more opportunity to coopt the school board through propaganda than those who remain more aloof. Consequently, we expect superintendent leadership to vary directly with the frequency of interaction and with the practice of indoctrination.

Gatekeeping

We found that the first of our gatekeeping indicators, agenda-setting, was heavily dominated by superintendent participation. In all but a handful of districts the superintendents participated in determining the school boards' agendas. Further, and of greater significance, in 70 percent of the districts the superintendent had the *primary* responsibility for setting the agenda; in two-thirds of the districts the superintendent was *solely* responsible for agenda-setting. These findings demonstrate that superintendents occupy powerful gatekeeping positions with respect to the definition of issues, and that they have the potential power to exert persuasive influences on the boards to define prosuperintendent educational political markets.

The second indicator pertains to superintendent control over the educational information the board receives. Board members were asked to name their four most important sources of "educational information of a technical or professional nature." The mean value of the individual scores equivalent to the proportion of all responses which included the superintendent or other members of the school administration was then computed for each school board. We found that the median proportion was 30 percent; that is, in half of the districts the mean value for superintendent information-giving was over 30 percent. The superintendent's potential influence is less prevalent in this area than it is in that of agenda setting, but it is clear that the educational information which passes through his hands on the way to the board constitutes a sizable proportion of the material which the board receives.

Although the logic of this argument would lead us to a contrary suspicion, we found no significant correlations between the extent of information control and any of the superintendent leadership variables.[18] Similarly, the overall correlation between information control and board role orientation was negligible ($r = -.02$). We did discover that higher status boards rely more strongly on the superintendent for educational information than do the lower status boards ($r = .17$). This finding is consistent with the view that higher status boards, by virtue of the habits they acquire in the course of their occupational and educational socialization, are more accustomed to relying upon specialists for information.

Recalling our previous findings concerning the differential effects of predictor variables within each of the three types of urban environments, we determined whether gatekeeping by the superintendent also operated differently according to urbanism. Table 10-2 contains correlation coefficients between superintendent gatekeeping power and indicators of superintendent leadership. In city districts, the effects of superintendent information control are in the same direction as for the whole sample, but show greater magnitude. Urban superintendents who serve as informational gatekeepers encounter more board opposition but have a better chance of overcoming it. The relationships in the suburbs are not only decreased but also their signs are reversed. Informational gatekeeping tends to reduce opposition to the superintendent while decreasing his chances of overcoming any opposition that does develop. Gatekeeping in small towns has the same directional effect as in the suburbs, but the correlations are so small that they are virtually meaningless.

TABLE 10-2
Correlations between Board Dependence on the Superintendent for
Educational Information and Board Opposition, by Urbanism

	Opposition to Superintendent	Probability of Board Victory
City	.23	−.18
Suburban	−.18	.10
Small Town	−.07	.07

What we may conclude from this analysis is that informational gate-keeping has only a modest effect on the leadership patterns that emerge in local school districts. What effects it does have differ according to the demographic characteristics of the community in which it is practiced, with the main impact in the city districts. It is in these heterogeneous and complex districts with infinitely more bewildering problems to solve that information control is more likely to lead to opposition while simultaneously helping contribute to a superintendent's victory over a recalcitrant board.

Propaganda

Each superintendent was asked to estimate the number of hours per week he spends "with school board members either in person or on the phone." The median number of hours per week is less than four. In one-third of the districts the superintendent spends more than five hours per week with board members. We also asked each superintendent: "In many districts the school superintendent meets individually with newly selected board members and introduces them to the workings of the school system and their responsibilities. Do you follow this practice?" This form of socialization was practiced in 80 percent of the districts.

Table 10-3 contains the overall correlation coefficients between the two propaganda-related indicators and the leadership variables. The direction of the associations is generally contrary to what one might expect. The most surprising aspect of the table is the strong association between rate of interaction and level of opposition; the more frequent the interaction, the *greater* the opposition. Socialization efforts, in contrast, have but a minor effect in the reduction of opposition. It would appear that superintendents who bear down hard on boards are engaging in self-defeating activity. In the board-superintendent exchange, as in other forms of human interaction, the heavy-handed approach is not an efficient persuasion technique.

TABLE 10-3
Correlations between Superintendent Communication
and Board Opposition

	Opposition to Superintendent	Probability of Board Victory
Hours Per Week Supt. Interacts With Board	.33	−.12
Supt. Socializes New Board Members	−.12	.02

The fascinating aspect of the interaction-opposition link is that inter-action does *not* produce a "normal" response, since it is apparently greeted with resistance. Interaction theory, as developed by social psychologists such as Homans,[19] would not have predicted such an outcome. Stated in its simplest terms, interaction theory tells us that if persons like each other they will interact; if they dislike each other they will cease the interaction.[20] Interaction is predicted by sentiment which, in turn, is a function of attitude *similarity*. In sum, those people who have similar values tend to like one another and to interact on the basis of this generalized positive sentiment.[21]

Why is this not true of the board-superintendent exchange? Partly, of course, it is because board-superintendent interaction occurs in a structured, nonvoluntary setting. Certain minimal levels of interaction are unavoidable. Going beyond that explanation, however, we may speculate that the opposition contrib-utes to the interaction, rather than the reverse. When conflict erupts, the superin-tendent tries to put out the fires. However, he does not succeed very handsomely: the correlation between interaction and probable board victory is low, albeit in the right direction.

The *level* of interaction, irrespective of its consequences, is substantially higher in urban and suburban districts than it is in small towns. Urban and suburban superintendents spend about seven and six hours per week, respectively, in com-munication with their boards compared to three and one-half hours per week in small towns. Socialization efforts are also somewhat higher, with 89 percent of the urban superintendents, 80 percent of the suburban superintendents, but only 69 percent of the small town superintendents making the effort.

The less intense nature of board-superintendent interaction in small towns would lead us to wonder if its adverse effects are less apparent in these districts. Or perhaps small town superintendents eschew such tactics because they have been proven unsuccessful. As Table 10-4 indicates, the adverse effects of frequent interactions are somewhat less pronounced in small towns, even though interaction is still associated with increased opposition. In small towns and suburbs superin-tendent interaction neither enhances nor detracts from the probability of board success. In urban areas, the interaction of the superintendent actually *decreases* the chances of victory at the same time that it raises the probability that a con-frontation will occur. With this exception, the costs of interaction exceed the benefits — from the superintendent's view.

The effects of meeting with new board members to explain how the system works have equally mixed benefits. Turning first to the question of board opposi-tion, we find indoctrination is associated with the lack of opposition in two of the three types of districts. Since a temporal sequence of socialization and opposition is implicit in the nature of the data, we can conclude that socialization depresses board opposition in cities and small towns. Additionally, there is a modest tendency for early socialization to decrease the probability that the board will prevail when opposition does occur in small town districts. Hence, although (or perhaps because)

TABLE 10–4
Correlations between Superintendent Communication
and Board Opposition, by Urbanism

	Opposition to Superintendent	*Probability of Board Victory*
Hours Per Week Superintendent Interacts with Board		
Urban	.31	−.20
Suburban	.33	.02
Small Town	.15	.04
Superintendent Socializes New Board Members		
Urban	−.31	.48
Suburban	.04	.38
Small Town	−.26	−.16

they practice it less, small town superintendents who socialize new board members stand a reasonable chance of winning. In small towns, then, the technique "works"; it both reduces opposition and the probability of board victory. Clearly it is not eschewed because of failure.

The same cannot be said of urban and suburban districts, however. In both of these environments, early socialization is significantly associated with an increased probability that the board will be able to prevail. This result is somewhat offset in large cities by the aforementioned tendency for socialized boards to engage in opposition less frequently. But in the suburbs no such effect on opposition is discernible.

These findings suggest that the complexity of the large urban district is such that the tactic of early socialization tends to forestall school board opposition to the superintendent regarding the educational program. However, in the event that socialization does not produce the desired effect and the board opposes the superintendent in spite of such efforts on his part, the board will probably prevail. Cooptation attempts in such instances are decidedly dysfunctional from the superintendent's standpoint.

Cooptation attempts are even more dysfunctional for the suburban superintendent, for he is unable even to avert opposition by employing them. Possibly the regard for quality schools that authorities typically attribute to suburban environments is sufficiently strong to cause the board to develop its ideas about the optimum educational program independently. In small towns, by contrast, the board may be unsophisticated enough to "allow" socialization to have its desired effect.

Political Cooptation: Building Support in the Community

Contrary to persuasive cooptation, building political support does not involve the direct manipulation of the board by the superintendent. Indeed, the actions of the superintendent which make building political support possible need not involve the board at all. He needs only to accumulate sufficient political resources within the district to counteract or supplement those commanded by the board.

In assessing the amount and type of support building engaged in by superintendents we first asked them, "Do you involve yourself in the creation of public support for the schools?" Given the central role of the superintendent in the school system's life, it is not surprising that every superintendent answered this question positively. Of more interest are the types of activities pursued. Very roughly these activities can be divided into those which are public, overt efforts — such as public addresses, statements to the press, and the like — and those which are more private and covert — such as talking to local influentials, trying to involve specific groups, and gaining a place in important local organizations. We are especially concerned with the latter type. Twenty-nine percent of the superintendents indicated that they engaged in private support seeking. The question for us is whether the presence of such activity strengthens or weakens the board's hand vis-à-vis the superintendent. Does his activity undercut the board's opposition potential?

Private solicitation of support has a modest dampening effect on board opposition (−.20). However, soliciation has only a trivial impact on the likelihood of board victory, and that effect is actually positive (.07). On balance, covert support building is of minor significance in board-superintendent confrontation.

Unlike our findings concerning propaganda efforts, the prevalence of seeking private support in the various urban environments hardly differs. Thirty-one percent of the city superintendents, 29 percent of those in the suburbs, and 28 percent of those in small towns report that they seek private support. But here the similarity ends, for once again we discovered unique patterns of association in each of the three environments.

The urban school district seems to be the most conducive to achieving the potential of political support (Table 10–5). There superintendent interaction with influential leaders of the community discourages the board from opposing the superintendent, perhaps because he is known to have the backing of powerful supporters. But such resources are not sufficient to help him overcome any opposition that should develop. Apparently, the urban school board is sensitive to the superintendent's political power to the extent that it issues fewer challenges as his private political support increases. But when it does challenge his views on the educational program, the board is confident that it has a fighting chance to win. The net result is that the urban superintendent who privately cultivates sources of political support staves off opposition but incurs a small risk of eventual loss.

This is not the case in suburban school districts. Whereas support-seeking

TABLE 10–5
Support Seeking by Superintendent
and Board Opposition, by Urbanism

	Opposition to Superintendent	*Probability of Board Victory*
Urban	−.42	.14
Suburban	−.32	.45
Small Town	.06	−.15

continues to be associated with a lack of board opposition, it also is related to a high probability of board victory. These relationships are in the same direction as those we observed in urban districts. Their principal difference lies in the much stronger likelihood that the superintendent will overcome whatever board opposition that may develop.

Pursuing this line of reasoning, let us assume that urban and suburban school boards are equally sensitive to whatever political resources the superintendent may develop. Let us further assume that private support-seeking enhances his political resources. We would then expect to find that superintendents who engage in such activity would encounter less resistance from their boards. But as we noted earlier with regard to the urban board, when boards which have support-seeking superintendents decide to challenge them, they do so with their eyes open and with the knowledge that they have a good chance of success. In other words, the calculation of relative *political* power is a task at which the urban board is proficient. When the superintendent initiates a political contest between himself and the board, he must be reasonably sure that he has sufficient political resources to outweigh the board's resources. If he does, board opposition is unlikely to result. If he does not and his views do not correspond to those of the school board, the board will probably win the "pure" political contest.

In the suburban districts, seeking political support, while minimizing opposition, maximizes the probability of a board riding over the superintendent should opposition develop. Perhaps this serious danger to the superintendent is a consequence of the costs he incurs in the use of his resources. Seeking political support is tantamount to renouncing his role as a neutral expert — to abandoning the sacred separation of education and politics. In the rough and terrible urban world, this tactic is not so damaging. However, in the more gentle world of suburban life, the sacrifice of neutral expertise can prove very nonproductive for the superintendent. Could it be that the suburbs contain the purest legacy of the reform movement?

Finally, the effects of support-seeking activity by the superintendents in small town districts are rather modest. To the extent that support-seeking has any discernible effect, it is one of *decreasing* the board's chance of victory. It is associated with neither increased nor decreased actual levels of opposition. If the small town is typified by a relatively simpler, concentrated influence structure, then it appears that the superintendent who seeks and gains the support of the "elders and high priests" enhances only slightly his chances of success with the school board.

INTRABOARD CONSENSUS

We have referred in passing to the role of board cohesion in board-superintendent interaction. At this point we take a more detailed look at that role. The internal consensus of the school board may have a direct bearing on its ability to function as an authoritative actor and on the ability of the superintendent to exert leadership. According to the official ideology of the various prescriptions for effective board-superintendent relations, factions are damaging to the health of a board. Unity, or government by consensus, is more thoroughly established in the literature of educational administration than in political science. The professional attitude, according to Gross, Mason and McEachern, is to avoid intraboard factions.[22] According to Salisbury, the quest for consensus is not without its political motivation:

> *Educators have tried very hard to achieve and maintain consensus among all those engaged in the educational enterprise. Unity is a prerequisite to a reputation for expertise and it thus adds to the bargaining power of schoolmen . . .*[23]

Consideration of the possible consequences of the various patterns of school board consensus suggests that they may affect the decision-making process in two ways. First, when internal conflict becomes intense and board members become polarized, the capacity of the board to act as an effective decision-making body may be diminished. In other words, dissension may markedly decrease the ability of the board to utilize its resources in the formation of educational policy. Second, the quality of the consensus that prevails within the board may affect the manner in which the superintendent's professional resources are evaluated.

In order to subject these propositions to empirical examination it was necessary that we first assign school boards a score reflecting intraboard cohesion. We constructed a threefold typology of school boards based on responses to the following two questions:

> *When a problem first arises, members of a board often find that they disagree about the best course of action. How true is this of your board?*

> *When the school board disagrees on issues would you say there is more or less the same division on the board? I mean, do some members seem to stick together from one issue to the next?*

Boards were classified as consensual if the majority of members reported little or no disagreement on the first question. The remaining boards, in which a majority of the members reported relatively frequent initial disagreement, were classified as factional if the majority indicated that there was "more or less the same division on the board" in response to the second question. If no consistent splits were reported by a majority of members of boards in which initial disagreement occurred, the board was classified as being pluralistic. One-half of the boards (54 percent) are pluralistic, with the remainder equally divided between factional (24 percent) and consensual (22 percent) types.

As expected, the highest levels of board assertion occur when the school board is pluralistic. Opposition to the superintendent averages 41 percent on pluralistic boards, 28 percent on factional boards, and 13 percent on consensual boards. Our suspicion is confirmed that such boards are both more willing *and* more able to muster the resources necessary to exert leadership over public policy. Pluralistic boards, however, differ scarcely at all from the other two types in their estimate of board victory. The deferential nature of consensual boards supports the proposition that the superintendent tends to be included within the prevailing consensus. Likewise, the hypothesis that factional boards find themselves unable to act in a decisive manner in the formation of public policy cannot be rejected.

Consensual boards are least able to distinguish between their responsibility to the public and to the school administration, whereas pluralistic boards are most capable of making this distinction (Table 10-6). This ability to make distinctions is reflected in their respective leadership behavior in the area of public educational policy and indicates that the quality of the consensus that exists in boards of the former type is professionally-oriented. Factional boards are also more adept than consensual boards at drawing the distinction. But since their behavior in the educational market is affected by their dissipation of resources in internal conflict, they are even less likely to be dominant in educational decision-making.

TABLE 10-6
School Board Cohesion and Professional Role Orientation
(Higher Scores Mean More Professionalism)

Cohesion Type	Mean Score
Consensual	71
Pluralistic	55
Factional	61

Our findings concerning consensual boards are not startling since a number of observers have depicted the typical dominated board as being highly consensual. Their view is that a relatively small group constitutes what may be called an educational elite within the district.[24] The elite member increasingly tends to depend on the superintendent for guidance, because in order to maintain their control they must rely upon expertise rather than public demand satisfaction in their interactions with the public. Since the superintendent is the acknowledged expert in the district, they cannot afford to antagonize him if they are to maintain their image. The educational elite theorists argue that since the educational system is governed by an oligarchy, whenever any challenge to its rule is articulated, the board reacts by presenting a united front in defense of its (the superintendent's) policies. Regardless of the existence of minor disagreements within the elite, they tend to display a consensual image to the public. Any internal conflicts are presumably resolved informally or in executive session.

We tested the validity of this portrayal of the consensual board by examining the extent to which such boards actually manifest tendencies toward closed decision making. Two indicators were used in this analysis. The first is the simpler of the two and is based on the superintendent's response to the question: "During public meetings, do board members nearly always agree with each other or is there usually some disagreement?" Consensual boards present a united front to their publics much more often than do the other types of boards: the average rate reported by consensual boards is 82 percent, compared with 35 percent for pluralistic boards and 32 percent for factional boards. Much of this difference can be accounted for by the fact that by definition there is less reported disagreement to start with in such boards. Nevertheless, we cannot discount the argument that they engage in the politics of concealment based on this evidence alone.

The second indicator to which we have alluded was based on responses of board members. Each was asked the open-ended question:

> *What differences are there between meetings of the board members which are open to the public and those which are closed? I mean in terms of the things that are discussed and the decisions that are made?*

Many board members said there were no differences. Typical of the answers in the category of nonpublic decision making were those which said that "the real work" or "getting down to hard cases" was done in closed sessions. The percent of the members of each board who responded in this fashion was calculated. A high score indicates a large proportion of members reporting private decision making or discussion. The univariate distribution of this variable is interesting in its own right, for it shows that relatively few respondents admitted to this type of activity. At the board level the mean percentage was only 22.

Given the level of attention that scholars have devoted to this phenomenon and the pervasiveness that they have attributed to it, one must wonder whether they could have been so wrong in their assertions or whether perhaps the personal involvement of our board members caused them to be somewhat less than accurate in their reports. Whatever the accuracy of the measure, consensual boards clearly eschew closed session decision making and unusual discussion. Whereas the means for pluralistic and factional boards were 31 and 21 percent, respectively, the figure was but 4 percent among the consensual boards. This contrast reflects the bland, issue-barren nature of their decision-making process. If there is nothing to dispute, there is no reason for an executive session.

The most we can confidently assert at this point concerning intraboard consensus is that consensual and factional boards are associated with stronger superintendent leadership; that they display a concomitantly weak ability to distinguish between their responsibility to the public and to the administration; and that pluralistic boards are both more likely to draw this distinction and more likely to dominate in making public educational policy.

As foreshadowed previously, there is a moderate inclination for consensual boards to develop in small towns and for factional boards to develop in cities (Table 10-7). Conversely, consensual city boards and factional small town boards occur infrequently. Pluralistic boards, which are the modal type in each of the three urban categories, exist in approximately half of the districts in each type of community. The high proportion of factional boards and the correspondingly low incidence of consensual boards in cities are what we would expect to find in heterogeneous districts with mounting problems and "politicized" boards. The weakest departures from the overall pattern occurs in suburban districts.

TABLE 10-7
Intraboard Cohesion, by Type of Urban Environment

	Con-sensual	Pluralistic	Factional	Total	N
City	12%	49%	39%	100%	24
Suburban	18	56	26	100	57
Small Town	30	55	15	100	25

The relatively high proportion of consensual boards in small towns, while lower than one might have expected, is consistent with the notion that small town boards are the products of more homogeneous, sacred communities. A key reason the proportion is not higher stems from our classification of small town districts which, it will be recalled, range from those in villages and townships to those in bustling medium-size towns.

We can now determine the joint effects of urbanism and board cohesion on the opposition behavior of the board. For this purpose we have combined the two variables of opposition intensity and probable victory into a single, standardized measure reflecting overall board strength.[25] Intraboard cohesion interacts with urban environment in a curious manner. Table 10-8 contains the mean board assertion scores for each category of urbanism within each of the three categories of intraboard cohesion. No consistent pattern in opposition scores appears when we examine the values *within* cohesion categories. In other words, when we read down the columns in Table 10-8, the relative ordering of leadership scores in city,

TABLE 10-8
Composite Board Opposition, by Urban Environment
and Intraboard Cohesion

	Consensual	*Pluralistic*	*Factional*	*Total*
City	$-.57^a$	-.07	-.02	-.11
Suburban	.28	.52	-.15	.30
Small Town	-.39	.27	-.91	-.11
Total	-.27	.26	-.33	.00

[a]Positive signs indicate higher opposition.

suburban, and small town environments varies according to the cohesion characteristic of the board, with each category being characterized by high leadership
scores in different kinds of communities. Thus city environments seem to be least
conducive to board leadership when the school board is consensual.

When we come to factional boards, it is the small town that seems to
provide the worst environment for board leadership. In fact, the lowest mean board
opposition score appearing is that for small town districts which have factional
boards. Perhaps the fact that small town boards seldom develop divisive factions
may account for this phenomenon. Such boards, inexperienced as they are in
conflict management techniques, may more readily become incapacitated by
factionalism when it does occur. The generally low status level of the small town
board lends some degree of credibility to this explanation, for lower status individuals tend to be less well-equipped with the skills required to handle highly
conflictual situations. It is ironic that the small town board, which is generally
thought to be the most jealous of its power, is the least able to retain it under
conditions of intraboard conflict.

Strangely enough it is the pluralistic suburban board which most effectively combines opposition plus confidence that it can prevail in a contest with
the superintendent over the educational program. Despite the mythology of
monolithic culture in the suburbs, it is precisely there that pluralism among the
educational governors is most instrumental. Perhaps pluralism in the suburbs does
not become submerged in the larger quagmire of the educational bureaucracy, as
it apparently does in the cities. The scale of suburban districts is more amenable to
pluralistic forces. At the same time pluralism may be less intimidated in suburbia
than in the more intimate environs of the small town.

NOTES

1. Neal Gross, *Who Runs Our Schools?* (New York: Wiley, 1958), p. 98.
2. T.R. Bowman, "Participation of Superintendents in School Board
Decision-Making," *Administrator's Notebook*, 11 (January, 1963), pp. 1–4.
3. Otis Dudley Duncan, "A Socioeconomic Index for All Occupations,"

Occupations and Social Status, eds. Albert J. Reiss, Jr., *et al* (New York: Free Press, 1961), pp. 109–138.

    4. Inasmuch as board members were asked only to indicate which of 14 categories their family income fell within, we assigned scores equivalent to the midpoints within each category.

    5. Factor loadings and factor score coefficients for each of the three status-related variables were:

Variable	Factor Loading	Factor Score Coefficient
Occupational Status	.92	.39
Education	.92	.38
Income	.84	.35

For further information concerning the relationship between factor loadings and factor score coefficients the reader is referred to the brief but readable discussion contained in Norman H. Nie, Dale H. Bent, and C. Hadlai Hull, *Statistical Package for the Social Sciences* (New York: McGraw-Hill, 1970), pp. 208–227.

    6. David Minar, "The Community Basis of Conflict in School System Politics," *American Sociological Review*, 31 (December, 1966), p. 832.

    7. Philip Selznick, *TVA and the Grass Roots: A Study in the Sociology of Formal Organizations* (Berkeley, Calif.: University of California Press, 1949), pp. 13–16, pp. 259–61.

    8. *Ibid.*, pp. 14–15.

    9. *Ibid.*, pp. 260–61.

    10. Norman D. Kerr, "The School Board as an Agency of Legitimation," *Sociology of Education,* 38 (Fall, 1964), p. 52.

    11. William A. Gamson, *Power and Discontent* (Homewood, Ill.: Dorsey Press, 1968), p. 79. We realize that for some purposes the superintendent would be considered one of the authorities in Gamson's scheme. For present purposes it seems important to distinguish the board as the authoritative body and the superintendent as "potential partisan" vis-à-vis the board.

    12. For a discussion of gatekeeping see David Easton, *A Systems Analysis of Political Life* (New York: Wiley, 1965), pp. 88–100.

    13. See, for instance: Archie R. Dykes, *School Board and Superintendent: Their Effective Working Relationships* (Danville, Ill.: Interstate Printers & Publishers, 1965), p. 153; David W. Minar, *Educational Decision-Making in Suburban Communities*, USOE Cooperative Research Project 2440 (Evanston, Ill.: Northwestern University, 1966), pp. 52–56; and Joseph Pois, "The Board and the General Superintendent," *Governing Education: A Reader on Politics, Power, and Public School Policy*, ed. Alan Rosenthal (New York: Doubleday, 1969), pp. 429–30.

    14. Elmer E. Schattschneider, *The Semisovereign People: A Realist's View of Democracy in America* (New York: Holt. Rinehart and Winston, 1960), p. 68. Similarly, Bachrach and Baratz have discussed the importance of issue definition in terms of the ability to keep certain issues from ever entering the decision-making

system. They refer to this as "nondecision making." The significance of this type of control for the student of educational government should not be overlooked. Peter Bachrach and Morton Baratz, "The Two Faces of Power," *American Political Science Review*, 57 (December, 1962), pp. 947–52. In this regard, also see: Robert S. Cahill, "Three Themes on the Politics of Education," *The Politics of Education in the Local Community*, ed. Robert S. Cahill and Stephen P. Hencley (Danville, Ill.: Interstate Printers & Publishers, 1964), p. 61.

15. Roland J. Pellegrin, "Community Power Structure and Educational Decision Making in the Local Community," a paper presented at the 1965 meeting of the American Association of School Administrators, Atlantic City, February 15, 1965, quoted in James D. Keorner, *Who Controls American Education: A Guide for Laymen* (Boston: Beacon Press, 1968), p. 138. See also Pois, *op. cit.*, p. 429.

16. *1973 A.A.S.A. Convention Reporter* (American Association of School Administrators), p. 27.

17. *Ibid.* See also Lloyd W. Ashby, *The Effective School Board Member* (Danville, Ill.: Interstate Printers & Publishers, 1968), p. 48.

18. For example, the product-moment correlations between this variable and our leadership variables are as follows:

Probability of Board Victory $r = -.01$
Opposition to the Superintendent $r = -.04$

19. George C. Homans, *The Human Group* (New York: Harcourt, Brace & World, 1950), pp. 11–12, 101–06.

20. Theodore M. Newcomb, "The Prediction of Interpersonal Attraction," *American Psychologist*, 11 (November, 1956), pp. 575–86.

21. Of course, one might just as easily argue that interaction is a *cause* of positive attitude.

22. Neal Gross, Ward S. Mason, and Alexander W. McEachern, *Explorations in Role Analysis: Studies of the School Superintendency Role* (New York: Wiley, 1958).

23. Robert Salisbury, "Schools and Politics in the Big Cities," *Harvard Educational Review*, 37 (Summer, 1967), p. 417.

24. For example, see Iannaccone and Lutz, *loc. cit.*; Raymond E. Callahan, *Education and the Cult of Efficiency* (Chicago: University of Chicago Press, 1962); and Ralph Kimbrough, *Political Power and Educational Decision Making* (Chicago: Rand McNally, 1964).

25. In order to combine the two opposition indicators into a single measure the square root of the sum of their squared values was converted into standardized equivalents.

Chapter 11

Opposition and the

Individual Board Member

For the next phase of our analysis, we will abandon boards as collective units and concentrate mainly upon individual board members. We will inquire into their recruitment, their change orientations, their ideology, and the correspondence between their attitudes and those of their superintendents.

Our interest in individual board members who find themselves in frequent opposition to the superintendent is dictated in part by a desire to understand deviant behavior. As we have seen, opposition to the superintendent, while occasionally vigorous and sustained, is not the normal pattern. Consequently, we might assume that opponents, since they are exceptional in the context of school board behavior, might also be exceptional in recruitment and ideology. Perhaps opponents provide the conduits for transmitting unorthodox and innovative ideas into the system. On the other hand, perhaps opponents to the superintendent are merely idiosyncratic and petulant, reflecting not the cutting edge of change but merely irritating, ineffective thorns in the side of the superintendent.

Are opponents outsiders who are isolated from sources of influence and frustrated at their ineffectiveness? Or are opponents situated within the mainstream of educational policy making? Obviously, given the paucity of sustained and successful opposition, the first explanation has initially more credibility. However, as we know, situations can develop in which the superintendent cannot contain a conflict. Under some circumstances, then, opponents may wield genuine influence. At the very least they can generate discussion.

Our analysis will continue to make use of the metropolitan-nonmetropolitan distribution. In addition, we will categorize boards into either high or low levels of opposition, depending upon whether at least one-fourth of the members qualify as opponents. These classifications are introduced to provide further clarification of the socialization functions and decision-making contexts previously described. Group pressures being what they are, we reasoned that the characterization of individual opponents might be appreciably different when opposition is a deviant point of view than when opposition is the norm, or is at least an acceptable way of behaving. In the first case, one might expect opponents to have the characteristics of the "outsider," while in the latter situation they may not.

The indicator of individual opposition is more general but also more stringent than the one used in the previous two chapters. Instead of dealing with opposition in the specific area of the educational program, we cast the net more widely and talk about opposition in any area. On the other hand, we restrict our definition to board members who identified themselves as "often" opposing the superintendent or who were identified by the superintendent as at least "sometimes" being in opposition.[1] To be classified as an opponent required, therefore, some degree of regularized contention with the superintendent. Board members labelled themselves as regular opponents at a rate of one in seven. To this total can be added an additional number of members named by the superintendent but not naming themselves. Altogether 18 percent of the members will be considered frequent opponents. High opposition boards consist of those where at least 25 percent of the members were classified as opponents.

RECRUITMENT AND OPPOSITION

Our major concern about recruitment centers upon the dimensions introduced in Chapters 2 and 3. We return, then, to the five dominant pathways to the board. The travelers on these pathways were called nonactives, civic notables, educational dilettantes, politicos, and diffuse actives. We suspect, given what we know about the behavior of boards at the aggregate level, that the political mode of entry is most likely to breed opponents.

Table 11–1 consists of a series of correlations based on whether the respondent is in opposition and on whether the respondent had traveled a particular pathway. Each of the pathways is essentially treated as a "dummy variable." For example, the correlations in the civic notables column state the relationship between being (or not being) a civic notable and being (or not being) a regular opponent.[2]

One of the important messages of Table 11–1 is that the overall level of board opposition makes a difference in the strength of background effects. Compared with parallel figures for low opposition boards, those in the high opposition half of the table are uniformly higher. Thus individual opposition on low opposition boards is much more idiosyncratic, although there are some continuities across the two levels. But the general pattern of stronger relationships among high opposition boards will be a recurring one throughout this chapter and it points

toward the more structured, integrated nature of opposition when there are
multiple opponents versus the more haphazard, idiosyncratic nature when opponents are alone.

TABLE 11-1

Correlations between Path to Board and Opposition to
Superintendent, by Level of Board Opposition
and Metropolitanism

	Non-actives	*Educational Dilettantes*	*Civic Notables*	*Politicos*	*Diffuse Actives*
Low Opposition					
Metro	−.10	−.16	.01[a]	.28	.12
Nonmetro	−.04	−.08	.02	−.01	.06
High Opposition					
Metro	−.17	−.26	−.18	.42	.30
Nonmetro	.14	.41	.32	.11	.21

[a]Entries are *tau-b* correlations. The higher the positive correlations, the higher the opposition.

Considering first the civic notables, one would assume that those who
reached the board via the "enlightened conservative" route of the civic associations
would have a healthy respect for unity and expertise. In low opposition situations,
such persons remain undistinguished. In high opposition situations, however, they
have clearly distinguishable responses to the superintendent. In metropolitan areas,
they are more loyal supporters. In these areas of teeming conflict and hostility,
they line up (along with the educational dilettantes and nonactives) against the
politicos and diffuse actives. In such areas, the superintendent-expert finds his
allies among the reform-oriented business and civic leaders who understand and
respect the need for a separation of politics and administration, and who appreciate
principles of solid business management. The educationally recruited, as can be
expected, also close ranks behind the superintendent in those settings.

Only those board members whose backgrounds interface with the community's manifest political process approach their responsibilities in a more
combative manner. The politically recruited, which includes the politicos and most
of the diffuse actives, are likely to oppose even when there is not much opposition.
They clearly make a major contribution when opposition is high. Significantly, the
only sizable relationship when board-superintendent conflict is low involves the
pure politicos. Once again, we learn the wisdom, from the superintendent's point of
view, of the traditional belief that politics and education do not mix.

The educationally recruited members and those without activist backgrounds are the most loyal supporters, remaining true in all cases except in high

opposition, nonmetropolitan districts. That the educationally recruited are loyal comes as no surprise. Experience within the educational "establishment" can certainly be relied upon to convince one of the need for unity. Yet even the stern blandishments of the educational-socialization process cannot keep such members from turning upon the superintendent in small towns when significant opposition appears. The consensus pressure of less complex environments is inevitable. When the superintendent runs into the immovable monolith in the "provinces," it is actually the educational dilettantes who lead the opposition.

In a related vein, the organizational involvement of board members is also related to opposition. For example, membership in school board associations also affects opposition levels. Whatever the context, there is a relationship between belonging to a school board organization and eschewing opposition. Such organizations enjoy a close working relationship with superintendents, conduct workshops and so forth, and in general contribute to loyalty. These organizations operate much like other professional associations.

Other educationally-involved groups have an impact that is less easily interpreted. Our respondents were asked to name the group, if any, which encouraged them to seek a board position. After removing those with obvious connections to the educational establishment (such as the PTA), we examined the extent to which supporters and opponents were "self-starters," or were linked to groups and possibly their demands. We found a modest pattern, depending upon the intensity of board-superintendent hostility. In low opposition contexts, opponents tend to be loners ($-.10$); but in high opposition contexts they are likely to have been propelled toward the board by groups ($.15$).

These brief comments on organizational support provide an introduction to a final and crucial comment upon resources. What we are really working toward is an understanding of the "so what" of opposition. Boards, like all decision-making units, have informal (as well as formal) leaders. Such opinion leaders assume a major role in swinging a decision in a desired direction. We asked our respondents to name that member of the board to whom they looked for guidance. Not surprisingly, opinion leaders are usually those with long tenure, high socioeconomic status, and important board positions.

Although influence within the board does not necessarily mean influence with the administration, it is likely that opinion leaders are at least respected (feared) by administrators. If opinion leaders are opponents, the superintendent's position may become untenable. In low opposition settings, whether in metropolitan or nonmetropolitan areas, opponents are not opinion leaders. Indeed, in metropolitan areas there is a modest negative association ($-.17$) between number of nominations as opinion leader and opposition to the superintendent.

Complexity of the environment becomes more crucial in high opposition areas. In metropolitan districts opponents tend not to be opinion leaders on the board ($-.13$). However, in high-opposition, nonmetropolitan districts, opponents are considerably more likely ($.29$) to be nominated as opinion leaders. Such a finding should come as no surprise, considering what we know about small town boards. The fact that the superintendent numbers among his opponents those that "count" reinforces the necessity to avoid raising dangerous issues. Such a configuration is distinguished largely by its exception to the rule. On the more customary board opponents are less influential. Especially when opposition is minimal, opponents are likely to be isolated and powerless.

OPPOSITION AND THE DESIRE FOR CHANGE

In Chapters 3 and 4 we addressed ourselves to the degree of policy differences surrounding school board elections and noted that elections at best are moderately competitive. Candidates typically cite few policy differences with opponents, and the differences that exist seldom relate directly to the educational program.

Given what we know about the superintendent's opposition, we suspect that these members are not typical in this regard. Opponents are not born overnight. It seems very likely that today's opponent to the superintendent was yesterday's change advocate in the election. The record against which or in favor of which candidates run is in substantial measure the record that the superintendent and the dominant portion of the board have put together. Therefore, the carryover between a call for change during the campaign may be expected to surface in board-superintendent interaction. Nor should the role of personality be ruled out. Some candidates and officeholders prefer to work in a mode which challenges ongoing practices, whatever the content might be.

Table 11-2, which displays the change and challenge orientation of opponents versus supporters, verifies our assumptions. The opponents to the superintendent approach their role with considerably more zest and desire for change than do his supporters. In both low and high opposition boards, opponents are more change-oriented, but the association is much stronger in high opposition boards. Supporters are committed to the status quo; opponents are not. Similarly, supporters are far less likely to express issue differences with their competitors during the election campaign.

The very strong commitments of opponents apply in all contexts, but especially in higher opposition, nonmetropolitan districts. There the correlations are robust on every indicator.

The extent to which ideology is a basis of competition with the superintendent can only be surmised. Surely in some districts, at some point in time, the lines of cleavage are formed around ideology. It is more probable, however, that the division of responsibility between the board and the superintendent plays a major role in separating opponents from supporters.[3] Some evidence for that probability is found in the last column of Table 11-2. While board candidates are concerned with a variety of issues, opponents to the superintendent are more likely than supporters, especially in nonmetro settings, to single out the definition of board roles as a campaign difference.

Perhaps one reason for this concern about board roles can be gleaned from

TABLE 11-2

Opposition Related to Desire for Change and Combativeness Prior to Board Service

	Proportion Desiring Change	Number of Changes Desired	Number of Differences with Predecessors[a]	Proportion Differing with Other Candidates	Number of Differences	Proportion with Differences on Board Roles
All Boards	.21[b]	.17	.20	.24	.11	.15
Low Opposition Boards						
Metro	.17	.12	.18	.09	-.09	.07
Nonmetro	.04	.07	.09	.28	.24	.18
High Opposition Boards						
Metro	.22	.15	.16	.23	.01	.05
Nonmetro	.52	.35	.41	.40	.32	.27

[a]For those originally appointed
[b]*Tau-b* correlations. Positive signs indicate that opponents score higher on the measure.

a consideration of the tendency of opponents to be "delegates" (Table 11–3). Opponents find the concept of a public for which they "stand in" more tolerable than do supporters. Such a role does not necessarily stem from any direct inter- action between the board member and a portion of the public. The significance lies in the existence of a reference group beyond the educational system. Opponents thus may see their job as one of supervising the superintendent according to the perceived expectations of the public.

TABLE 11–3
Opposition and the Role of the Board Member

	Subscribe to "Delegate" Role	Feel Conflict in Responsibility to Administration and Public
All Boards	.18[a]	.08
Low Opposition Boards		
Metro	.20	.14
Nonmetro	.08	.16
High Opposition Boards		
Metro	.19	.19
Nonmetro	.29	−.16

[a]*Tau-b* correlations. Positive signs indicate higher scores for opponents.

One barometer of the potential conflict between sets of expectations is given by the response to the inquiry of whether board members feel any conflict between their responsibility to the public and their responsibility to the school administration (Table 11–3). With the exception of nonmetro opponents in high opposition districts, the opponents more often feel such a strain, suggesting that they have at least one set of cues which originates outside the educational system.

Our comments about board roles and opposition preface our examination of the perception of the appropriate functions of board and superintendent, which we scrutinize to see if the opposition takes the form of resistance to superin- tendent domination. Table 11-4 reports the correlations between being in opposi- tion and views on board functions; Table 11–5 does the same for superintendent functions.

Turning first to board functions, we find no consistent or appreciable differences between opponents and supporters among low opposition boards. Differences between opponents and supporters tend to be greater when the level of opposition is more intense, particularly in nonmetro districts. In these situations opponents prefer a more active role for the board. They believe the board creates public support for education — evoking a position consistent with their "delegate" role. But they do not see the creation of support as necessarily involving increased expenditures. Indeed, they consider it substantially more important to *reduce*

TABLE 11-4

Opposition and the Role of the Board

	Create Support for Education	Increase Financial Support	Hear Parental Complaints	Hear Teacher Complaints	Reduce Expenditures	Supervise Superintendent
All Boards	-.02[a]	.00	.07	.03	.16	.17
Low Opposition Boards						
Metro	-.15	-.08	.14	.04	.06	.16
Nonmetro	.06	.03	.08	-.02	.17	.02
High Opposition Boards						
Metro	-.14	.01	-.07	.01	.14	.12
Nonmetro	.14	.01	.16	.12	.30	.35

[a]*Tau-b* correlations. Positive signs indicate that opponents are more in favor of the measure.

expenditures. In this case, the desire to reduce expenditures is a consistent characteristic of opponents, especially in less complex settings. In terms of their "watch-
dog" role, opponents in these areas emerge as the most watchful. It is they who
assert the necessity of keeping an eye on the superintendent and of not letting
expenditures get out of hand. They are also slightly more receptive to hearing the
complaints of parents and teachers. At least in regard to their desire to assert
authority, nonmetro boards provide reinforcement to the currently popular idea of
decentralization. In these smaller, more homogenous districts publics can be heard
(through individuals more than groups, as we pointed out in Chapter 5) and the
board will probably respond, if their voices become loud enough.

    We find the response pattern on appropriate superintendent roles to be
consistent with this interpretation. Opponents on high opposition boards emphasize the ideally subordinate position of the superintendent, who should be a business manager and an executive secretary (Table 11-5). Compared with supporters,
opponents generally react negatively to the notion of the superintendent representing a group or serving as an intermediary. When opposition is heated, the ideal
role of the superintendent as executive secretary, business manager, or *instrument*
of the board, receives its sharpest support. Such an emphasis is decidedly lacking
in low opposition boards, suggesting a salient point of friction in high opposition
boards.

    The saliency of the superintendent's behavior can be observed from the
final column. Derived from answers to an open-ended question asking what a
superintendent ought to do in order to be effective, the column lists the association between the number of responses and posture toward the superintendent.
Opponents in high opposition areas have slightly more notions of the appropriate
behavior of the superintendent than do supporters, especially in smaller places,
where opposition tends to be more intense once established. On balance opponents
in high conflict situations more often want to keep the superintendent "in his
place."[4]

The Role of Ideology

Our interest in the ideology of opponents is partly simple curiosity, but more a
consequence of our desire to understand the basis of opposition. Do board members
and superintendents clash over the big questions or are their disputes more idiosyncratic and based upon personality? Do opponents manifest consistent ideologies
in various contexts, or are their values unrelated to their relationship with the
superintendent?[5]

    It would be unrealistic to expect opponents to differ consistently with
supporters across all districts. The specific nature of differences is highly conditioned by the regional, state, and especially local environment. Thus there is no
strong reason to suspect that opponents will always be more liberal, for example.
Rather, the nature of the potentially controversial topic, its salience, and the
environment in which it arises will all help determine the juxtaposition of oppo-

TABLE 11-5
Opposition and the Role of the Superintendent

	Public Relations Expert	Teacher Representative	Intermediary between Board and Teachers	Business Manager	Executive Secretary	Number of Prerequisites for Superintendent
All Boards	-.14[a]	.08	-.16	-.15	.12	.04
Low Opposition Boards						
Metro	-.16	-.15	.02	-.25	-.18	-.09
Nonmetro	-.05	-.22	-.30	.06	.04	.03
High Opposition Boards						
Metro	-.12	.10	-.16	.30	.10	.06
Nonmetro	-.07	-.18	-.17	.16	.45	.15

[a]*Tau-b* correlations. Positive signs indicate that opponents are more in favor of the measure.

nents and supporters of the superintendent. It is with these constraints in mind that we turn toward the issue orientations of opponents and supporters.

We have examined three domains in considering a range of potential ideological disputes: 1) reference groups; 2) national issues; and 3) teacher behavior. We selected evaluations of two teacher groups and two community groups, each having a "liberal" or "conservative" image.[6] We chose two controversial national issues, prayers in public schools and federal intervention to achieve integration, and two more general issues, expansion of the federal role in society and the place of the federal government in the governing of education. Six teacher activities of varying levels of controversy were submitted for evaluation.

We will continue the division of boards according to metropolitanism. Because ideology is often associated with region, this section will also introduce a set of regional controls as appropriate. We present the full results only for high opposition boards because, for the most part, differences between opponents and supporters are either minor or erratic among low opposition boards. Correlations between issue positions and stance toward the superintendent appear in Table 11-6. Each entry represents a cross tabulation of the attitudes of opponents and supporters with the ideological items as the dependent variable. Positive signs indicate a favorable attitude on the part of opponents. The size of the correlation indicates the degree of difference between opponents and supporters.

Concerning reference groups, the first thing that comes to our attention is the more favorable attitude of opponents toward the American Federation of Teachers (AFT), which represents a challenge to the traditional distribution of authority in the educational system. One might interpret this finding as a further sign of AFT's assault upon tradition. This interpretation is bolstered by the less favorable views expressed about the AFT's older rival, the National Education Association (NEA).

But this view does not presage a uniformly liberal mode of thought. Taxpayer associations, with the exception of large city Southern boards, do not fare too badly. The NAACP does moderately well, also suggesting a more receptive attitude on the part of opposition to community groups, irrespective of the nature of the groups.

The NAACP does better among Southern opponents than among Northern opponents, and a shade better in nonmetro than in metro districts. This finding is contrary to the image of attitudes associated with these areas. Perhaps opponents are likely to adopt an attitude which is in contrast to the dominant mode of thought in the community. Consider, for example, large city Northern opponents. While they support the AFT they are relatively hostile to the NAACP. Their liberal attitudes appear to be confined to approval of a teachers' organization which challenges the authority of the administration.

Turning to national issues, we find additional glimmerings of the above pattern. The prayer issue, which essentially measures agreement with the Supreme Court decision "outlawing" prayers in public schools, produces relatively few differences between opponents and supporters except in the metro South. The

TABLE 11-6
Individual Opposition and Issue Positions on High Opposition Boards, by Region and Metropolitanism

	Reference Groups				National Issues						Teacher Behavior			
	NEA	AFT	Taxpayer Groups	NAACP	Prayers in School	Federal Role in Integration	Federal Government Power in Society	Federal Control of Local Education	Join Civil Rights Group	Speak on Civil Rights	Allow Atheist to Address Class	Speak in Favor of U.N.	Allow Distribution of NAM Literature	Speak in Favor of Socialism
South														
Metro	-.01[a]	.06	-.49	.17	-.27	-.24	-.27	.28	-.16	-.15	-.10	.28	.10	.33
Nonmetro	-.29	.32	.44	.22	-.06	.09	-.47	-.68	.13	.15	.16	.49	-.06	-.17
Non-South														
Metro	-.03	.15	.12	-.14	.03	-.35	-.29	-.13	-.09	-.01	.00	-.21	.19	-.04
Nonmetro	-.02	.14	.04	.01	.09	.52	-.16	.02	-.01	.20	.03	.29	-.16	-.11

[a]Entries are *tau-b* correlations. Positive signs indicate that opponents are more in favor of the objects than are supporters.

deviant position of opponents is highlighted in that context. It is on the integration issue that the ideological difference between opponents and supporters becomes more consistent. In every case, including the low opposition boards (not shown) large city opponents are more inclined to favor a slowdown of federal efforts to achieve integration and small town opponents are more inclined to support such efforts. The disparity between large city and small town is especially apparent in the high opposition North, where the conservative attitude of metro-area opponents stands in vivid contrast to their substantially more liberal country cousins.

Opponents are uniformly more dubious than supporters about the role of big government in American society, a skepticism which extends in much reduced magnitude even to the low opposition boards (not shown). There is some indication throughout our materials that opponents worry more about control from above than do supporters. That tendency is most noticeable among nonmetro, Southern boards. Opponents there express the most opposition to "big government," and they also express the most concern about the amount of federal control over local education.

So far our findings point toward some regularities of ideological differences between opponents and supporters of the superintendent, but the results do not form a tight pattern. As we suggested at the outset, the peculiarities of each district and the larger environment within which it operates preclude generalization of a high order. This intractability is manifested in the last set of objects evaluated, those of specific teacher behaviors. The opinions of opponents regarding teaching behavior vary according to the behavior being proposed. To the extent that there is a pattern, however, it lies in the small town opponents adopting the more liberal stance — in this case, a more tolerant approach to teacher activities inside and outside the classroom. The most glaring exception to that pattern occurs in the greater reluctance of opponents to condone speaking in favor of socialism. The other apparent exception is their lesser enthusiasm about the distribution of materials from the National Association of Manufacturers (NAM). Here the opponents were cross-pressured, because the behavior would result in a "conservative" action, since the NAM could be expected to dispense conservative information.

Despite some gnawing inconsistencies, there is a general conclusion to be drawn from the results presented in Table 11-6. Small town (nonmetro) opponents when compared with supporters in the same settings are more liberal than large city opponents when compared with supporters in the same settings. The interpretation of this overall finding, which was tentatively advanced earlier in the chapter, is that opponents represent the deviant point of view within a system. For larger environs, where people are more liberal, opponents often appear to be conservative or reactionary.[7] In smaller environs the reverse is true. The small town opponents pick up and articulate the liberal dissent, thus representing a potential attack from the left on the superintendent. In larger, more complex settings the assault will more probably originate from the right. Whatever their ideologies, opponents *tend* not to fit into the established patterns of thought and action.

ISSUE CONGRUENCE BETWEEN THE SUPERINTENDENT AND HIS OPPONENTS

Illustrations of the nature and substance of disputes between board members and superintendents can also be achieved by focussing upon conflict within each district. Since the interviews with superintendents included many items identical to those asked of board members, it is possible to match board member and superintendent responses. Although such data deserve a fuller airing, at this time we can only offer a glimpse into what they reveal.

We computed average scores for the opponents on each board and then matched these aggregated scores with the superintendent's score on the identical item. Only five issues were considered: the federal government's role in integration, two forms of teacher activity, and two indicators of appropriate roles for the board and the superintendent. All of these issues have been introduced before.

As the top row of Table 11–7 shows, there is a negative relationship between opponents' scores and superintendent's scores on four of the five issues. As we shall see momentarily, there are interesting variations on each one of these issues within certain kinds of districts. For the moment, we might first ask why the opponents do not show higher disagreement with the superintendent. The major reason, of course, is that these five issues are only a sample (and probably not a representative one) of the myriad number of issues over which opponents might disagree with their administrative chief. Some of these so-called issues may not be issues at all in many districts. The lines of cleavage probably lie elsewhere.

On the other hand, the two highest instances of disagreement suggest the most likely sources of cleavage. We have seen already that opponents have different ideas than supporters about appropriate roles for board members and superintendents and that these differences date back even to the preboard stage. It is precisely in these areas that opponents show the most disagreement with the superintendent's views, as seen in the last two columns of Table 11–7. Virtually all of the contribution to these two negative correlations derives from situations in which the opponents more often favored emphasizing the superintendent as an executive secretary and in emphasizing the board's role in supervising the superintendent. These findings underscore others throughout this study that tension over role definitions and power allocations make up a good part of the struggle between the professionals and the lay governors.

We looked at superintendent-opponent congruence with categories of districts. On low-opposition boards there are scant differences between opponents and superintendents on these five issues. On high-opposition boards the opponents are more likely to take issue with the superintendent, although there are exceptions and many of the associations are trivial (Table 11–7). Of the twelve correlations larger than .10, ten indicate disagreement between the two sets of actors; two show that opponents tend to agree with the superintendent. These results are not surprising considering the multidimensional nature of opposition. Opponents will not necessarily disagree with their superintendent on each issue presented to them.

TABLE 11-7
Board Member-Superintendent Congruency, by Region and Metropolitanism

	Federal Role in Integration	Teachers Join Civil Rights Groups	Teachers Speak on Civil Rights	Superintendent as Executive Secretary	Board Supervises Superintendent
All Boards	-.13	-.09	.08	-.19	-.29
High Opposition Boards					
South					
Metro	-.23[a]	-.16	-.11	.08	-.11
Nonmetro	-.11	-.26	.03	.01	.02
Non-South					
Metro	-.38	-.09	.15	-.10	-.14
Nonmetro	.52	-.28	.01	-.01	.06

[a]Entries are *tau-b* correlations. Negative associations indicate that opponents disagree with the superintendent.

To return to a theme which has been advanced throughout the book, it is probable that members adopt a stance in contrast to that of the superintendent partly as a consequence of the political environment of the board-superintendent exchange. The legal constraints and competition structure, which we found to be effective links between tension and opposition, should serve a similar function in the development and maintenance of members who oppose the superintendent. Such assumptions prove correct. If we abandon the classification scheme that depends upon level of opposition, region, and complexity, in favor of a classification of districts according to the structure of elections and the extent of genuine competition, we find that the more political the structure the more serious the opposition (Table 11-8).

We find, for example, that in partisan election systems opponents differ more severely with superintendents in all issues than in nonpartisan election systems. Similar findings hold for other types of political structures. Ward elections accentuate the difference between the opponents and the superintendent whom they oppose. What seems to happen is that unreformed institutions offer up winning candidates who are basically distrustful about the superintendent's preeminent role. This posture is, in turn, more easily maintained in the unreformed settings. Support for this line of reasoning comes in the very large disagreement registered with respect to the superintendent and board roles (last two columns, Table 11-8). Although opponents in partisan and ward districts also disagree more with the superintendent on the other three issues, the magnitudes are not nearly as large.

Two measures of electoral competitiveness yield results compatible with those just described. If anything, the findings are more uniform in revealing the elevating effect of livelier political environments. Districts with electoral opposition in the immediate past and forced turnover exaggerate the ideological differences between opponents and the superintendent. Such a finding is hardly surprising, but it provides yet again a warning to the superintendent: keep out of politics. It appears that the superintendent can become a focus for electoral disputes, with the focus carrying over into board behavior. In heated political climates opposition is not idiosyncratic; it is serious.

In determining what factors lead to more individual opposition and in discussing the policy stances of opponents we have implied that opposition is good in and of itself. As stated previously, we do not hold that view. Cantankerous and spiteful opposition ordinarily has few, if any, salutary consequences. Yet given the necessarily different perspectives and mandates of the professional administrators versus the lay representatives of the public, it seems highly unlikely that all the relevant needs and interests of the public are being considered when boards docilely follow the leadership of the superintendent. Regardless of his astuteness and perspicacity, it is the rare superintendent who can unilaterally perceive and translate into action the needs and demands of a varied constituency. We shall return to these very central problems in the concluding chapter.

TABLE 11-8

Electoral Variables and Board Member-Superintendent Congruency

	Integration	Teachers Join Civil Rights Groups	Teachers Speak on Civil Rights	Superintendent as Executive Secretary	Board Supervises Superintendent
Election Area					
At-large	.04[a]	-.08	.10	.04	-.12
Wards	-.10	-.16	-.14	-.41	-.45
Partisanship					
No	.10	.14	.01	-.05	.09
Yes	-.14	-.10	-.09	-.50	-.37
Electoral Opposition					
No	.03	-.06	.10	.11	-.13
Yes	-.39	-.12	-.16	-.28	-.41
Forced Turnover					
No	.15	.07	.03	-.09	-.13
Yes	-.32	-.19	-.13	-.24	-.40

[a]Entries are *tau-b* correlations. Negative associations indicate that the opponents disagree with the superintendent.

NOTES

1. The question put to board members read: "Does one person or group on the board often oppose the superintendent?" If the answer was affirmative, the member was asked: "Would you consider yourself one of these persons?" Superintendents were asked: "Does any person or group on the board sometimes oppose you?" Affirmative answers were followed by asking for the names of the individuals. The self-identification and superintendent identification appear quite compatible. However, we define an opponent as one named by either source.

2. Throughout this chapter we will be using Kendall's *tau-b* as our measure of association. It is a statistic designed for ordinal-level data and involves fewer assumptions than the correlations and regressions used in previous chapters.

3. See J.C. Walden, "School Board Changes and Superintendent Turnover," *Administrators Notebook*, 15 (1957), pp. 1–4.

4. Talcott Parsons, "Some Ingredients of a General Theory of Organization," *Administrative Theory in Organization*, ed. Andrew Halpin (Chicago: Midwest Administrative Center, 1958), pp. 40–72.

5. David Minar, "Community Politico and the School Board," *American School Board Journal*, 154 (March, 1967), pp. 33–38.

6. Opinions about reference groups were assessed by means of a "feeling thermometer." A response from 0 (low) to 100 (high) was recorded for each reference group.

7. Louis Masotti, "Political Integration in Suburban Education," *The New Urbanization*, ed. Scott Greer (New York: St Martins Press, 1968).

Chapter 12

Racial Problems as an Example of

the Board-Superintendent Interaction*

Racial conflict is the "external" or public issue par excellence. One is tempted to describe racial conflicts as episodic, but in this case the episodic has become almost routine. The racial issue in public education has always been a question of how the school system will respond to external demands. The court system, followed belatedly by Congress and the U.S. Department of Health, Education, and Welfare, has required that schools achieve integration, even if pupils must be bused from one school to another. The issue is one that superintendents and school board members would not have raised, but one that they must respond to. Racial conflict arouses fierce antagonism, propels interest groups into the educational policy-making process, and provides little opportunity for professional resources to be exchanged. Racial problems, along with school financing, stimulate more intense interest group activity than do any other issues (see Chapter 6). Unlike most issues, furthermore, the federal government is providing, through the judicial system, a serious challenge to the insularity of school systems. Superintendents see federal intervention as a seriously disruptive force, even more of a threat than militant civil rights organizations.

The division of responsibility between the school board and the superintendent and the impact of the community on school decision making have a major bearing on the resolution of the racial issue in the schools and the success of the civil rights movement. The school board and the superintendent are not equally sensitive to the racial issue. The boards reflect a more political perspective; the superintendent, a more educational one. Moreover, the two are likely to respond

*This is a revised version of an article that first appeared in *Sociology of Education*, Vol. 47, (Summer 1974), Michael O. Boss, co-author.

to the racial issue differently, boards with both substantive and symbolic policy outputs and superintendents primarily with substantive policy outputs.[1]

We attempt to examine the issue area from the perspective of the policy maker. Our analysis focuses on three principal variables: 1) policy maker perceptions of racial problems in the schools; 2) policy maker perceptions of the political environments surrounding the schools; and 3) the policy responses evoked, given the problems and political environments. Throughout our analysis, we treat the school board and the superintendent as two separate policy makers. Thus we can examine the racial problem from the perspective of both the school board and the superintendent, in order to trace separate paths of influence to the school board and the superintendent, and in order to link both individually to the policy response.

Our data for this chapter is based upon the augmented sample of districts (see Appendix A). However seven school districts with entirely white student populations are excluded from the sample for this analysis. The sample thus includes 503 school board members (weighted $N = 1033$) and 80 superintendents (weighted $N = 167$) in 81 school districts (weighted $N = 169$).

THE NATURE AND IMPORTANCE OF THE RACIAL PROBLEM

Our first concern is with the school board member and the superintendent's perceptions of racial problems in the schools. Two open-ended questions in the interview schedule tap this area. The first asks about major problems that affect education in the school district, and the second asks specifically about racial problems that affect education in the school district.[2]

Before considering these specific replies, we should set the overall pattern of board and superintendent responses. Table 12-1 indicates whether the superin-

TABLE 12-1
Racial-Problem Recognition by Boards and Superintendents

| | | Superintendent | | |
		No Problem Recognized	Problem Recognized	Total
School Board	No Problem Recognized	45%	8%	53%
	Problem Recognized	11%	35%	47%
	Total:	56%	43%[a]	$N = 166$
				Tau-b = .36

[a]Percentages do not add up to totals due to rounding error.

tendent perceived a problem and whether at least one board member within the district perceived a problem (the marginal figures). These responses are then cross-tabulated (internal cell entries).

Differences or conflicts between the superintendent and the school board in the recognition of racial problems are relatively minor (Table 12-1). The superintendent and the school board appear similar at the aggregate level in their sensitivity to racial problems. The differences in problem-type marginal totals are minor. The school board and the superintendent also seem to be in high agreement with each other (paired by district). Partial problem agreement, as indicated by the diagonal figures, is evident in four-fifths of the cases. In these terms, then, there is broad agreement between superintendent and board recognition, but it should be borne in mind that this agreement is established with the minimal criterion that at least one board member perceives a racial problem.

Let us turn now to the specific kinds of problems mentioned. The replies to the racial problem questions were coded into five categories. An examination of Table 12-2 indicates that the most frequent problems cited by both board members and superintendents are the general problems of integrating the students, integrating the students and faculty, integrating the schools, or just integration. We at first suspected that the preponderance of replies in the general integration category might be a function of an overly broad coding system. After reexamining the data and coding system, however, we feel this is not the case. Rather we are inclined to believe that the majority of school board members and superintendents are not able to identify the substantive nature of racial problems and therefore deal with such problems in very vague and general terms. But conversely, we should also note that the civil rights movement is highly symbolic and has raised relatively diffuse demands.[3] Consequently, school policy makers may approach the racial problem with a low level of information from within the school system and ambiguous cues from outside the school system.

Superintendents are much more likely to see federal forced integration as a

TABLE 12-2
Racial Problems Recognized by School Policy Makers

	School Board Members	Superintendents
No Problem	53.0	49.8
General Integration Problems	32.5	34.0
Black Militancy and Demands	8.6	12.7
White Opposition to Integration	4.1	0.6
Federal Forced Integration	3.8	9.4
Other	4.6	5.5
Total[a]	106.6%	112.0%
	N = 1033	*N = 167*

[a]Total percentages exceed 100 due to multiple responses.

problem than are school board members. Indeed, in only a few districts did a majority of school board members agree that forced integration was a problem. We are not surprised, however, if we consider that the entry of a dominant actor — the federal government — tends to resolve or displace any conflict.[4] Consequently, the political conflict with which the school board must deal is reduced and the task of complying with integration orders is left for the superintendent.

School policy makers citing problems in the remaining categories were distributed so irregularly among the school districts that further analysis of these problems was judged to be highly tenuous. Moreover, problems in the general integration category were cited by policy makers in all but 13 of the school districts in the sample. The frequency of response and the distribution of response suggests that the general integration problem best describes the racial problem for most school policy makers. This category will therefore be used in the analysis as the basic racial problem variable.

A measure of racial problem intensity for each individual policy maker was constructed within the general integration category by recoding replies according to the following schedule:[5]

	code
no problem noted	0
problem but not major	1
major problem	2

At the individual level 62 percent of the board members saw no problem, 24 percent saw a problem, and 15 percent saw a major problem. Superintendent perceptions were almost identical: 61 percent, 24 percent, and 12 percent, respectively. Racial problem intensity was then summarized at the board level by taking the mean of all individual board member scores for each school board. The means and standard deviations for board racial problem intensity and superintendent racial problem intensity for all school districts are given in Table 12-3. Although we will

TABLE 12-3
General Racial Problem Intensity

	Board Racial Problem Intensity		Superintendent Racial Problem Intensity	
	Mean	*S.D.*	*Mean*	*S.D.*
All Cases	.50	.51	.55	.74
North	.40	.45	.45	.68
South	.72	.57	.73	.83
Urban	.84	.40	1.02	.74
Suburban	.35	.36	.44	.71
Small Town	.38	.57	.31	.63

not discuss their implications, it is important to note the striking differences by region and urbanism also presented in the table.

Structural Antecedents of the Racial Problem

Major differences in racial problem intensity exist among the school districts in our sample with scores ranging from 0.0 or no problem to 2.0 or the maximum score possible. These differences may in part reflect the variation in policy maker sensitivity to racial problems, an issue we shall consider in the next section. A more fundamental consideration in explaining these differences, however, is the variation in racial structure or composition among the school districts.

The relationship between board racial problem intensity and the size of the nonwhite[6] student population expressed in absolute terms is only moderate ($r = .26$). The proportion of nonwhite students in the school district provides a standardized measure of racial structure. The relationship between the percent of nonwhite students and board racial problem intensity for the school districts in our sample is a moderately strong ($r = .54$). We suspected, however, that the relationship between racial problems and racial structure was probably curvilinear. Board racial problem intensity and the percent of nonwhite students were therefore entered into a polynomial regression analysis.[7] The resulting function explains 60 percent of the variance in board racial problem intensity among the school districts and takes the form of the "J" curve illustrated in Figure 12-1.

The most significant feature of the characteristic curve is the rapid rise (high slope) at the lower end. Racial problem intensity rises to two-thirds of the peak magnitude within the first 15 percent of nonwhite student level. It is evident that policy makers would experience the most severe rise in problem level or "problem shock" with the initial increases in nonwhite student population.

A second significant feature of the characteristic curve is the reversal at about the 38 percent nonwhite student level. We cannot offer a complete explanation for the reversal. However, as the proportions of white and nonwhite students in the school district equalize, more even and complete integration may occur through weight of numbers and thus reduce the problem of integration through policy. On the other hand, as the proportions of white and nonwhite students in the school district equalize, polarization of races may occur and thus transform the general problem of integrating the schools into a more crucial problem of direct and open racial conflict. Our data are incomplete but indicate that either conclusion may hold.

In contrast to the school board, superintendent perception of racial problems in the schools does not appear to be as directly linked to the racial structure within the school district. The relationship between superintendent racial problem intensity and the percent of nonwhite students in the district, ($r = .24$), for example, is about one-half of that for school boards. The relationship between individual board member racial-problem recognition and district racial structure is .34, lower than the aggregate correlation, but still higher than the superintendent correlation.[8]

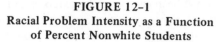

FIGURE 12-1
Racial Problem Intensity as a Function
of Percent Nonwhite Students

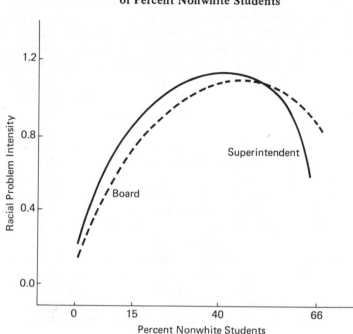

A partial explanation for the lower superintendent-based correlation may lie in the professional education ethos. First, superintendents define the function of the schools quite narrowly, with stress on the educational rather than the social or political functions. They, therefore, do not directly associate the racial problems evident in the general community with the school system. Second, superintendents hold highly universalistic norms and tend to see no color lines. They therefore approach day-to-day difficulties and routine problems in the schools without regard to the racial overtones that might be involved. As a consequence of these two trends, superintendents are less sensitive to racial problems when they first arise in the schools.[9]

Community Impact on the Racial Problem

Two elements in the community have particular bearing on the sensitivity of the school policy maker to racial problems in the schools: civil rights activity and white concern or tension over racial matters. We do not attempt to unwind the sources of the civil rights movement but assume that civil rights activity is an exogenous variable which affects the school policy-making process. Our measure of civil rights activity is constructed from school board member replies to two open-ended questions asking what groups from the community had been active in school district affairs or had been critical of the school board. Each school district is scored on the level of civil rights activity according to the proportion of board members which mentioned civil rights or other related groups in their replies. Our measure does not indicate the objective level of civil rights activity in the community, but rather the effectiveness of civil rights groups in reaching the policy maker. Interestingly, we found that board members with strong attitudes toward civil rights groups, whether positive or negative in tone, were the most likely to respond positively to civil rights demands.[10] And it is, of course, the effectiveness of civil rights activity that is of concern in analyzing the policy process. Civil rights activity scores have a range from 0 to 86, a mean of 13.2, and a standard deviation of 23.9.

Our measure of white racial tension is constructed from school board member replies to an open-ended question asking what issues or problem areas were sources of tension or concern among the people in the school district. Each school district is scored on the level of white racial tension according to the proportion of board members mentioning that white groups or individuals were concerned over racial issues. As in the case of civil rights activity, our measure does not indicate the objective level of tension but rather the policy maker's perception of the state of the community. Further, our measure does not necessarily indicate anti integration or racist feelings but rather a broad complex of concern, anxiety, and fear over racial issues in general and the impact of racial problems on the welfare of children in the schools and the welfare of the community.[11] White racial tension scores have a range from 0 to 100, a mean of 19.7, and a standard deviation of 7.2.

Board racial problem intensity and superintendent racial problem intensity were individually entered into two regression equations, one with civil rights activity and one with white racial tension, while controlling for percent nonwhite students in the school district. The results, in the form of simple correlations (*r*) and standardized regression coefficients (*beta*) are given in Table 12-4.

It is evident from the data in Table 12-4 that the factors underlying board racial problem intensity and the factors underlying superintendent racial problem intensity differ. In the case of the school boards, the percent nonwhite maintains its strength even when the political variables are also considered. School boards thus appear to draw cues concerning the nature and importance of racial problems from the racial structure within the school and, to a smaller extent, from community activity and feeling outside the schools. In the case of superintendents, however, the significance of the percent nonwhite student level is reduced to virtually nothing if we control for either of the political variables. Superintendents appear to draw cues concerning the nature and importance of racial problems more from community activity and feeling outside of the school than from the racial structure within the system. Our earlier argument that superintendents show initial insensitivity to racial problems is supported further. The disquieting element is the implication that superintendents do not recognize and respond to routine racial problems in the schools until they balloon into major public issues.

TABLE 12-4
Racial Problem Intensity as a Function of Civil Rights
Activity and White Racial Tension

	School Boards		Superintendents	
	Simple r	*Beta*	*Simple r*	*Beta*
Percent Nonwhite Students	.54	.48	.24	.08
Civil Rights Activity	.36	.11	.36	.31
Percent Nonwhite Students	.54	.40	.24	.06
White Racial Tension	.47	.26	.39	.36

Civil rights activity and white racial tension both appear to excite school policy maker awareness of racial problems. There is a strong relationship between civil rights activity and tension ($r = .78$), however; thus we cannot directly interpret their relative impact on the policy maker. There is a strong indication in the data that white racial tension arises as a direct consequence of civil rights activity rather than as a result of a growing nonwhite population. If we control for the size of the nonwhite population in the district, the relationship between white racial tension and civil rights activity is not significantly changed (.73).[12] In contrast, if we control for civil rights activity, the relationship between the size of the nonwhite population and white racial tension is reduced to an insignificant level ($r = .14$).[13] This causal link suggests that civil rights activity (1) excites the policy maker directly and (2) excites white racial tension. White racial tension further excites the policy maker. The results of the regression analysis of racial problem intensity with civil rights activity, white racial tension, and the percent nonwhite student population are presented in diagrammatic form in Figure 12-2 with this causal link included. It is evident that the impact of civil rights activity would be grossly underestimated if consideration of the indirect causal effect were not taken into account. Moreover, it indicates the extent to which the effectiveness of civil rights activity in exciting policy makers to racial problems is tied to mobilizing the white community.[14]

Policy Responses to the Racial Problem

We have discussed the nature and importance of racial problems in the schools in some detail. Our second concern is with the nature of policy responses to these problems. The policy response variable is constructed from school board member and superintendent replies to an open-ended question asking what action the

FIGURE 12-2
Three Factors Underlying Racial Problem Intensity
Values given are standardized regression
coefficients for predicting Board Racial
Problem Intensity. Values in parentheses
are for predicting Superintendent Racial
Problem Intensity.

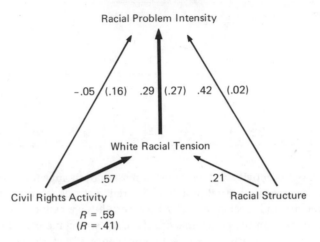

school district had taken or what policies the school board had adopted to deal with racial problems in the schools. The replies were recoded into five categories:

1. *Specific action to integrate schools including busing programs, altering school boundaries, and integrating faculty.*
2. *General policy of integrating schools but no indication of specific action.*
3. *Passive response restricted to discussing problem or investigating problem further (including the formation of committees).*
4. *Other action not classifiable in the above.*
5. *No action or policy.*

The distributions of board member and superintendent replies in which either the superintendent or a school board member recognized problems are given in Table 12-5.

We noted earlier that school policy makers tend to treat racial problems in the schools in general terms. An examination of Table 12-5 indicates that policy makers are similarly general in their response to racial problems. Of the policy makers noting any policy response at all, less than one-fifth identity specific action to cope with the problem of integrating the schools. The apparent ambiguity of school integration policy is further indicated by the large number of contradictions among the policy makers within each school district with regard to what

TABLE 12–5
Responses to Racial Problems Reported by
Governors in Problem School Districts

	School Board Members	Superintendents
Policy of no Action Ignored problem.	43.2	35.2
Passive Policy Discussion or investigation of problem but no indication of action.	20.6	23.6
General Policy Policy to integrate schools or improve race relations but no indication of specific action.	25.1	38.1
Specific Action Policy Action to integrate schools including busing, altering boundaries, integration of faculty.	11.6	12.9
Other Not classifiable in the above, including action to avoid integration.	9.1	6.4
Total[a]	109.6% N = 783	116.2% N = 114

[a]Total percentages exceed 100 due to multiple responses.

policy might be in effect. In nearly 70 percent of the districts, contradictions over policy were evident. For instance, one policy maker would state that the policy was to integrate the schools, another would state that the district had no policy and had done nothing. We have no objective measure of the effectiveness of the school districts in dealing with racial problems in general or in dealing with the integration problem specifically. However, we suspect that most policy, by design or by default, is woefully inadequate, which may in part account for and is substantiated by the general failure of integration plans in most school districts today.[15]

Each school district in our sample was classified according to the type of policy that had been adopted to deal with the general integration problem based upon the distribution of the policy replies by a majority of the policy makers in that district. Three general categories of policy response were utilized: (1) no response or no action; (2) a response to the issue including discussion and investigation but no action; and (3) a direct response to the problem in the form of some integration plan. The classification scheme employed is illustrated in Figure 12–3. It will be noted that some overlap exists between policy categories as a result of conflict in replies. Questionable cases were resolved by weighting the superintendent double. The distribution of school districts in each of the policy response categories is given in Table 12–6.

TABLE 12–6
The Distribution of Policy Types in Problem School Districts

	No Policy	Problem Policy	Issue Policy	Total	N
All Districts	22%	36%	41%	99%	115
North	24	36	40	100	68
South	19	37	44	100	47
Urban	07	72	21	100	47
Suburban	28	19	53	100	33
Small Town	36	06	57	99	36

There is a major conceptual difficulty in our classification of policy responses that warrants comment. The issue response encompasses two types of policy behavior, both of which have nearly identical outward characteristics. The issue response may be an intermediate stage of information gathering and planning prior to dealing positively with the integration problem and, therefore, should be treated theoretically and methodologically as part of a serial order or policy responses. But the issue response may be an attempt to delay or avoid taking a

FIGURE 12–3
School District Policy Classification Scheme

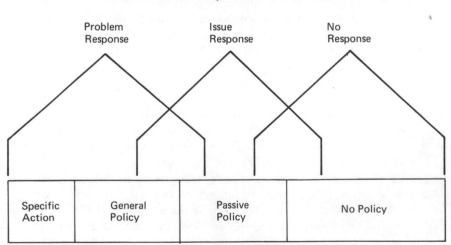

position on integration, particularly under conditions of actual or potential community conflict, and should thus be treated theoretically and methodologically as part of a nominal order of policy responses. Unfortunately we cannot separate the two components of the issue response and must treat the response as confounded. Our analysis is thus severely complicated. Initially, response districts will be pooled and no-response versus response district differences examined. Then as a second step, issue response versus problem response district differences will be examined. This does not solve the problem of confounding but does allow us to work around it.

Problem and Policy: The Linkage

In order to explore the linkage between policy maker perceptions of the problem and subsequent policy response, the policy responses for each school district were recoded as a dummy variable (0 for districts with no policy response, 1 for districts with a policy response regardless of type) and entered into a regression equation with board racial problem intensity and superintendent racial problem intensity. The analysis included only problem school districts.[16]

The relationships between policy response and both board racial problem intensity and superintendent racial problem intensity are quite strong ($r = .33$ and .55, respectively). Note that the attenuated distribution of problem districts only reduces the measured correlation. The true relationship between policy response and problem intensity is thus much higher than indicated by the correlations. Our analysis may mask the effect of feedback from policy response to problem intensity. However, the strength of the linkage suggests that this effect is minor.

The linkage between problem and policy suggests that school policy makers act primarily in response to problems rather than to prevent problems. The responsive, rather than innovative, character of school policy making is further indicated by a finding that policy makers in only one school district in our sample acted to deal with the racial problem before it became a public issue. A significant paradox about school policy making is that school policy makers argue that they are unable to follow innovative policies in the schools because of public pressure, and yet school policy makers do not appear to take innovative action to deal with problems until such problems become public issues and public pressure is, indeed, really brought to bear.[17]

The linkage between problem and policy allows us to make an assessment of the relative importance of the school board and the superintendent in the school policy-making process with regard to a public issue like race. We have treated the school board and the superintendent as separate actors to this point. Our analysis of their relative importance in policy making, however, must assume that the two actors work at least in part as a team. We should, therefore, control the contribution of each type of policy maker to policy outputs for the effect of the other. With such a control, the contribution of superintendent racial problem intensity to policy response is considerably greater than that of school board racial problem intensity to policy response (*beta* = .50 and .11, respectively). We can speculate that if the school board ever asserts its policy-making authority, it will be in an episodic kind of public issue such as racial problems. But even in this kind of policy-making situation, the superintendent emerges as the dominant actor. We suspect that when more routine policy-making situations arise in the schools system, the dominance of the superintendent is even more marked.

Civil Rights Activity and the Nature of Policy Responses

In order to explore the factors that might influence the nature of the policy response, the policy responses for each school district were recoded as a second dummy variable (0 for districts with an issue response, 1 for districts with a problem response, and excluding districts with no response) and entered into a regression equation with board racial problem intensity, superintendent racial problem intensity, civil rights activity, and white racial tension. The results of the regression analysis are given in Table 12-7.

TABLE 12-7
Policy Response Type as a Function of Racial Problem Intensity,
White Racial Tension, and Civil Rights Activity, Controlling
for District Racial Structure

Variable	Simple r	Beta
Civil Rights Activity	.42	.29
White Racial Tension	.35	.15
Board Racial Problem Intensity	.20	.09
Superintendent Racial Problem Intensity	.17	.21
	$R = .57$	

The goals of the civil rights movement within the schools include the attainment of varying mixtures of symbolic and substantive policy outputs. In many cases, civil rights leaders are as much interested in the legitimation of civil rights demands by school policy makers as in making gains in the integration of the schools. Consequently, the effectiveness of civil rights activity is not necessarily linked to a problem policy response by the school district. It is clear from Table 12-7, however, that civil rights activity is the most important factor influencing the type of policy response (*beta* = .29).

To explore the impact of civil rights activity on policy response further, we divided the sample into two groups: (1) districts in which civil rights activity was evident and (2) districts in which civil rights activity was not evident. The differences in issue-problem responses attributable to the level of civil rights activity within the first group are greater than the differences in issue-problem responses attributable to the presence or absence of civil rights activity between the first and second group.[18] Moreover, within the first group the likelihood of a problem response increases as the level of civil rights activity increases (r = .44).[19] The impact of civil rights activity on policy response is also significant among the 16 districts in our sample in which the federal government had intervened to force integration. Of the districts, eight were classified as problem response and eight were classified as issue response. In 13 of the districts, the type of policy response could be predicted solely from the level of civil rights activity and in all eight of the problem response districts, civil rights activity was markedly higher than in the issue response districts. We should note, however, that the social and political conditions within the district that give rise to a successful civil rights movement may also permit school policy makers to adopt integration plans with less fear of community backlash. We doubt that civil rights activity, in itself, is sufficient in most cases to bring about integration within the schools. The level of civil rights activity does appear to have a significant bearing on the policy outcomes.[20]

We suggested earlier that white racial tension represents concern over racial problems in the schools and not necessarily opposition to integration of the schools. Assuming this generally neutral perspective, we might expect white racial tension to evoke assurances from policy makers that problems in the schools are under control but to have little impact on eventual integration action. The data in Table 12-7 lend support to this argument, for it is evident that white racial tension, if anything, has a positive bearing on the nature of the policy response (*beta* = .15). One caution is necessary here. Over the total range of districts with some policy response, the effect of white racial tension on the type of policy response may balance out to be neutral. In any single district, however, white racial tension may give rise to strong support for or opposition against integration plans and affect the type of policy response.

We remarked in the introduction that school boards and superintendents are likely to respond to the racial issue differently; the school board is inclined to symbolic policy outputs, or in this case, an issue response.[21] This characteristic of policy behavior is evident in the data in Table 12-7. Board racial problem intensity has little bearing on the type of policy response (*beta* = .09), indicating that the school board is equally disposed to both the issue response and problem response. In contrast, superintendent racial problem intensity does have some bearing on the type of policy response (*beta* = .21), indicating that the superintendent, to the extent that he is involved in racial policy making, is more disposed to a problem response. A dilemma for civil rights groups appears; although the school board appears to be more sensitive to racial problems than the superintendent initially, and although the school board appears to play a more important role in racial policy making than the superintendent, action by the superintendent is more likely to lead to a positive integration effort within the schools.[22]

INTEREST GROUP ACTIVITY AND RACIAL POLICY MAKING

To maintain simplicity, we have limited our analysis thus far to two variables relating to community influence on school policy making: civil rights activity and

white racial tension. In this section, we expand our analysis to examine briefly
the impact of interest group activity of school racial policy making. Our interest
is twofold. First, we are interested in the specific question of the effect of interest
group activity on policy maker sensitivity and responsiveness to racial problems
in the schools. And second, we are interested in the general question of the extent
to which interest group activity sets the political climate and establishes the
informational, cue-taking systems in which policy makers operate.

The variables we use refer to the distribution and intensity of board-
interest group interaction over a broad range of issue areas common to most
school districts. As we noted earlier with regard to civil rights activity, the measure
does not indicate the objective level of interest group activity but rather the
effectiveness of interest groups in reaching the policy maker. Further, with the
exception of civil rights groups, our measure is one of general political activity
rather than issue-specific activity. (See Chapter 6 for the measures of interest group
perception by board members and Table 12–8 for the listing of groups.)

Board racial problem intensity and superintendent racial problem intensity
were entered into regression equations with the set of interest group variables.
Civil rights groups, as we would expect, have singular importance in exciting policy
maker awareness of racial problems in the schools (*beta* = .50 for boards, .57 for
superintendents). Only right-wing groups have much additional impact on board
members (*beta* = .21). Service clubs serve that function for superintendents
(*beta* = .20).

If white racial tension is brought into the equation, the impact of civil
rights groups on policy makers drops markedly (*beta* = .25 and .41 for the board
and superintendent, respectively). Community reaction to and concern over racial
issues tend to be channeled through informal protest as well as through formal
interest groups. Introducing racial tension does not change the impact of most
other interest groups on policy makers to any significant degree. Formal interest
groups are failing to capitalize on any white racial tension or discontent that might
be evident in the community. The exception to this is right-wing groups. If white
racial tension is brought into the equation, the impact of right-wing groups on
board members is reduced by about one-half (*beta* = .11). Right-wing groups thus
appear to take advantage of racial discontent for their own purposes.[23]

In order to explore the impact of interest group activity on policy
response, the policy responses for each school district were recoded as a set of
two dummy variables (the first indicating an issue response or no response, the
second indicating a problem response or no response) and entered into a canonical
correlation with the set of interest group variables while controlling for racial
problem intensity.[24] Canonical correlation is an extension of the multiple-correlation method that allows prediction from a set of independent or predictor variables
to a set of dependent or criterion variables. The method further allows the compu-
tation of successive orthogonal prediction equations from the predictor to criterion
sets of variables. The results of the canonical correlation analysis are given in
Table 12–8.

TABLE 12-8
Canonical Correlation of Interest Group Activity and
Policy Responses, Controlling for Problem Intensity

Interest Group	First Canonical Coefficients	Second Canonical Coefficients
Civil Rights	.349	-.287
Taxpayers	.230	-.033
Service Clubs	.179	.417
PTA	-.149	.228
Citizens Advisory Committee	.113	-.009
League of Women Voters	-.114	-.220
Religious	-.081	-.095
Labor	-.081	-.179
Right-wing	-.079	.464
Left-wing	.066	-.728
Political	.066	-.157
Teachers	.038	.250
Business and Professional	.030	-.010
Neighborhood	.028	-.226
Policy Response:		
Problem Response	.853	-.351
Issue Response	.521	.936
	$R_c = .86$	$R_c = .54$

As indicated, there are two prediction equations, each represented by a set of canonical coefficients (interpretable as standardized regression coefficients). The first equation predicts principally problem response and to a lesser extent issue response with a canonical correlation of .86 (interpretable as a multiple-correlation). This equation does not distinguish between the two types of responses (the coefficients of both variables in the criterion set are positively signed), an indication of the confounded elements in the issue response that we discussed earlier. The second equation predicts principally issue response and only partially problem response with a canonical correlation of .54. This equation does distinguish between the two types of responses (the coefficients of the variables in the criterion set are opposite in sign), an indication that under some conditions the issue response is a distinct type of response from the problem response. Each equation can be interpreted as representing a significant and different pattern of interest group activity that influences the policy process.

The first equation or pattern is marked by a relatively low level of interest group impact and suggests a rather conflict-free or routine policy process. Civil rights groups, as we would again expect, are singularly important. The other significant interest groups are all rather orthodox or establishment in tone (i.e., service clubs, PTA, League of Women Voters). The curious exception is the taxpayer groups. We can offer no explanation for this exception except perhaps that taxpayer groups tend to sensitize school policy makers to political issues in general, thus resulting in more timely policy responses. The most important feature of this pattern is that civil rights groups appear to have the most effective impact on policy outcomes when the pattern holds.

The second pattern, in contrast to the first, is marked by a relatively high level of interest group impact and suggests a rather conflictual policy process. Under these conditions of high interest group conflict, the impact of civil rights groups on the policy process is diminished in both relative and absolute terms. Left-wing groups, right-wing groups, and taxpayer groups emerge as the dominant political actors and overshadow civil rights groups. The relative weights of the coefficients of the variables in the criterion set are an indication that under conditions of conflict an issue response is much more likely to occur than a problem response (coefficients = .936 and – .351 for issue response and problem response, respectively). There are two important features of this conflictual pattern. First, civil rights groups do not appear to have a very effective impact on policy outcomes. And second, policy makers are much more likely to respond to the controversy than to the root racial problem.

We are limited by our approach in what we can conclude about the direct impact of any single interest group on racial policy outcomes. It is clear, however, that the level of civil rights group activity does increase policy maker awareness of racial problems in the schools and can increase the likelihood that some kind of integration policy will be adopted in the system. Further, we cannot translate our findings into conclusions that are applicable to the whole range of issues that school policy makers confront. It is also clear, however, that interest group activity does increase policy maker sensitivity to some kinds of problems and can influence the type of policy response to some kinds of problems. Thus interest group activity definitely appears to influence the school policy-making process, both in its direct impact on the racial issue and in setting the tempo of the political climate in which school policy makers operate.

Our principal finding in this chapter highlights a major difference between school board and superintendent response to racial problems. Whereas the board is more sensitive to racial problems than is the superintendent, the board is as likely to respond to the controversy associated with racial stress as to the substantive problem. The less sensitive superintendent, however, will respond substantively to the educational issue at hand. It would appear that civil rights groups can best gain symbolic rewards by directing their energies toward the school board; for progress in integrating the schools, they must address themselves to the superintendent.

Both white racial tension and civil rights agitation heighten the policy maker's awareness of racial problems, but only civil-rights agitation affects the nature of policy responses. Further, high levels of group activity, regardless of the ideological orientation of the groups involved, decrease the effectiveness of civil rights groups and increases the likelihood that school policy makers will respond symbolically to the controversy and conflict evident rather than substantively to the racial problem. The effectiveness of civil rights groups can perhaps be increased by mobilizing informal support and concern in the white community but may be reduced by bringing other interest groups of any political persuasion into the conflict.

We have found that district governors perceive and respond to racial problems in the schools in a very vague and general fashion. We can see a high sensitivity to racial problems but a low understanding of the substantive nature of the problems or how best to respond to the problems. Here may be one of the most important factors involved in both resolving racial problems in the schools and in the continued self-governance of the schools. Unfortunately it is an area where we have offered the least clarification, and indeed, an area that social science as a whole has just begun to explore. Our findings suggest several areas where further research is required. However, the effectiveness with which the governors recognize and respond to problems in the schools and the effectiveness with which they anticipate and act to prevent problems in the schools may be the most important in the immediate future.

NOTES

1. Murray Edelman, *The Symbolic Uses of Politics* (Chicago: University of Chicago Press, 1964) is an incisive work on this point.

2. The questions are:

"In your opinion what is the most important problem facing education in this school district? Would you tell me more about that? Now what do you think is the second most important problem? And would you tell me more about that?"
"What kinds of racial problems or issues have come up in this school district?"

Multiple replies to both questions were coded (see note Table 12-2).

3. Robert L. Crain and David Street, "School Desegregation and School Decision Making," *Urban Affairs Quarterly*, 2 (September, 1966), pp. 65-67, examine this point in more depth.

4. E. E. Schattschneider, *The Semisovereign People: A Realist's View of Democracy in America* (New York: Holt, Rinehart, and Winston, 1960).

5. White opposition to integration, black militancy, and general integration were pooled to form the general integration variable. Responses citing racial problem as one of the most important problems facing school district were coded as a major problem. Responses noting racial problem (i.e., second question) but not recognizing racial problem as one of most important problems were coded as a problem but not major.

6. We use the term nonwhite throughout this chapter, in part because our data refers specifically to nonwhite students in the schools, and in part because we feel our analysis is applicable to the broad range of racial problems, and not just to those relating to blacks.

7. Two districts, one with 87 percent nonwhite students and the other with 97 percent nonwhite students, were excluded from the analysis because of discontinuity in the data.

8. It is a well-known psychometric finding that the mean of several individual estimates is generally more accurate than any individual estimates. Hays, for instance, writes, ". . . pooled estimates are actually weighted averages of the estimates from the different samples. The big advantage lies in the fact that the sampling error will tend to be smaller for the pooled estimate than for any single sample's value taken alone." William L. Hays, *Statistics for Psychologists* (New York: Holt, Rinehart, and Winston, 1963), p. 209.

9. Robert L. Crain, *The Politics of School Desegregation* (Chicago: Aldine, 1968), pp. 116–117, offers an excellent treatment of the point under the rubric of "color-blindness."

10. The specific data is part of another forthcoming study and is not included here.

11. This is evident in the works of both Crain, *op. cit.*, and B.T. Edwards, *School Desegregation in the North* (San Francisco: Chandler, 1967). See also Paul P. Sheatsley, "White Attitudes Toward the Negro," *Daedalus*, 95 (Winter, 1966), pp. 217–238.

12. Our data only cover the student population. Our analysis assumes that the proportion of nonwhites in the community is similar to the proportion in the schools.

13. The remaining correlations are: civil rights activity and percent nonwhite, $r = .55$; civil rights activity and percent nonwhite controlling for white racial tension, $= .22$.

14. This tends to support a model proposed by Michael Lipsky, "Protest as a Political Resource," *American Political Science Review*, 62 (December, 1968), pp. 1144–1158.

15. See, for example, the recent report "School Desegregation: How Far will the Country Go?" *Congressional Quarterly*, 28 (December 11, 1970), pp. 2953–2957.

16. Problem school districts are those districts in which at least one school board member or the superintendent report racial problems.

17. Neal Gross, *Who Runs Our Schools?* (New York: Wiley, 1958), argues that community pressure interferes with school policy making while Roscoe C. Martin, *Government and the Suburban Schools* (Syracuse, N.Y.: Syracuse University Press, 1962), argues that political control of the schools is necessary to evoke policy changes in an otherwise static system.

18. The proportional reduction in error within the first group was 20 percent compared to an adjusted proportional reduction in error between groups of 13 percent.

19. The r is based on an attenuated distribution which masks its total significance.

20. Crain and Street, *op. cit.*, reached the opposite conclusion. Civil rights activity did, however, appear to be quite high in the cities studied.

21. We add that token integration plans are equally symbolic.

22. Bert E. Swanson, *The Struggle for Equality* (New York: Hobbs, Dorman, 1966), provides an excellent example of a case in which the superintendent emerged as the key figure in implementing integration plans in the New York schools.

23. This supports the concept of interest group entrepreneurial activity developed by Mancur Olson, *The Logic of Collective Action* (Cambridge: Harvard University Press, 1965), and Robert H. Salisbury, "An Exchange Theory of Interest Groups," *Midwest Journal of Political Science*, 13 (February, 1969), pp. 1–32.

24. The treatment of policy responses as a set of variables is the best means of dealing with the effect of confounding discussed earlier, but at a cost of methodological simplicity.

Chapter 13

The State of

School Governance

This study was undertaken in the 1960s, a period in which demands for participation, condemnations of unresponsive public institutions and vigorous dissent from long unchallenged policies became commonplace. Schools, like most public institutions, were targets of the drive toward democratization. Not only in the popular rhetoric of the new left, but also in the more sober assessment of such prestigious institutions as the Ford Foundation, schools were condemned as overly bureaucratized, rigid, and nonresponsive.

     Now that the tumult and shouting has subsided, we are in a position to assert that schools — like most public institutions — weathered the storm. We began this book with a discussion of the dilemma of school governance. On the one hand, schools provide an expert service, the quality of which the client has traditionally been judged incompetent to assess. On the other hand, school district governments are legally established in such a way as to provide the expectation of responsive and responsible governance. The presence of elections and other mechanisms of accountability means that school district governance can be judged against the standards of traditional democratic theory.

     An essential element of representative democracy is a responsive and active legislative assembly. There are three components involved at the school district level. First, there is the selection process. Second, there are ongoing linkage relationships between the board and the public. Finally, there is the interaction between the board and the superintendent. Ideally, the board is selected in accordance with constituency preferences; in response to community demands and needs the board formulates policy; and the superintendent, as the legal "clerk", administers the policy. The board then performs an oversight func-

tion with respect to this administering. Hence, educational policy is made congruent with constituent needs and demands. Obviously, the ideal is not fully realized in school districts nor in other similar governing structures.

SCHOOLS AS COMMONWEAL ORGANIZATIONS

Whatever the difficulties of obtaining the impossible, and however inadequate the performance of the governmental units, we make two fundamental assertions: (1) democratic theory is an appropriate standard by which to judge educational governance; (2) educational governance receives a mixed report card.

The first point involves a return to our discussion of experts and representatives. Schools, we believe, produce "public goods," are subject to collective decision-rules, and are a commonweal institution. Schools also produce private benefits, have a developing expertise (at least as reliable as that of, say, psychiatry, but not as reliable as other technologies), and hence can be judged as service institutions. Schools, then, are a mixed form of institution. Judging them as service institutions is not our major objective as political scientists, though clearly political scientists should not be excluded from the fraternity of cost-benefit analysis.

At the risk of oversimplification, the available evidence is that as service institutions, schools perform somewhat better than they do as commonweal institutions. For many Americans, the principal utility of education has been thought of in terms of its effects on economic productivity. They measure the value of education in terms of the present value of the extra lifetime income one can expect to receive as a result of education. Education supposedly increases an individual's general skills, and as a result, individual productivity and the productivity of the entire economy. Consequently, national achievement tests are widely assumed to be appropriate as indicators of service performances. There should be only mild complaint here, albeit there are distressing indicators that basic skills are sometimes not taught as effectively as they should be. Moreover, all Americans do not have equal opportunity to gain access to technical skills. However, one solution to that problem is simple, namely, busing.

The deliberately callous way in which busing is introduced as a solution leads us to our major concern: schools are commonweal in that the goals they distribute allegedly benefit the entire community. Thus equality of access is presumed. With regard to busing, however, decisions were generally made without regard to either community expectations or anticipation of the consequences for the quality of education. The thrust for busing came primarily from the U.S. Commission on Civil Rights, using the Coleman Report as its justification. While the Coleman Report found that the functions traditionally associated with quality of education (per pupil expenditures, curricular innovations, etc.) were unrelated to achievement, there was some evidence that the best learning experience took place in middle class white schools.[1] Hence, the Commission called for an end to neighborhood schools, and the busing of children to racially balanced schools began.[2] In other words, the control of the school (insofar as control involves a choice of attendance areas) was not subject to community preferences. Soon, of course, political opposition became rampant, and busing as a panacea has been dying a violent but slow death.

The entire debate involved, in reality, minimum concern with the performance of service functions by schools. Although whites fretted about the alleged decline of educational standards, there is no reliable evidence to support these fears — indeed, the evidence of the Coleman Report is to the contrary. Further, the effect of racially desegregated schools on blacks is far from certain. The available, skimpy evidence indicates only that "if desegregation continues over a fairly long period it usually raises black students' scores slightly. But the gains are usually small, and they depend on factors that nobody fully understands."[3]

While the Coleman Report was used to support busing, it was also used to defend decentralization and neighborhood schools: "of all the variables measured in the survey, the attitudes of student interest in school, self concept, and sense of environmental control show the strongest relation to achievement."[4] Consequently, it was argued that the only way one could maximize student interest and sense of control was to create a governing structure more proximate to the client. This single technical report provided ammunition both for the elimination of neighborhood schools *and* for the creation of more neighborhood schools. The fact of the matter is that the basic issue is not the relation of busing, or neighborhood schools, to the performance of the clients (students). The bone of contention is the ancient political question: who has effective control? Indeed, the expansion of Coleman's theme by Jencks *et al.*, who conclude that school quality has little effect on achievement, does not reduce the urgency of this question.[5] People *believe* that education is the key to success, and occasionally (when they perceive they are not getting what there is to get), try to influence the conduct of school governance. Whether various governing structures have any consequences for learning, they clearly have consequences for control of public institutions.

Here is where our judgment as political scientists begins. What have we learned about educational governance that allows us to assess its performance against the standards of democratic theory? A review of the findings would be cumbersome, but some of the main points stand out as particularly relevant. We will speak now of overall trends, blurring for the moment the distinctions which are contained in our analysis. Our first concern is with how the school district governors came to occupy their seats of authority.

It is patent that, when measured against the yardstick of a classic democratic theory of leadership selection, school district governance hardly comes through with flying colors. There are, indeed, certain broad prerequisites which might well be considered discriminatory. Competition is limited, sponsorship and pre-emptive appointments common. Challenges to the status quo are infrequent; incumbents are but rarely challenged and more rarely still defeated. There are often no issue differences at all in an election, and when there are they seldom deal with the educational program, per se.

Although it would be easy to interpret such results within a "conspiracy-establishment" framework, such a view belies the truth in most districts. In the first place, board members seldom see or use the board membership as a vehicle for political ambition. We tend to view that as a liability rather than an asset, but the point in the present context is that board members seldom reap political or personal profit from their service. A second, and related point, is that positions on the school board often go begging for occupants. If the establishment or ruling elite is keeping control on succession, it does so with a marvelously hidden and light touch, bringing it to the point of near disaster when candidates are scraped up at the last moment. Third, even though we clearly established that certain credentials by way of social background and public service characteristics marked the profile of board members, it was equally clear that the pool of potential board members in any community is enormously large. Moreover, especially in smaller areas, people can become board members with but a modicum of "relevant" background characteristics. Finally, the self-perpetuating aspects of board composition stem as much from a genuine desire for successors with some sort of public service record as from a desire to restrict the inner circle to those with the correct virtues.

Open, recurrent, and content-filled competition are relevant democratic criteria for the selection of board members. We argued that these criteria are but weakly satisfied in general. But there should also be relevant standards for judging how leaders interact with their constituents. Unlike the criteria for attaining office, however, those for elite-mass interaction achieve less consensus. Indeed, they constitute the battleground for longstanding debate about representative governments.

We adopted the standard of representatives acting in a responsive manner to constituents to mean, primarily, paying attention to and interacting with constituents and, secondarily, to mean sharing their preferences. By the standards of a vital, mass-elite interaction model the school boards would measure up only moderately well. We had glimpses of that in seeing how office is attained. Public involvement in recruitment and campaigns as gauged by board member reports (and by turnout figures, though not reported here) is on the low side. Turning more directly to ongoing interaction, the verdict is not appreciably improved. By extending the concept of responsiveness to include ad hoc, "individualized" interaction we were able to invest most districts with at least a modest amount of responsiveness. Yet the more potent form of elite-mass interaction — that including group expression — was surprisingly weak. Ironically, there was evidence that interest groups were important actors when they did assert themselves.

Our other assessment of linkages compared board member preferences with those of their constituents. Neither we nor democratic theorists hold that responsiveness means simply replication by the elite of the precise will and preferences of the masses (assuming that could be done). Nevertheless the extent of congruity between the board and its constituents is a matter of concern. Where congruence is low, boards would at least be held responsible for having a good reason as to why it is low.

As with the shortcomings in the area of leadership selection, those in the domain of mass-elite linkages would seem not to be the result of willful, deceitful, and self-serving motivations on the part of board members — though those elements are undoubtedly present in some measure. Rather, the path of least resistance is followed. The public, while declaring it wants delegates rather than trustees, nevertheless scarcely exerts itself to instruct the delegates. Communication is sparse, often one-sided in either the supportive or nonsupportive mode, and ad hoc. For its part the board feels threatened when any but harmless group activity flourishes because that has come to mean that all is not well in the district, that the natives are restless.

THE SALUTARY EFFECTS OF POLITICS

Failures in both the selection and linkage functions of the school system are primarily a manifestation of unused resources and opportunities for influence. Yet it is clear that certain conditions and structures facilitate the use of these resources so that they might be used in satisfying the criteria of democratic selection and responsive representation. These are not simply matters of chance.

We saw two main sources of structural antecedents. The first of these has to do with the scale of social and political life. In general, the more complex and diverse the socioeconomic environment, the more likely would the criteria of democratic selection and responsiveness operate. Political life is simply more vibrant, more competitive, more articulated, somewhat more "professional," and (inevitably) more divisive in such environments. While there are some social costs to this, that may well be the price exacted if the criteria of governance we have suggested are to be met. On the other hand, some complex environments do not develop the components of political vitality, and other less complex environments do.

A second set of structural features is manifestly political in nature. Nearly all of the failures outlined above are ameliorated when variables traditionally associated with political processes are introduced: ward elections, partisan appeals, more intense competition, and the like. These processes sometimes operate in direct fashion, as in improving the quantity and quality of electoral competition. At other times they function in a mediating, indirect fashion, as in strengthening the connection between metropolitanism and group responsiveness. Clearly, political competition — conflict, debate, elite turnover — strengthens the selection and linkage processes. As Dahl and Lindblom, Eulau and Prewitt, and numerous others have argued, political competition is essential to the control of the leaders by the led.[6] If one wishes to address the problem of change, it can safely be asserted that institutionalized politicization — undoing the work of the reformers — is a prerequisite to strengthening the linkage mechanisms between the board and the public. Of particular interest here is the slight improvement in attitude congruence in politically impregnated districts. Since such districts are also the most socially heterogeneous, the fact that they are even slightly more representative is of considerable significance.

Our findings on the relationship of responsiveness to reform are corroborative of the findings of recent studies of urban policy. In their study, Lineberry and Fowler found that reformed cities (those with manager government, at-large constituency, nonpartisan elections) were relatively unaffected in their taxing and spending policies by differences in the income, occupational, religious, or ethnic characteristics of their populations. In contrast, unreformed cities (those with traditional political institutions) were more reflective of the varied needs and interests of the community. Reformed governments "are associated with a lessened responsiveness of the cities to the enduring conflicts of political life."[7]

It should be noted that these analyses are generally based upon policy outputs, making them not directly comparable to the conclusions reached by us. However, one might argue that two studies of different governmental units, using different indicators, which nevertheless reach similar conclusions, provide compelling corroboration of the nature of response in reformed decisional structures.

This apolitical stance was, as we have noted, the ethos of the reform movement, and it was by no means limited to schools. Agger, Goldrich and Swanson find that the "community conservationist" ideology, one of "a-political" politics, rejects traditional notions of the legitimacy of interest group cleavages in much the same fashion as does the ideology of school administrators.[8] Mayor Richard Lee of New Haven, whose political career has been so widely documented, was a classic community conservationist, stressing benefits to citizens in general, rather than appealing to class or group cleavages. Lee, a powerful political leader, was in no sense subservient to experts. Indeed, he successfully mobilized expertise in the cause of his dominant goal: urban renewal. Although Lee's skillful building of a coalition in favor of urban renewal was politically adept, the issue itself united those traditionally identified with urban reform: the educated, activist, middle class. The coalition, as was typical of reform in general, and urban renewal in particular, did not include blacks. The impact of urban renewal was most visible in the downtown business district, and in middle-income apartment developments, not in improving the lives of ghetto residents. Despite, or because of, its progressive orientation, New Haven fell victim to the riots of the 1960s. In a sense, the neglect of minorities in urban renewal is ideologically comparable to the neglect of minorities in favor of efficiency in education.

The justification for the centralization within and consolidation across school districts — which helped lead to the counterdemand for the return of schools to "the people" — was efficiency. Systems planners demonstrated that the smallest efficient unit of operation was one of approximately 50,000 students.[9] Nowhere in the equations of systems planners is there a consideration of the human cost of centralization. The fact that nearly half of American cities have adopted the council manager plan lends additional credence to the notion that expertise, the relegation of as many questions as possible to the level of a technical problem, is a very pervasive political philosophy. If "the end of ideology" was prematurely declared, it is nevertheless the case that there has been a relentless move (with cyclical counterrevolutions, as in the 1960s) towards a society so complex that the competence of amateurs is seriously challenged.

It is exactly this question of competence which produces the dilemma of the expert in school governance. Dahl argues persuasively about the value of what he calls the "criterion of competence."[10] Some decisions should *not* be made democratically. Would one, for instance, want to be a patient in a democratic hospital, with majority vote determining diagnosis? Or fly across the Atlantic in an airplane in which the pilot abided by the decision of the passengers? Such examples sound absurd, but a glance at the real world renders them less so. For instance, loyalist units in the Spanish Civil War elected their officers and, occasionally, voted in support or opposition to their decisions. An examination of the referenda issue regularly submitted to voters may raise equally absurd questions of competence. For instance: should there be a vote on capital punishment? Legalization of marijuana? Both issues have been recently voted on, and perhaps they should be. But certainly the technical expertise of criminologists and pharmacologists was irrelevant to the decision of most people.

From the perspective of democratic theory, the problem is one of balance. To what extent can the public and its representatives determine when a decision is beyond their competence? There is no hard and fast rule, nor should there be. As we noted in the first chapter, many countries regard educational governance as beyond the competence of the average citizen. In America we theoretically do not. Ours is the model of lay control toward which many European educators look with envy. In fact, as we have seen, we have a commonweal institution behaving largely as though it were a service organization. But, given the mixed nature of the school, how can we sort out the mix? To begin, substantial portions of the "services" provided by schools are hardly so precise or value free as to make them understandable only to experts. Excluding for the moment the technical skills normally expected to be accrued by those who attend them, schools also assume the responsibility of teaching "good citizenship," history, the humanities, and other subjects which make little, if any, pretense toward the consensus of truth and knowledge characteristic of a science.

With regard to the teaching of basic skills, another problem exists. There is no knowledge base, about which practitioners can achieve consensus, unique to the teaching-learning process. Innovations abound, as education is faddish. Yet the evidence continues to mount that there is no appreciable link between the way a subject is taught and the way a subject is learned.[11] Teaching remains more of a craft, rather than a profession. The services provided by teachers sometimes succeed, sometimes fail. No one really knows why: "After a century of psychological research, educators still know little about how children learn."[12]

Given the fact that the experts have not demonstrated that they know extraordinarily more about education than laymen, the response to lay demands certainly should not create any fear of the reduction of quality. Polyarchy would probably not make a great deal of difference in output, though it might make a substantial difference in the processes through which the outcomes were achieved.

If we wish educational governance to perform in the manner of a commonweal institution, a polyarchy, or a representative democracy, we will have to provide it with the institutional linkage to the political process which it currently lacks. Such ideas are conspicuously absent in proposals for either decentralization or community control.

The myriad of proposals for various methods of creating a countervailing power to the superintendent and his bureaucracy generally coalesce around the notion of proximity. The smaller the decision-making unit, the greater the opportunity for participation. With considerable justification, traditional political organizations were as distrusted as administrators. The consequence is that, while the cast of characters in community schools, or decentralized schools, has shifted, the link between new elites and constituents has not been strengthened. Participation in elections is as low as (or lower than) in the elections of "centralized" school systems. Consequently, the new elite — those who sit on the new boards of education — share an insulation with the older elite. Recruitment paths are different: board members are typically recruited from various antipoverty organizations and established social welfare agencies. However, the same filtering process occurs. Poverty and welfare agencies are to community schools what civic and business associations are to the "normal" board.[13] Ideologies differ, conformity to dominant values does not. Linkages are no more apparent. For instance, many of the new elite call for deemphasis on achievement and development of a noncompetitive ethos. However, the residents of the areas represented by the new elites feel strongly that the purposes of school are vocational, and their images of appropriate learning environments are often traditional to authoritarian.

As we noted, there are three essential links in the chain of governance. When we turn our attention to the final third of the governance chain, the ability of the board to control the behavior of the superintendent in the name of the public, our mixed assessment continues. The majority of boards see no conflict between their responsibilities to the public and their obligations to the school administration. Members of boards cluster toward the "professional" role, one of deference to the superintendent. Deference is, of course, only the norm: complexities in the board-superintendent relationship abound. One of the most striking is the effect of board status upon its interaction with the superintendent. Higher status boards, presumably reflecting the ideology of the separation of policy and administration, are more likely than their lower status counterparts to stay clear of the day-to-day administrative problems of the superintendent. They wish to devote their attention to the educational program, and to avoid "meddling." Such boards, however, are more likely to oppose the superintendent regarding educational programs. Lower status boards do not seem to be able to develop a consistent opposition faction. Ironically, the higher status boards, while more willing to challenge the superintendent, are also more likely to defer to him when he responds to opposition.

Lower status boards — which are more likely to be unimpressed by the superintendent's professional credentials — are relatively scarce. Other sorts of factors which contribute to the development of opposition are similarly scarce. For example, boards whose recruitment process and competition structure are intertwined with the broader political process are more inclined to develop an independence from the superintendent. An open, competitive selection process reduces insularity, while the tendency of boards to engage in self-perpetuation contributes to isolation. Unfortunately, from the point of view of democratic theory, the majority of boards does not appear to be very political in this sense.

The urban school board, with its myriad of problem solving opportunities, is a particularly acute example of the problem of controlling the superintendent. The relation between community tension and opposition is stronger in big cities than in small towns. In spite of the more diffuse influence structure of metropolitan areas, the translation of community tension into board behavior is more apparent. Such a translation is even more immediate when the complexity of the demand structure is enhanced by institutional arrangements and a competition structure which links the school system to the larger political framework of the community. However, once again, such situations are the exception rather than the rule. Our overall conclusion is that boards are likely to become spokesmen *for* the superintendent *to* the community; their representational roles are reversed, and the superintendent becomes the dominant policy maker. Here is, of course, a serious gap in the chain of governance with a remedy far from apparent. Again, the dominance of experts is not an isolated phenomenon; it is not peculiar to schools.

If we apply the same reasoning to board-superintendent relations as we did to board-community relations, we would offer our usual prescription: large doses of politics. However, the same political processes which enhance the *responsiveness* of the board do not necessarily encourage an active *policy-making* role for the board. Although public involvement either through the electoral process or through group-related activities does lead to greater willingness on the part of the board to question the superintendent's priorities, the board's attempts to play an active role in the policy-making process are frustrated by the complexity of educational problems and by its inability to gain control of a sprawling educational bureaucracy. The more conflictual and political the system, the more active the board is in opposing the superintendent. However, the translation of community diversity and tension into resistance to the superintendent (a translation enhanced by institutionalized political devices), makes the probability of a superintendent victory more likely. A divided board is easy prey. The most *effective* opposition to the superintendent is the consensual elite of the small, nonpolitical district. Here challenges occur rarely, but they are more likely to succeed. Ironically, then, this portion of the governing process is inhibited by the very factors which enhance other aspects.

Is the situation we have described unique? Are school boards more removed from their publics and less in control than is true in other units of government? If so, is their relative insulation and weakness defensible? If not, why the cry for school reform? Our evidence in these matters is necessarily fragmentary.

Until that Utopian moment of total replication, we can muster only partial evidence. A basic source of evidence is the city council study directed by Eulau and Prewitt. We find that a majority of city councils are recruited in much the same fashion as school boards, have the same class bias, the same sort of issueless competition, and the same limited contact with nonsupportive groups. Prewitt, for instance, speaks of the strong norm of "volunteerism" present in city councils. He argues that city councils enter and leave office "not at the whim of the electorate," but according to their own schedules. Incumbent return is high (as is the case with most legislative bodies), recruitment is not group-oriented, but is on the basis of *noblesse oblige*: "They [city councilmen] treat council service as a 'citizen duty' in much the same manner as they treat service on the Chamber of Commerce, the PTA, the Library Board, and other such community service organizations."[14] They, like school board members, are inclined to view their role as "trustee," e.g., standing aloof from community opinion. Nearly half the councils studied are categorized as "unresponsive." Further, the groups to which they are likely to respond are the Chamber of Commerce, merchant groups, civic affairs groups, and the like. Reform or protest groups are rarely heard.[15]

On the other hand, city councils seem to play a larger policy leadership role than do school boards.[16] Although city managers are correctly compared with school superintendents as experts dealing with amateurs, a more appropriate balance seems to have been struck in the former case. One could hardly deny that managers are policy makers. Numerous studies have shown them to be major participants in policy formation: indeed, in many cases the chief initiator of policy.[17] There are, of course, some significant differences in the two arenas of government. Most school districts resemble the council-manager plan, with no elected chief executive. Most of the cities in the Eulau-Prewitt study have this form of government. About half the cities in the country, however, (even those with managers), have an elected executive. Very few school districts have elected superintendents, and efforts to eliminate the few remaining elected district heads continue.

There is, then, no political equivalent within the school system to the mayor. Since the chairman of the school board is normally chosen by his colleagues, he does not serve as a focus of representative balance against the bureaucracy. This independence from popular representation may strengthen the hand of the superintendent. There are, of course, other reasons why expertise appears to have been more successful as a resource in school management. There is some evidence that school policy decisions normally do not arouse the public as much as municipal policy decisions.[18] The main client of schools — the child — is clearly a "sacred object." Thus there is more fear that "normal" politics will disrupt the service to the client. Such a fear may be less a threat when the issue is zoning, garbage disposal, or budgeting. We assert, however inconclusively, that school experts have been somewhat more successful in insulating themselves than have experts in other governmental units. This is not to deny that conflict over school policy can occasionally become heated. Indeed, the very sacredness of the client virtually guarantees that emotions will occasionally become aroused. When the arena of

conflict expands — as in busing, sex education or similar issues — the climate of
conflict is hardly restrained. It is simply that routinized decision making — denying
the legitimacy of conflict — is the accepted norm. Conflict is equated with crisis.

THE CONSEQUENCES OF CHANGE

We are reluctant to engage in speculation about the future, but there is
some evidence that the isolation of schools is being reduced. The recognition of
the educational process as a political one is, however gradually, coming to pass.
Efforts to decentralize school districts, more radical demands for community
control, the controversy over the voucher plan, the increasing unionization of
teachers, and the reluctance of taxpayers to pungle up all provide evidence in
support of our suspicion. Our purpose is not to recommend appropriate ways of
coping with increased politicization. We do suggest that any reform movement
must deal simultaneously with the relationship between the representatives and the
public and the interaction of the board and the superintendent. Whether or not
schools are decentralized, it is highly likely that the issue of representation (as
opposed to citizen participation) will remain central. Most people do not want to
participate on a day-by-day basis in educational decision making, even if it is taking
place in a neighborhood school.

One model of governance suggested as appropriate is the worker's council,
as used in Yugoslavia and some Western European countries. Such a model is
normally associated with decision making at a rather decentralized level. However,
if such a model is followed, we plunge back into the dilemma with which we began.
Worker councils, elected by workers, seem reasonable enough except for two
problems: (1) workers are *not* the clients of the institution; (2) the output (profit)
of the institution is a consensual goal. Neither condition applies to schools.

Other suggestions for reform come readily to mind. If we want legislators
to be responsive, why not give them the tools to do the job? Making board membership a full time paid position, or furnishing a full time staff would provide more of
an opportunity to balance the distribution of influence between board and superintendent, but would probably not strengthen the link between the representatives
and represented. Another possibility is to convert the superintendent into a mayor,
that is, make the superintendent an elective office. As is done in some large cities,
he could be provided with a "chief administrative officer" to handle administrative
duties. The superintendent of today's schools might be ideally suited to become
the chief administrative officer. It appears that an elective superintendent is an
unlikely feasible alternative. There is simply too much tradition against it, to say
nothing of the opposition which mayors and other elective officials would mount
against the plan.

Suppose, then, that — by whatever means — we create "responsive"
school governance. What then? Will the *content* of policy change? If people ought
to be able to participate in decisions that affect their lives, and if decisions regarding
schools fall into this category, then we can ask closer questions of political science:

To *whom* should the school respond? *Who* should make the response? What *kinds* of decisions would be made at what level of governance? Suppose, for instance, that a researcher decided to measure the quality of education in responsive, politically robust districts in contrast to the normal district and found that, sure enough, the reformers were right: "educational" achievement is less in our "good" districts. Such an outcome is not necessarily improbable. Politically open districts would probably respond more to the needs of children from the nonprofessional classes, who typically score lower on achievement tests.

Yet we have no evidence that any structure of education — open classrooms, community schools, team teaching, or any of the various innovations tried and abandoned in the last twenty years — has any sustained impact upon what is learned. If the reformers were proved right, it is a reasonable conclusion that factors not associated with the school would prove the most reliable explanatory factors.

In terms of the ability of students to achieve what adults have decided they should achieve, responsive schools would change very little. However, there is a *process* question to be researched. Most people are concerned with discipline, and the assurance that their child will "make it."[19] If these people prevail, would schools simply become caricatures of what they now are? Most of the demands for alternative education are university-based rather than community-based. If educational elites were to reflect mass preferences, there is a reasonable probability that the children would be given even stronger doses of "education for docility." The process of education might become less innovative. Might the cost of narrowly-conceived responsiveness be too great?

However one answers this question, the future will surely see a continuation of the debate over the proper relationship of technical decisions to political decisions.[20] As we move into a society more concerned with conservation than distribution of resources, more and more reliance upon experts appears inescapable. As of this writing, the technology of teaching is primitive compared to, say, the technology of medicine. But it may not always be so. Perhaps someday there will be an educational technology (behavior modification?) which will be as powerful as the technology which created nuclear weapons. Should such a technology be "responsive"? An analogous situation is the technology of euthanasia, abortion, or even cloning. Should such technologies be untrammelled by political decisions?

The example of uncontrolled technology which is most frequently cited is the decision to use the atomic bomb. Should there have been some ratification by Congress? Should there have been a plebiscite? Under either circumstance it is probable that the decision would have been the same. Indeed, it is likely the people would have "voted" to use even more nuclear weapons! Similarly, an educational technology which could create a generation of children who learned at or near their capacity would probably be eagerly seized upon by a grateful citizenry irrespective of the methods employed.

In spite of the obvious perils, political decisions are — as long as we remain committed to democracy — logically superior to technical decisions. If we are going to maintain the trappings of democracy in education, then the realities of democracy should be achieved. School boards should govern or be abolished. In spite of occasional proposals for abolition, they will probably remain a visible part of educational governance. It is possible that boards will become merely ceremonial, a "vestigial remnant of past government."[21] Such a result can — and should — be avoided. Boards are the mechanism whereby schools can be made more responsive to their constituents. Whatever the perils that more responsive schools may bring, the costs of insulation from the community are greater.

NOTES

1. James S. Coleman, *et al., Equality of Educational Opportunity* (Washington, D.C.: Government Printing Office, 1966).

2. U.S. Commission on Civil Rights, *Racial Isolation in the Public Schools*, 2 volumes (Washington, D.C.: Government Printing Office, 1967).

3. Christopher Jencks, *Inequality: A Reassessment of the Family and Schooling in America* (New York: Basic Books, 1972), p. 102.

4. Coleman, *op. cit.*, p. 319.

5. Jencks, *op. cit.*

6. Robert A. Dahl and Charles E. Lindblom, *Politics, Economics, and Welfare* (New York: Harper and Row, 1953); Heinz Eulau and Kenneth Prewitt, *Labyrinths of Democracy* (Indianapolis: Bobbs, Merrill, 1973).

7. Robert L. Lineberry and Edmund P. Fowler, "Reformism and Public Policy in Cities," *American Political Science Review*, 61 (September, 1967), p. 716.

8. Robert Agger, Daniel Goldrich, and Bert Swanson, *The Rulers and the Ruled* (New York: Wiley, 1964).

9. Larry St. Louis and James McNamara, "Economics of Scale for a State System of Public School Districts," Center for the Advanced Study of Educational Administration, University of Oregon, Eugene, Oregon, 1971.

10. Robert A. Dahl, *After the Revolution* (New Haven: Yale University Press, 1970).

11. See, for example, Sidney Tickton and Sherwood Kohn, *The New Instructional Technologies: Are They Worth It? A Statement and a Technical Report* (Washington, D.C.: Academy for Educational Development, 1971).

12. Daniel E. Griffiths, "Intellectualism and Professionalism," *New York University Educational Quarterly*, 5 (Fall, 1973), pp. 5–6.

13. Two excellent assessments of the distribution of influence in such schools are: Joseph M. Cronin, *The Control of Urban Schools* (New York: Free Press, 1973); and George R. LaNoue and Bruce C.R. Smith, *The Politics of School Decentralization* (Lexington, Mass.: Lexington Books, 1973).

14. Kenneth Prewitt, "Political Ambitions, Volunteerism, and Electoral Accountability," *American Political Science Review*, 64 (March, 1970), p. 11.

15. Betty H. Zisk, *Local Interest Politics: A One Way Street* (Indianapolis: Bobbs-Merrill, 1973), pp. 10–58. For a strong statement questioning the uniqueness

of educational politics see Paul Peterson, "The Politics of American Education," *Review of Research in Education* (forthcoming).

16. Robert Eyestone, *The Threads of Public Policy: A Study of Policy Leadership* (Indianapolis: Bobbs-Merrill, 1971), pp. 122–123.

17. For a convenient summary, see Ronald O. Loveridge, *City Managers in Legislative Politics* (Indianapolis: Bobbs-Merrill, 1971).

18. R.J. Snow, *Local Experts: Their Roles as Conflict Managers in Municipal and Educational Government* (Ph.D. dissertation, Northwestern University, 1966).

19. In addition to our evidence, see Jeffrey A. Roffel, *Responsiveness in Urban Schools: A Study of School System Adaptation to Parental Preferences in an Urban Environment* (Ph.D. dissertation, MIT, 1972); and Paul Hill, "Public Views on the Objectives of Secondary Education," (National Institute of Education, 1973).

20. The literature on this subject is growing exponentially. For three cogent statements of the issues see Daniel Bell, "Technology and Politics," *Survey*, 16 (Winter, 1971), pp. 1–24; Heinz Eulau, "Technology and the Fear of the Politics of Civilization," *Journal of Politics*, 35 (May, 1973), pp. 367–385; and Victor C. Ferkess, "Man's Tools and Man's Choices: The Confrontation of Technology and Political Science," *American Political Science Review*, 68 (September, 1973), pp. 973–980.

21. Laurence Iannaccone, "The Future of State Politics of Education," *Struggle for Power in Education*, ed. Frank W. Lutz and Joseph J. Azzarelli, eds., (New York: Center for Applied Research in Education, 1966), p. 66.

Appendix A

Study Design

and Execution

Planning for this study began in 1967 as an outgrowth of previous work and interest at the Institute for Social Research of the University of Michigan and at the Center for the Advanced Study of Educational Administration of the University of Oregon. Depending upon the stage of the study, one or the other of these research centers was bearing the leadership role through Jennings in Michigan and Zeigler in Oregon. More specifically, the inception of the study, its funding (via the U.S. Office of Education), and the preliminary instrumentation came from the Oregon center; the full development of the instrumentation, the pretests, final field work, coding, and preparation of data were carried out at Michigan, primarily through the Survey Research Center (SRC); and the bulk of the analysis has been performed at Oregon.

Sample Design

We sought a body of data which would enable us to range in depth and breadth, one which would be representative in a statistical sense but which would also produce enough intensive information about a variety of school districts to capture the full flavor and richness of school district governance. Although deficient in some respects, an appealing and immediately usable sampling scheme emerged from the political socialization study which was being carried out by Jennings at the University of Michigan.[1] That inquiry included a national sample of high school seniors, their parents, social studies teachers, and school principals. Because of the interlocking nature of these data sets and the potential further enhancement of adding school board members and superintendents, it was very tempting to use as our sample of school districts those districts within which the high schools were located.

Before doing this, however, it had to be determined that the loss of representativeness was not too great. The main problem was that some school districts cover the elementary years (or high school years) only. If that proportion was too great, then basing our sample of districts on high school enrollments (which lay at the basis of the probability proportionate to size rationale of the socialization sample) would seriously affect the bias toward districts with high schools. Fortunately, approximately 90 percent of the K-12 school population was embraced by districts combining both elementary and secondary grades. Consequently, the bias is small.

Another problem of representativeness was the fact that we intended to enter the field in 1968, whereas the socialization study had been carried out in 1965 and was based mainly on a sampling frame resting on 1964 data. Thus any changes between that data and the time of our field work would possibly cause mis-estimates. Although we recognize that changes were occurring during that short period, it was our judgment that they would be relatively slight and the possible gains were compelling.

It should be stressed that this sample is designed to cover school districts *proportionate to the size of the school population.*[2] This means, for example, that the average size of the school population in our sample would be much larger than that in a straight, unadjusted probability sample of all school districts. As noted below, some further addition was made in our sampling plan in order to ensure the inclusion of large city school districts.

The School Board Sample

Working from the list of schools contained in the socialization study, we first eliminated the 11 nonpublic schools out of the total of 97. Of this total of 86, three pairs were in the same school district, leaving a total of 83 districts for which school board interviews would be sought. However, two districts refused to cooperate in the study. In one instance another district in the same SRC Primary Sampling Unit (PSU) was substituted. It had very similar characteristics to the declining one. For the second district that refused, a district in the same PSU which was included in the study was double weighted in the analysis. A key point here is that had either of the schools included in the 1965 project which were located in the declining districts chosen not to participate, then replacement schools under the jurisdiction of the substitute and doubleweighted school districts would have been used. In any event the refusal of only two districts cannot be judged to have had a major impact on the results. Altogether, of the original 83 boards which might have been included, 81 are actually included. The substitute board increases the total to 82.

For some purposes, it would not have been necessary to interview all

members of the boards serving these districts. But there were some compelling
reasons for doing so. As Leigh Stelzer has noted in another place:

> First, we were interested in studying the internal politics of the board.
> We wanted to know how the board members related to one another and
> to the superintendent. Furthermore, we hoped to gain insight into these
> relationships through an understanding of each member's background
> and attitudes. Using only a few board members as reporters would
> likely have introduced perceptual biases as well as incomplete information.
> Second, we wished to get as complete information about the board as
> possible. By putting the accounts of all members together, we thought we
> would get the most complete picture of the board. Again, using a few
> members as reporters could have introduced bias and created an incom-
> plete picture.
>   It is important to note in relation to our choice to interview
> all members that we were interested primarily in opinions, attitudes, and
> behavior. Answers to factual questions about the school district were
> obtained from the superintendent or his staff. Furthermore, the foci of
> these opinions were the local school districts and local politics, not
> national or general education policy.[3]

The response rate was exceptional. Out of a potential pool of 541 board
members, successful interviews were obtained with 490, for a response rate of 91
percent. Complete coverage was accomplished in 52 districts, and all but one
member of an additional 21 boards were interviewed. In only one district did we
interview less than a majority of the board. Interview time lasted well over an hour,
on the average.

For most purposes these 82 boards constitute the ingredients of our
analysis, whether the focus is on the individual board member as the unit of
individual analysis, or — as is more frequently the case — the focus is on board
member data aggregated to the level of boards as the unit of analysis. Thus Chapters
2, 3, 6, and 9–11 rely mainly on data from these districts.

Partly because of the enormous public policy problems raised by education
in large city school districts, partly because of the pace-setting nature of these
districts, partly because of minor underrepresentation of such districts in the
original sample, and partly to insure having enough cases for analytical purposes
we augmented this sample by oversampling in the 13 largest Standard Metropolitan
Statistical Areas (SMSA). This oversampling generated an additional 91 board
member interviews spread across 13 additional boards. Interviewing rates were
approximately the same as for the above sample, but a considerably shortened
interview schedule was used. Having oversampled from this stratum (which is
one of the criteria by which the SRC establishes its PSU's), it became necessary to
adjust for the contribution of the districts in the other three strata (suburbs in large

SMSAs, all other SMSAs, and non-SMSAs). More details are presented in the weighting section, below.

Another adjustment was required, however, because a few of the districts in the unaugmented sample had actually been included because of noncooperation of high schools in the original socialization study. A minor shuffling operation ensued, wherein seven districts in the primary sample were deleted from the data file. The net result is to make the augmented sample slightly more representative than the basic sample. But since the range of variables is severely circumscribed, only limited analysis can be carried out with the augmented sample. Overall, the raw number of boards used in the supplementary analysis is 88, and the raw number of individual board members is 550. Great use is made of this supplementary data set in Chapters 4, 5, 7, and 12.

Superintendent Sample

The rationale for including superintendents in the study is spelled out in Chapters 1 and 8, as well as being referred to elsewhere. Selecting the superintendents for study flowed automatically from the selection of boards. Again, we were very fortunate in having an extremely high response rate. In the regular, unaugmented sample all but one of the eligible superintendents was interviewed; the same was true of the additional thirteen districts. In addition to the direct use of the superintendent interviews for analytic purposes, as in Chapters 9–12, great reliance was also placed on the superintendents for accounts of a strictly factual nature about the conduct of school district governance (for example, how often the board meets).

Mass Public Sample

Chapter 7 describes the rationale and procedures used for incorporating respondents from the 1968 Survey Research Center election study into our analysis. It should be borne in mind that the sampling errors for the districts with a low number of respondents is quite high. The range of respondents across the districts in no instance exceeded 23, and the average was 8.5. Consequently, extrapolations to the universe of school board (and superintendent) — mass public matrices should be made with considerable caution. Two arguments persuade us that our undertaking was worthwhile despite the statistical problems. First, experimentation with districts with a large mass public sample versus those with a small sample tended to produce similar findings. Our confidence in the small N situations was thereby increased. Second, we are working with the best data available in an enormously important area. The choice was whether to proceed with what were admittedly less than 14-carat data, or not to proceed at all. It was our decision that even if the analysis produced only tantalizing propositions for further study, it would have been worth the effort.

Weighting of Cases

Two types of weighting schemes are used. The first, and most important, derived from the fact that the earlier socialization inquiry had employed weights. In neither that study nor the current one does the use of weights generate more than minor differences when compared with results from unweighted data. Nevertheless, in the interest of approaching the true parameters as well as possible, we have used weights throughout our analysis. Thus the weights assigned the high schools in the socialization project were assigned to the corresponding school board members. In the case of the unaugmented board sample this means a weighted N of 638 instead of the raw N of 490, for an average weighting increase of 1.30. At the board level this means a weighted N of 106, instead of 82, for an average increase of 1.29. Superintendents were given the same weights as the boards to which they were attached. Again, it should be stressed that even though all results reported in this book are based on weighted cases, the difference between those results and those obtained by using unweighted data are overwhelmingly trivial. In percentage terms, for example, one seldom found differences of over 5 percent comparison categories when using weighted versus unweighted data.

In the case of the *augmented sample* the weighting assumed an additional complexity. Because the large city stratum was oversampled, it would have assumed too much prominence in the analysis unless compensations were made in the other strata. In practice, this means "weighting up" the districts in the other three SMSA strata (see below) so that they would occur in their proper proportion. This procedure necessarily inflated the computational N considerably, but we have not let this inflation give us the illusion of having more cases than are actually present. The weighting merely adjusts for the oversampling of one stratum. To put the matter in perspective in Table A-1 are the raw N's and the weighted N's in the *augmented sample* for each of the four classes of PSU's, by board members and by boards.

TABLE A-1
Weighting the Augmented Sample

	Raw N		*Weighted N*	
	Members	*Boards*	*Members*	*Boards*
Largest Cities in 13 Largest SMSAs	95	13	95	14
Suburbs in 13 Largest SMSAs	84	13	181	28
All Other SMSAs	171	30	358	59
Non-SMSAs	200	32	505	85
Totals	550	88	1139	186

Other Sources of Data

In addition to the personal interviews we have utilized a number of other mechanisms in order to categorize school districts. Two forms, often filled out by aides in the superintendent's office, were especially valuable. One asked for the electoral history and electoral structure of the district covering the five years before the study date, which was summer, 1968. For appointed districts information was sought concerning the record of appointments over the same period. Another form solicited information about the history of any financial referenda. A third form sought information about important district characteristics, including the size of school system population, proportion nonwhite, expenditures per pupil, and the like. Much of the credit for the successful efforts to obtain information of this kind rests with the persistence and ingenuity of the Survey Research Center interviewers.

The basic data files and accompanying codebooks for this study are available through the Inter-University Consortium for Political Research, the University of Michigan, Ann Arbor, Michigan.

NOTES

1. For a description of the earlier study see M. Kent Jennings and Lawrence Fox, "The Conduct of Socio-Political Research in Schools: Strategies and Problems of Access," *School Review*, 76 (December, 1968), pp. 428–44; and M. Kent Jennings and Richard G. Niemi, *The Political Character of Adolescents* (Princeton, N.J.: Princeton University Press, 1974).

2. Strictly speaking, the sample should be defined as those public school boards having jurisdiction over a national probability sample of high school seniors as of 1965.

3. Leigh Stelzer, "The Receptivity of School Board Members: A Study of Reform and Representation" (Ph.D. dissertation, University of Michigan, 1971), pp. 97–98.

Appendix B

Descriptions of Variables

Comprising Public Tension Factor

(1) Intensity of Organizational Activity with Respect to Education.

Board members were asked eight open-ended questions in which they were to respond by listing the organized groups in the district which met the criteria of the questions. The maximum number of responses coded varied between 2 and 3 on each item. These questions concerned:

(a) Organizations most interested in the board.
(b) Organizations from which the board seeks support.
(c) Organizations working for passage of financial referenda.
(d) Organizations critical of the board.
(e) Organizations which attempt to influence teacher behavior in the classroom.
(f) Organizations which defend teachers when the latter are criticized.
(g) Organizations which attack teachers.

The maximum possible number of specific organizations mentioned was 19. In constructing our organizational intensity measure, we calculated the mean number of groups mentioned by the members of each board. The resulting scores range from .20 to 11.14. The mean is 3.92, and the standard deviation is 2.74.

(2) General Approval of Board by Groups within District.

The percent of board members responding that no groups in the district were critical of the school board was calculated for each board. The result was taken as our measure of group approval. Scores range from 1 to 98.[1] The mean is 56, and the standard deviation is 3.497.

(3) Composite Indicator of the Level of Educational Problems.

This measure is described in Chapter 6. The composite problem index ranges from 0 to 100. Its mean is 40.20, and its standard deviation is 23.10.

(4) Diversity of Organizations Active with Respect to Education.

This summary measure was constructed from the same basic items on the board interview schedule as (1) above. Instead of treating each organization mentioned as a separate entity, however, they were categorized according to the titles in Table 6-2.

Each district was given one point for each type of group mentioned by board members in their responses to the eight open-ended questions. The resulting sum for each district was taken as an indicator of the diversity of educationally active organizations it contained. Scores range from 1 to 12. The mean is 6.57, and the standard deviation is 2.78.

(5) The Level of Consensus regarding education.

This is a straight percentage of the members of each board who replied negatively to the question: "Is there any tension or conflict among people in the district on questions having to do with school policies?" Scores range from 1 to 98. The mean is 45.08 and the standard deviation is 27.93.

(6) The Extent to which Groups Contact the Board.

This measure, too, was based on a single question and reflects the percent of board members on each board who responded affirmatively to the question: "Do any representatives of community groups or organizations ever contact you personally or seek your support for their position?" Scores range from 1 to 98. The mean is 64.14, and the standard deviation is 25.19.

(7) Role Consensus between Board and Public.

Board members were asked which of the following points of view best approximated the way they approach their job:

(a) The board member "should do what the public wants him to do even if it isn't his own personal preference."
(b) The board member "should use his own judgement regardless of what others want him to do."

They were also asked:

How do you think the people of the district feel about the two points of view? Do you think they want you to follow their wishes even if you disagree with them, or to use your own judgment?

The percent of members on each board who felt that their approach to the job was consistent with what the public wanted (regardless of which view that may have been) was taken as our indicator of role consensus. Scores range from 1 to 98. The mean is 52.74, and the standard deviation is 24.66.

(8) Popularity of Board Policy Positions.

The proportion of the members of each board who indicated that rarely or never did they "take a stand that the majority of the public seems to disagree with" was computed. Scores on this variable run from 1 to 98. Its mean is 64, and the standard deviation is 25.19.

These eight variables and their respective factor loadings are listed in Table B-1.

TABLE B-1
Variables Significantly Loaded on the Tension Factor

Variable	*Factor Loading*
Intensity of Organizational Activity with Respect to Education	.76307
General Approval of Board by Groups within District.	−.88936
Composite Indicator of the Level of Educational Problems.	.78065
Diversity of Organizations Active with Respect to Education.	.76307
The Level of Consensus Regarding Education.	−.75550
The Extent to Which Groups Contact the Board.	.73116
Role Consensus between the Board and the Public.	−.52817
Popularity of Board Policy Positions.	−.49135

NOTES

1. Due to technical problems in the computations of scores on this variable, no scores of 0, 99, nor 100 were assigned. A score of 1 was assigned to districts that would otherwise have been scored 0. Likewise, 99s and 100s were assigned the score of 98. This procedure was also used in computing variables (5), (6), (7), and (8) discussed in this appendix.

Index

265